CHILDREN

of the

DREAM

CHILDREN

of the

DREAM

The Psychology of Black Success

*Audrey Edwards and
Dr. Craig K. Polite*

Doubleday

New York London Toronto Sydney Auckland

PUBLISHED BY DOUBLEDAY
a division of Bantam Doubleday Dell Publishing Group, Inc.
666 Fifth Avenue, New York, New York 10103

DOUBLEDAY and the portrayal of an anchor with
a dolphin are trademarks of Doubleday,
a division of Bantam Doubleday Dell
Publishing Group, Inc.

Book design by Chris Welch

Library of Congress Cataloging-in-Publication Data
Edwards, Audrey.
Children of the dream : the psychology of Black success / Audrey
Edwards and Craig K. Polite. — 1st ed.
p. cm.
Includes bibliographical references and index.
1. Afro-Americans—Psychology. 2. Success—United States.
I. Polite, Craig K.   II. Title.
E185.625.E29   1992
155.8′496073—dc20   91-26791
                                                              CIP

ISBN 0-385-24268-9
Copyright © 1992 by Audrey Edwards and Craig K. Polite

To the ancestors

CONTENTS

Acknowledgments   xi

Introduction: Children of the Dream   1

1. BLACK SUCCESS IN AMERICA: A PROGRESS
   REPORT   9
   The New Black Upper Class   12
   Black Wealth in America   13
   John H. Johnson: From $500 to $200 Million   14
   Madame C. J. Walker: The Stuff of Dreams
   and Fortunes   17
   Reginald F. Lewis: Leveraging a New Deal   19

PART 1   GETTING READY

2. A REUNION IN LITTLE ROCK   27
   "Blood in the Streets"   29
   "The Beast in Us . . ."   31
   Walking into War   33

3. FROM SEPARATE TO EQUAL   37
   From Separate to Inferior   40
   The Psychological Charge for Integration   42

4. THE INTEGRATION GENERATION   48

Success and the Black Family:

Richard Mays, Les Hollingsworth, and Lottie
Shackelford   50

Ernest Green: The First Black to . . .   57

PART 2   GETTING OVER

5. TO BE YOUNG, GIFTED AND QUALIFIED   69

Carolyn Sawyer: Breaking into the Business   71

In the Matter of Being Qualified   77

People Get Worthy   80

Arnold F. Roane: Ready to Go at All Times   81

Arlene Roane: On the Daddy Track   86

6. ACTING YOUR COLOR   92

Maxine Waters: The Color of Power   94

Lloyd Gite: The Color of Strength   100

James Russell: The Color of Style   105

Kathleen Knight: The Color of Image   108

7. GETTING MAD, GETTING EVEN   112

Ellis Gordon: Angriest Black Man in America   114

Getting Over   115

Succeeding Beyond Anger   123

Gerald B. Smith: Taking the Larger View   124

8. A CREDIT TO THE RACE   129

Dan Gasby: Exceptions and the Expectations   132

The Grooming Process   137

Ramona Tascoe Burris: Playing by the Rules   138

Learning to "Eat It"   142

9. SUCCESS AND THE BLACK WOMAN 151

    Julianne Malveaux: Feeling Fulfilled 152

    Up Off Her Knees 155

    Of Race and Gender 157

    Jennifer Lawson: The Life and Times of the
        Movement People 160

    Having It All 161

    Loretta Johnson: A Success in Her Own Time 166

    Barbara Britton: Dealing with the Brothers in the
        Struggle 169

    Anne Ashmore: Woman Power 172

    Susan L. Taylor: The Essence of Success 175

10. SUCCESS AND THE BLACK MAN 180

    Kweisi Mfume: Against the Odds 183

    Black Men, Black Power 188

    Haki Madhubuti: The Warrior as Artist 190

    Ramon Hervey: Amazing Grace 194

    Christopher Edley, Jr.: Presumptions and the
        "Smart-Ass White Boys" 199

    Gregory T. Baranco: The Master Dealer 203

    Les Payne: Shooting the Wounded 206

    Jamil Sulieman: The Revolution Will Not
        Be Televised 210

PART 3   GETTING DOWN

11. A DREAM DEFERRED? 217

    Paying the Price of the Dream:

    Janet Cooke, Leanita McClain, and Edmund Perry 217

    Charles Morrison: Integration and the Real Thing 222

    Winning at Race 227

Craig and Gloria Smith: Taking Affirmative Action   229
Earl G. Graves, Jr.: The Dream Continues   234

12. HOW WE HAVE OVERCOME: THE PSYCHOLOGY
OF BLACK SUCCESS   240
Note 1: Personal Responsibility/Integrity   241
General Fred A. Gordon: Taking Command   242
Note 2: GOPAS (Goals, Organization, Planning,
and Action Sequences)   245
Bert Mitchell: Giving an Accounting   246
Note 3: Managing Others' Racial Perceptions and
Reactions   249
Alfred E. Woods: Managing at the Top   250
Note 4: Pioneering   251
Shellie Ferguson: Breaking New Ground   252
Note 5: High Degree of Self-reliance   255
Rhonda Strivers: Brewing It Her Way   256
Note 6: Positive Self-acceptance   258
*Clarence O. Smith: Reaping the Rewards of the
Risk*   258
Note 7: Balance in Life   262
Ed Welburn: Designing the Dream   262
Note 8: Giving Back, Reaching Back   264
Betty Winston Bayé: Coming Home Again   266
Note 9: Faith   270
Thomas Watson: Doing God's Will   271
Note 10: Transcendence of a Racial-Victim
Perspective   273

Conclusion: Reaching the High Note   274
Bibliography and References   277
Index   281

ACKNOWLEDGMENTS

An undertaking of this kind would not have been possible without the invaluable assistance of many people. We would like to first thank our agent, Marie Brown, and our editor at Doubleday, Martha Levin, two people whose belief in and support for the book kept us going. We are especially grateful to Lucretia Santapria, Carolyn Porter, Shere Crute, Beverly C. Lewis, Ann Marie Crenshaw, Kay Reese, Gordon Chambers, Ruth Delores Manuel, Benita Allison, and Joseph Hayden, who were indispensable to much of the administration involved with the book: transcribing interview tapes, doing research, mailing correspondence. A special thanks to our computer guru, Stephen Miller, who got us linked up and modem-ized. And to the two righteous brothers in the U.S. Census Bureau, statisticians Dwight Johnson and Robert Cleveland, who helped us give meaning to numbers.

Thank you, Emile Milne, Roland Alston, Curtis Bagley, Pat Charbonnet, and Laura Randolph, who were invaluable in providing leads on subjects to interview; and Lena Sherrod, Michael Smart, Gerald Gladney, and *Essence* editors Stephanie Stokes Oliver and Valerie Wilson Wesley, who so generously gave of their time and good counsel in reading the manuscript-in-progress; and *Essence* art director Marlowe Goodson. We also thank Arlene Hawkins. Last but certainly not least, we are most grateful to our respective "significant others," C. Obalewa Scott and Cheryl Polite, whose love, encouragement, and support created the best possible working conditions.

And finally, we would like to offer a special acknowledgment to the subjects we interviewed whose profiles were not included in the book, yet whose accomplishments further document the triumph of modern African-American success. We thank them for so magnanimously letting us into their hearts and their confidence.

In Atlanta: Diane Rawley, M.D., an epidemiologist with the Centers for Disease Control, and her husband, Bill Jenkins, Ph.D., also an epidemiologist at the CDC; John Leak, president of Central Atlanta Progress; and Rafael Battine, senior trial attorney with the U.S. Department of Labor, Office of the Solicitor.

In Houston: city councilman Anthony Hall; Melanie Lawson, television news anchor on Channel 13, and her husband, Gary Broadnax, a photographer with the *Houston Post.*

In Los Angeles: real estate developer Marlene Charbonnet; actress Berlinda Tolbert and her husband, Bob Reid, television producer; television producer and script writer Winifred Hervey Stallworth; and writer Bebe Moore Campbell. In Oakland: dentist Kathleen Carney Sulieman.

In Chicago: Carolyn Shelton, a counselor with the Chicago Mental Health Foundation; Thomas Elzie, budget director for the City of Chicago; and John Rogers, president of Ariel Financial Services.

In Detroit: Mark Cocroft, public relations manager, and Barbara Sanders, director of advanced technology, both of General Motors Corporation; Robert Holland, president of Gilreath, Inc.; Rhonda Welburn, president of Welburn Buick Inc.

In Boston: Laval Wilson, superintendent of schools. In Cambridge: Linda Hill, assistant professor of business administration at the Harvard School of Business.

In New York: Caroline Jones, president of Caroline Jones Advertising; Bernard Thomas, a vice president at the Chase Manhattan

Bank; Jackie Lewis, owner of The Grand Hotel boutique; Randy Daniels, press secretary to former Manhattan borough president Andrew Stein; Nancy Lane, director of corporate affairs at Johnson & Johnson; Monte Trammer, publisher of the *Saratogian* newspaper in Saratoga Springs, New York; Kevin Nelson, a graduate student in the Yale School of Public Health; Dwayne Gathers, formerly assistant vice president for National Westminster Bank; Rafee Kamaal, producer of "In the Black"; James Obei, president of the Obei Insurance Agency, a unit of the Equitable Life Assurance Society; Edna Wells-Handy, formerly Brooklyn assistant district attorney and now corporation council for the Health and Hospital Corporation; and Patricia Tyner, senior vice president and Merchandising Manager of The Petrie Stores Inc.

In Denver: Raymond Jones, judge of the Colorado Appellate Court; and Janis Powell-Rollins of the Mountain Bell Corporation.

In Hartford: Dr. Paul Copas, superintendent of schools of Bloomfield, Conn.; and Gerald Peterson, director of the Hartford Civic Center.

In Washington, D.C.: Captain C. A. "Pete" Tzomes, U. S. Navy, former commander of the fleet submarine *U.S.S. Houston* and currently director of Navy Equal Opportunity; and Paula H. J. Cholmondeley, vice president with Faxon International Corporation.

Introduction

CHILDREN
OF THE DREAM

*The bottom line for us is that every morning for
nine months we got up, polished our saddle shoes—
and went to war.*

Melba Beals, speaking at the reunion
of the Little Rock Nine,
October 23, 1987

*I*t had been thirty years. And all nine returned for the reunion.
Middle-aged now. But all nine still alive, present, and accounted
for. That alone was a singular victory. Only one remained in Little
Rock. Two lived abroad. Three had married white. All had gone to
college and were considered successful. The oldest, most visible,
and generally considered most successful of the group was an investment banking vice president in Washington, D.C. One had
become a radio talk-show host in northern California, another a real
estate broker in a Colorado suburb; the fourth a magazine editor in
the Netherlands, the fifth lived on a farm in Canada; another was a
home economics teacher in East St. Louis, yet another had become
an assistant dean in southern California; the eighth was an accounting technician for the Department of Defense, and the one who had
remained in Little Rock was a housewife and Army veteran.

When they integrated the Little Rock, Arkansas Central High
School as teenagers in September 1957, they were known collec-
tively as the Little Rock Nine. In another era the name might
evoke rap groups. But in 1957 the label applied to the nine black

teenagers who would help reshape a generation and define a civil rights movement.

Social movements are typically fired if not led by the youth of any given generation. It is the young's capacity for change and innocent optimism that make real the notion of possibilities. And the modern American Civil Rights Movement was certainly as much a movement of black youth as it was of the black clergy. The Student Nonviolent Coordinating Committee, the youth branch of the National Association for the Advancement of Colored People, and the Black Panther Party were all organizational catalysts that propelled a generation of young people into a future marked by unprecedented economic, social, and political opportunities.

The black youth who came of age during the modern civil rights era between 1954 (the year the Supreme Court outlawed segregation in public classrooms) and 1968 (the year Martin Luther King, Jr., was assassinated) also formed the vanguard of what might be termed the "integration generation," a generation shaped by the belief that the key to black success in America lay in assimilating into the very culture that had long denied it opportunity and equality. The integration of Central High School in 1957, then, like the Montgomery Bus Boycott, begun a year earlier in Alabama when Rosa Parks refused to give up her seat on a bus to a white man, became one of the warning shots that put America in mid-century on notice: a black movement for civil rights had begun that would transform a nation.

For a race convinced that education was the unassailable cure for all its ills, the integration of the American public school system became the logical line of scrimmage in the competition to gain access to American opportunity. Thus the thirtieth reunion of nine blacks who as teenagers helped lead the charge for integration became a logical place for us to begin a book examining the impact of the Civil Rights Movement on black success during the last three decades and to assess what has happened to the black generation of "integrationists" who emerged from the fallout of the cataclysmic sixties.

For the Little Rock Nine, who spent one brutal year of their youth fighting what at the time amounted to a nascent civil war, their reunion was to be a bittersweet triumph, a tribute and a legacy to the black baby-boom "success" generation they had come to represent: a generation that has been the prime beneficiary of integration's successes and in some ways the most damaged by its failures. It is a black American generation more technically prepared than any that has gone before to solve the problems still gripping its community. This "black success" generation in many ways resembles the "yuppie" phenomenon of contemporary America: it is young, professional, affluent, and struggling to forge an empowering sense of identity in an increasingly perplexing society. Nearly a hundred years ago W. E. B. DuBois named this class the Talented Tenth: that segment of the black American population which represents its success and leadership class, the best and the brightest of the race.

Success has always been a relative phenomenon in black America, however, often measured as much by what has been overcome as by what has been achieved. For black achievement inevitably remains a triumph over odds, a victory over struggle. Whether it be in overcoming the debilitating effects of racism or the accompanying destructive pathology of low self-esteem and self-hatred, black success is almost always the result of a peculiar kind of drama that gets played out first in the psyche.

So what exactly do we mean by black success? During the last thirty years it has meant the realization of an American promise: access to equal opportunity. For our purposes here we will use both economic and occupational frameworks to assess the phenomenon of success on a generation of blacks who grew up in an era defined by the concept of integration. No other social force has so helped shape a people's expectations or fuel its ambitions. And no other social force has exacted a more severe toll on the very group seeking to assimilate.

Yet the successes of today's black baby boomers have been real and remarkable. In 1967 less than 5 percent of the black families in America could be counted in the middle class, having annual household income of $15,000 in 1987 dollars. By 1987 the figure had grown to 36 percent having middle-class annual incomes of $25,000 or more. However, income is but one measure of individual worth. Professional occupations, status, and influence are perhaps more significant barometers to gauge shifts in power. And here the shifts have been dramatic indeed. Black baby boomers can now be found in positions of power and influence just about everywhere in the American workplace: in the boardrooms of major corporations, at the heads of labor unions, in the halls of Congress and state legislatures, running major cities, on television commercials pitching everything from aspirin to hamburgers. No other generation of African-Americans has come so far so fast.

But if this generation's "Talented Tenth" has had more advantages and successes than previous ones, it has also had to contend with the old demon of racism speaking in a new forked tongue. "Downsizing," "glass ceilings," "retrenchment," "last hired, first fired," and "twofer" are all new terms in a business vocabulary ostensibly describing the state of American industry during the past twenty-five years, but in truth actually characterizing the declining state of black advancement into the American corporate mainstream. As the vocabulary suggests, much of the black employment gains made during the economic boom times that coincided with the Civil Rights Movement began to be eroded once economic prosperity started to wane.

Much like the era of reprisals and repression that marked the end of Reconstruction following the Civil War, today's black baby boomers increasingly operate in a climate of economic and social backlash. More ominously, the climate has unleashed a growing underclass among the remaining "ninety percenters" of the black race, whipped by a ferocious media with its lust for the sensational trying to make pathology the salient descriptive of black American life. Female-headed households, drug abuse, infant mortality, AIDS, crime, poverty, and racism have all come to characterize a "black crisis," a race in trouble.

A focus on pathology, however, tends to disturb rather than illuminate. Our contention, and hence the premise of this book, is that it is much more useful to focus on the success stories within the black race to identify the special strengths and skills it takes to prevail in the face of persistent racism. Our success subjects, encompassing the thirty-year span of a generation, are black men and women born between the years 1935 and 1965 who represent both a post-Depression and a baby-boom civil rights era. Though many were born poor, all have reached the upper middle class, having in 1990 either household incomes of at least $75,000 or individual incomes of at least $40,000, and all are employed in professions and hold positions that were closed to most blacks prior to the Civil Rights Movement. Some are well known. Most are not. Their stories reflect the status of their lives at the time they were interviewed. They come from all over America, though where they currently reside is most likely to be different from where they were born—the latter most often being the first variable that has helped shape their destiny.

Whether they came of age at the beginning of the Civil Rights Movement in the late fifties or at its peak in the mid-seventies, all our interview subjects have had the edge of integration as a force driving their success. Affirmative action, equal employment opportunity, set-asides, mentors, networking, training programs—these became the buzzwords of a generation who grew up possessing something no generation of blacks before had ever experienced: a sense of entitlement, a belief in the right to have access.

We have deliberately chosen to omit interviews with black entertainers and athletes (though their impact on black wealth is the first thing mentioned in Chapter One) from our examination of black success—first, because their sizable incomes skew any meaningful discussion of black economic gain over the past thirty years, and second, because entertainment and sports were relatively accessible arenas of employment for blacks prior to the Civil Rights Movement.

Primary emphasis is on the professional class of blacks who comprise DuBois's old notion of a Talented Tenth. We spent three years between 1987 and 1990 traveling the country to talk with nearly a hundred men and women on the subject of their individual success. We observed them in their public and professional postures, sometimes for days, other times for only hours. We were privy to their private reveries, heard their painful confessions, saw them shed new tears from old hurts, heard them reveal fears never voiced and slights never avenged; and we heard them recount successes unparalleled as well. Interviews were done in offices and living rooms, around tables in the kitchen or in a hotel lounge or quiet pub; in cars, on airplanes, in restaurants, in backyards; beginning in Little Rock, then moving on to Atlanta, Louisville, Houston, Los Angeles, San Francisco, Oakland, Denver, Chicago, Detroit, Boston, Hartford, New York, Washington, D.C., West Point, and Ft. Lauderdale. The intention was to obtain not so much a geographic sampling of the black American middle class as a representative depiction of a distinctly black American psychological experience: a view of what the journey looks like and feels like for a historically disenfranchised class moving to that elusive place called freedom, success—inclusion in the American mainstream.

In the end we chose forty-one subjects to examine as profiles in black success. Their stories are no more remarkable than those we chose not to include, just more representative of a particular black experience for a particular generation at a certain point in American social history (integration and the Civil Rights Movement), stories that also happen to most dramatically reveal the various and distinct interactive styles that successful blacks have typically used in order to achieve.

Whatever the personal behavioral styles, the one common trait that emerges from all the interviews presented here is that successful blacks are first and foremost affirmed and empowered by a positive sense of racial identity. They fully understand that as blacks they will encounter obstacles, prejudices, and inequities, but *they never view their race as the cause of the problem.* They understand it is the perverse reactions of others to the black race which constitute the deficiency. It is this essential recognition that grounds the thinking of achieving blacks, enabling them to successfully operate out of a "positive sense of blackness," a positive sense of who they are—and to gain a powerful measure of spiritual strength from the physical and psychological struggles that racism inevitably demands.

Not surprisingly, success is a subject that makes even the most accomplished blacks a bit uncomfortable. For a people whose history has been uniquely shaped by oppression, the idea of success carries some ambivalence and a certain degree of guilt. Indeed, most of those interviewed said they did not consider themselves really successful—either because they had not accomplished all they would like to, or because the black race as a group is still not successful. "As long as the rest of my people have not made it, I haven't really made it," was a frequent litany.

It is perhaps the nature of the oppressed to measure life against a standard of minuses: to view the glass as half empty rather than half full, to discredit achievement by pointing to that which is still undone. And while many of the subjects of this book exhibited such tendencies initially when asked to articulate what they did that set them apart, the very key to their success has been their resilient ability to overcome the power of negative thinking; to affirm who they are in a society that at best usually ignores them, or at worst actively tries to deny them their very humanity.

How have successful blacks managed to attain their success? And what has been the price? What do they bring that's old and what do they bring that's new to the arena of work and competition? What have been the particular mindset and motivating psychology behind their achievements?

Chapter One gives an overview of the peculiar route the development of black American wealth has taken (and includes three profiles based on second-source references), showing how the rise in black income has become a useful gauge to measure the rising fortunes—and thus the rising success—of black Americans over the last twenty years. The rest of the book is divided into three parts: "Getting Ready," "Getting Over," and "Getting Down." "Getting Ready" begins with the integration of Central High School in 1957, and examines how and why education (both formal—schooling; and informal—family training and background) became an almost obsessive preoccupation among blacks whose strivings for success meant first overcoming the devastating effects of racism on self-esteem and feelings of self-worth. "Getting Over" examines both the emotional price blacks have paid to successfully integrate America's professional arenas as well as the intraracial psychic damage successful blacks have frequently had to overcome to achieve. It also examines what success has come to mean for black women and for black men. "Getting Down" assesses the downside of integration and lists success characteristics and psychology of adaption achieving black men and women have ultimately developed in order to be effective.

All of our success subjects have agreed to go on record using their real names as they tell their personal stories of struggle and triumph, of pain and progress. These pre- and current black baby boomers, the oldest of whom are now entering their fifties, are consolidating the gains made in the early days of integration, while the youngest, in their twenties, are just finishing school or starting careers—some already on a fast track that will take them past the greatest successes attained by the older peers of their generation. The thoughts and insights of this generation help illuminate just what it takes to be a successful black living in white America. For whatever successes blacks have achieved are the results of battles hard fought and hard won, the legacy of many thousands gone who lived and died fighting to ensure that their children would "live to see a better day"—that, in the words of the prophet who had a dream, "little children will one day live in a nation where they will not be judged by the color of their skin but by the content of their character." These are the children of the dream.

Audrey Edwards and Dr. Craig K. Polite
May 19, 1991

One

⚞

BLACK SUCCESS IN AMERICA: A PROGRESS REPORT

*I*n 1987 one of the highest-earning individual blacks in America was neither a producer nor manufacturer of goods and services, nor a business executive in the classical sense. He was an entertainer—a comedian, to be precise. The formidable Bill Cosby emerged to head *Forbes* magazine's first annual list of the top 10 American entertainers and was estimated to have earned nearly $100 million in 1987 alone. In point of fact he made only a little more than half that—$57 million—though his two-year total for the years 1987–88 came to $92 million. The next year he had been booted to the number 2 position on the list and replaced by a 30-year-old pop singer named Michael Jackson, who earned $60 million in 1988, giving him a two-year total of $97 million. Moreover, the *Forbes* list now ticked off the earnings of the top 40 entertainers, including athletes. And ten of those, *a full 25 percent of the total,* were black Americans: in addition to Jackson and Cosby, there was the actor-comedian Eddie Murphy (number 5, earning a two-year total of $62 million); boxer Mike Tyson (number 8, $61 million in two years); television host and producer Oprah Winfrey (number 14, $37 million); pop singer Whitney Houston (number 17, $30 mil-

lion in two years); boxer Sugar Ray Leonard (number 21, $27 mil-
lion); singer Tina Turner (number 24, $25 million in two years);
pop singer Prince (number 29, $24 million); and boxer Michael
Spinks (number 38, whose two-year earnings came to $17 million).

The two-year combined earnings of these ten entertainers and
athletes came to nearly half a *billion* dollars. The collective revenues
of the top 100 black-owned industrial and service businesses listed
in *Black Enterprise* magazine every year came to $6.75 billion in
1988. Clearly, a staggering share of the wealth in black America
has become concentrated among an enormously successful few who
sing and dance and talk and fight for a living. It is an aberration
with profound implications. The fact that a black can now grow up
to become the number one entertainer in America, though not yet
President, reveals both the success of integration and its failure. On
the one hand, America has become comfortable and literally color-
blind in its acceptance and adoration of the blacks who entertain,
but it is still stubbornly racist in conceding equitable power to
blacks in most other arenas. That shouldn't be surprising. The
power to entertain is not quite the same as the power to control.

To be sure, black performers today have more control over their
productions than at any other point in entertainment history, but it
is a power diminished by the same economic reality that limits the
rest of the race: most do not *own* the means of production or distribution. It is the classic proletarian dilemma, one that has kept the
majority of blacks, whether they be millionaire superstars or ordinary schoolteachers, in the position of wage earners—employees
rather than entrepreneurs.

Yet the wages of man (and woman) still remain the best barometer of the economic well-being of a society's citizens. As Theodore
Cross writes in *The Black Power Imperative:* "Whenever income is
transferred to another person, some form of economic power is
working—either in the form of skills, hard work, ingenuity, persuasion, coercion, or proprietary advantage. Moreover, income is
easily quantifiable, requiring no value judgments or subjective in-
terpretations." Given this, income has traditionally been the yard-
stick for measuring success and achievement. And it doesn't matter
much whether that income is derived from salaried employment or

independent enterprise. What counts is the value of an individual's labor—the worth that has been assigned to a particular skill or talent as measured by money. The more money an individual earns, the more valued and successful he or she is considered to be.

It is precisely for this reason that when comparisons are made between how well blacks and whites are doing, income is invariably the gauge. Such comparisons are inevitable in a society in which there is still persistent inequality. All things being equal there would be no reason to make comparisons based on race, gender, age, geographical location, or occupation if such differences didn't have an impact on success. And for the African-American, race continues not only to make a critical impact on success and achievement, but also to skew how black success and achievement are viewed: inevitably it is in relation to white success. What is the per capita income of a black family of four as compared to that of a white family of four? What percentage of black households are headed by females and how does this compare with the number of white female-headed households? How does the black male unemployment rate stack up against white male unemployment? How many black families can now be considered in the middle class, and how does this compare with the number of white families? What is the median income of blacks and of whites? Is the gap between the two narrowing or widening?

The comparisons, contrasts, and constellations are endless, and while they are typically used to assess how far a disadvantaged group has come and how far it has yet to go, statistics also have a tendency to reduce reality to number-crunched data that tells only part of the story. In the case of blacks the data is most often used to tell a story of continuing inequities: of a growing underclass, a middle class under siege, a loss of the ground gained during the past thirty years. This is certainly not untrue, but the danger of such an emphasis is that it too often only serves to reinforce a collective sense of inferiority by suggesting that blacks never quite measure up.

THE NEW BLACK UPPER CLASS

If a key measure of success is income, a telling measure of black success is the growth of upper middle class income during the post civil rights era of the last three decades, a period marked by the kind of economic, social, and political opportunities that for the first time in their history gave blacks a certain advantage.

Indeed, during the twenty years between 1970 and 1989 the percentage of blacks who had upper middle class household annual incomes of $50,000 or more grew by 182 percent. In 1970 only 6.9 percent of the black American population, or roughly 426,000 households (adjusted for inflation in 1989 dollars), had annual incomes of $50,000. By 1989, the figure had grown to 11.5 percent, or 1.2 million households, representing an increase of 182.2 percent in real terms, nearly double the increase among white American households in which annual incomes of $50,000 or more grew 93.6 percent between 1970 and 1989. Interestingly, the percentage of black households that have now reached upper middle class status slightly exceeds the "Talented Tenth" of the black American population which W. E. B. DuBois described nearly a century ago as representing the race's talent and leadership class. DuBois was then referring to an elite professional class (10 percent of the black American population, he estimated) characterized less by income and more by education, occupation, status, and aspirations. Today's talented tenth is also now defined by economics, and represents a generation of blacks with the kind of expanded opportunities during the last two decades that allowed it to successfully "cross over" from poor or working-class origins to the upper middle class.

To be sure, much of the increase in black upper middle class income reflects two wage earners in a household, though black women have traditionally always worked outside of the home, so the gain also reflects real increases in earnings among both black men and women during the last twenty years. Such gains, however, have been tempered by the growing class of blacks disenfranchised economically. According to a 1988 Census Bureau study on net worth as a measure of wealth, the median net worth (calculated by subtracting total liabilities from total assets) of black households in the top 20 percent of the income distribution (having household incomes of $40,000 a year or more) came to $47,160, while the median net worth of total black households in 1988 was only $4,169. And 29 percent of black households had a zero or negative net worth.

The discrepancy between black wealth and white wealth is startling, for while blacks in the top 20 percent of the income distribution had a median net worth of $47,160, white households in the top 20 percent of the incomes distribution had a median net worth of $119,057. So although the over-$50,000-a-year black upper middle class has increased nearly two hundredfold during the last twenty years and even almost doubled the rate of increase for whites in this income category, the gap between white wealth and black wealth is still more than two-and-a-half to one.

Race obviously continues to be a determining factor in one's ability to attain wealth in a society where whites have had a 200-year economic head start. Yet the fact remains that a growing segment of the black race has nevertheless managed to attain upper middle class status despite the historical disadvantage of race discrimination. Much of this is certainly due to the expanded opportunities that resulted from the Civil Rights Movement, but just as much is due to the skill, resourcefulness, and attitude of those blacks who have achieved success. For in a society that still more often thwarts black ambition than encourages it, black success is rarely accidental or ever a matter of simple blind luck.

BLACK WEALTH IN AMERICA

Money, like sex, is one of those loaded issues that frequently compels lies, exaggerations, half truths, and some degree of guilt.

Among blacks the issue is a particularly sensitive one, regardless of at which end of the spectrum they find themselves—rich or poor. Poor, however, has come to almost characterize the black condition. Grim statistics point to a third of the race living in poverty, a fact that has led economic pundits to redefine the meaning of class by eliminating the black poor from such categorizations entirely. They are consigned to no economic class at all. So intractable and enduring is their poverty that they have attained a status *beneath* class: the underclass.

Black wealth, on the other hand, is a different matter. There are no economic descriptives that define the black monied class in America. Indeed, before *Black Enterprise* magazine started compiling and publishing the annual list of the top 100 black companies in 1973, there were not even any reliable estimates as to who or how many constituted such a group. And while the *Black Enterprise* list gives an accounting of black business earnings, it doesn't reveal individual wealth or even the earnings of the individual company CEOs. Since nearly all 100 black companies listed are privately held enterprises, such financial information is not publicly disclosed and when made available cannot always be verified.

John H. Johnson: From $500 to $200 million

For several years in a row the Johnson Publishing Company in Chicago headed the *Black Enterprise* list. John H. Johnson, founder, chief executive officer, and sole owner, may or may not be the richest black in America, but he certainly is rich. It is a distinction he seems to relish, as he unabashedly asserts in the sweeping title of his book, *Succeeding Against the Odds: The Inspiring Autobiography of One of America's Wealthiest Entrepreneurs.* The assertion is not unfounded. Johnson was the first black ever to be cited on *Forbes*'s annual roll call of the 400 richest Americans, and with a personal net worth estimated to be about $200 million, he is also, as he says, "the only former welfare recipient in my tax bracket."

Born in Arkansas City, Arkansas, in 1918, Johnson migrated north to Chicago with his mother at age 15. There he would become a rags-to-riches success without benefit of either integration or affirmative action. When he launched his first publishing venture, *Negro Digest,* during World War II in 1942, he recalls in his autobiography, "Black men and women were struggling all over America for the right to be called 'Mr.' and 'Mrs.' In that year we couldn't try on hats in department stores in Baltimore, and we couldn't try on shoes and dresses in Atlanta. We couldn't live in hotels in downtown Chicago then, and the only place a Black could get a meal in the downtown section of the nation's capital was the railroad station. It was a world where the primary need, almost as demanding as oxygen, was recognition and respect."

It was into this milieu that Johnson introduced *Negro Digest* on November 1, 1942, at the age of 24, with a stirring editorial that read in part, *"Negro Digest* is dedicated to the development of interracial understanding and the promotion of national unity. It stands unqualifiedly for the winning of the war and the integration of all citizens into the democratic process."

Johnson's financing of that first issue revealed the kind of vision and daring that characterizes many success stories, but was all the more remarkable given the peculiar handicaps a young black man faced in segregated America in 1942. At the time he conceived an idea for a magazine that would highlight the achievements of black Americans, Johnson was working as a clerk for the Supreme Liberty Life Insurance Company in Chicago, then one of the largest black-owned insurance companies in the nation, with assets of $27 million. He had been assigned the task of going through black press articles and preparing a digest of what was happening in the black world for Supreme Life president Harry Pace.

It didn't take long for Johnson to spot the potential "black goldmine" in a publishing venture that would highlight on a consistent basis positive, uplifting articles on black life and black success stories. Such stories almost never appeared in the white press, and Johnson claims in the South "there was an unwritten rule . . . that a black's picture could not appear in the press unless in connection with a crime."

Of course financing a black magazine venture in 1942 would take some ingenuity. For more than two months Johnson went the traditional route, scouring the black business community of Chicago for investors, but as he explains, "Most people had seen *Reader's Digest* and *Time,* but nobody had seen a successful black commercial magazine. And nobody was willing to risk a penny on a twenty-four-year-old insurance worker."

The key to the fortune turned out to be right on the premises of the Supreme Liberty Life Insurance Company. Another job of Johnson's as insurance clerk was to run the office Speedaumat, an addressing machine that kept the names and addresses of Supreme Life's 20,000 customers. Johnson hit upon the idea of sending a solicitation letter to every customer on the list asking for a two-dollar prepaid subscription to a new black magazine. His reasoning was that if he got even a 15 percent response rate, he would raise $6,000, enough to publish the first issue. He got permission from Supreme Life president Harry Pace to use the company's mailing list, but now he needed $500 to pay for the 20,000 two-and-a-half-cent stamps it would take to mail the letters. He went to the one financial institution in Chicago that would make loans to "colored people" in 1942, the Citizens Loan Corporation. The only snag was that Johnson had to come up with collateral to secure the loan. Here the answer lay with family: Johnson prevailed upon his mother to let him pledge the new furniture he had helped her buy to secure the $500.

It was this final stroke—a mother's love and belief in a son's dream—that turned the tide or, as Johnson puts it, turned a $500 loan into millions. That first solicitation letter netted 3,000 prepaid subscriptions, raising the $6,000 Johnson needed to publish the first issue of *Negro Digest.* Within eight months the magazine was selling 50,000 copies a month nationally. In 1945 Johnson launched his second magazine, *Ebony,* a picture magazine modeled on the size and format of *Life* and *Look.* It became an instant success and today still ranks as the number one black magazine in America, with a circulation of 1.6 million. "We've never seen ourselves before in large photographs presented in a positive light unrelated to crime, and we love it," said Johnson in explaining the *Ebony* appeal.

Madame C. J. Walker: The Stuff of Dreams and Fortunes

Unlike the Vanderbilts and Rockefellers, Carnegies and Mellons whose fortunes coincided with the industrial revolution of the late nineteenth century, black wealth in America is largely a twentieth-century phenomenon. The first 244 years of the black experience in America was one of slavery—forced labor without income, wealth producing without wealth accumulation. And the half century following emancipation witnessed a people's slow, painful trek toward elusive freedom—an era marked by the promises of reconstruction, the betrayal of the Hayes Compromise, the apartheid of Jim Crow legislation, the terror of cross burnings and lynchings, and the viciousness of race discrimination which created an inferiority-breeding caste system within a democracy that left the black race free only in name, but in all other ways—economic, social, and political—virtually powerless.

Yet despite such daunting circumstances, by 1916 America could claim its first black millionaire, a woman: Madame C. J. Walker, who built an empire and a fortune selling black beauty products door-to-door. Born Sara Breedlove in Delta, Louisiana, in 1867, four years after emancipation, Walker began her working life like most blacks of that period: as a menial laborer—in her case working fourteen-hour days as a washerwoman for wealthy whites in St. Louis, where she had fled following her husband's murder by a lynch mob.

The daily assault of hot steam, vapors, fumes, and harsh soaps in her laundry work took its toll on Walker's skin and hair (which was beginning to fall out). By contrast Walker noted the numerous lotions, skin creams, and ointments her white employers used to keep their skin smooth and their hair styled. She began experimenting with preparations of her own that could similarly be used to care for black skin and hair. The formula for her bestselling Hair Grower preparation came to her in a dream, she would later insist. "One night I had a dream; a big black man appeared to me and told me what to mix up for my hair. Some of the remedy was grown in Africa, but I sent for it, mixed it, put it on my scalp, and in a few weeks my hair was coming in faster than it had ever fallen out. I tried it on my friends; it helped them. I made up my mind that I would begin to sell it."

Such dreams may be the stuff legends are made of, but two years after Walker had moved north to Denver, Colorado, she had gained so many customers she was able to quit working as a laundry-woman and devote all her time to her burgeoning business: preparing and selling her hair products and also training sales agents to sell for her. By now her beauty system included the hot comb (for straightening black hair), Wonderful Hair Grower, Glossine hair oil, Temple Grower, and a Tetter Salve for psoriasis of the scalp.

When she died in 1919 at age 52, Madame C. J. Walker's personal fortune was in excess of a million dollars. Her holdings included property in the South and Midwest, two townhouses in Harlem, and her showpiece, Villa Lewaro, a sprawling quarter-of-a-million-dollar estate in New York's Irvington-on-the-Hudson. At its height the Madame C. J. Walker sales force numbered more than 2,000 agents selling hair and skin products door-to-door, pioneering the direct sales marketing concept that would make Avon and Mary Kay Cosmetics even greater fortunes in the latter half of the twentieth century.

America's early black wealthy class were invariably entrepreneurs, and their enterprises were inevitably rooted in the delivery of vital services to the black community—the kind of services that the white community was either unable or unwilling to deliver to its black citizens. Early black fortunes, then, were built on such industries as insurance, undertaking, banking, media, and health and beauty. In a segregated society where the majority race would neither insure, bury, lend money, portray fairly in the press, nor market health and grooming products to its minority population, these needs were quickly filled by enterprising black businessmen and -women.

It is not surprising that John Johnson built his wealth on media, for the press performs not only a vital information function, but a powerful psychological one as well. In explaining the impetus for *Negro Digest,* Johnson has said, "In a world of despair, we wanted to give hope. In a world of negative black images, we wanted to provide positive blacks images. In a world that said blacks could do few things, we wanted to say they could do everything. We believed then—and we believe now—that you have to change images before you can change acts and institutions."

Reginald F. Lewis: Leveraging a New Deal

In 1988 the Johnson Publishing Company lost its number one ranking on the *Black Enterprise* list of top 100 black businesses to a billion-dollar company that epitomized just how much black images, white acts, and American institutions had changed in the 45 years since Johnson hocked his mother's furniture to go into business. The company was TLC Beatrice International Holdings, Inc., and its CEO was a 44-year-old Wall Street attorney named Reginald Lewis. In what was touted as the largest leveraged buyout of an overseas operation in the history of American business, Lewis had, in two daring entrepreneurial strokes, acquired the former international division of a giant food conglomerate for $985 million. The acquisition made Lewis personally worth $100 million and marked the triumph of an entirely new kind of black businessman: the pure capitalist.

Unlike the typical black business owner, represented by John Johnson or Madame C. J. Walker, who starts a business from scratch, building wealth from the ground up with his or her own hands, sweat, and talent, Reginald Lewis successfully did what only whites had done before him—buy a business empire outright. It was a stroke of the boldest force and typified the heady, high-rolling kind of transactions that glamorized the game of American business in the eighties: mergers and acquisitions, corporate raiders, white knights, hostile takeovers, leveraged buyouts, divestiture, junk bonds, insider trading. The very terms of the deals conveyed the drama of the action.

Lewis's coup not only marked the entry of a black man as a

player in the game, but it earned him admission as a proven winner into the ranks of an elite and previously all-white capitalist fraternity: the rarefied world of the Wall Street financier, those professional money men—"masters of the universe," novelist Tom Wolfe has called them—skilled in the art of raising capital to finance the mammoth business undertakings that bring vast wealth and bestow world hegemony. For what made the Reginald Lewis BCI deal historic was not just the color of its key player, but the sheer size and scope of the undertaking, the dizzying enormity of the stakes —and the sheer magnitude of the profits.

Reginald Lewis was neither a retailer, a wholesaler, a distributor, nor a manufacturer when he finalized the deal for the purchase of BCI Holdings, the former international division of Chicago-based Beatrice Foods in the winter of 1987, yet his new, far-flung business operations encompassed all of that: meat processing in Spain, soft drink manufacturing in China, grocery wholesaling, retailing, and distribution in France, a chocolate business in Venezuela, dairy producing in Singapore and Malaysia, ice-cream manufacturing in Ireland, Italy, and Denmark. BCI Holdings comprised a total of 64 companies operating in 31 countries at the time Lewis purchased it from the investment firm of Kohlberg Kravis Roberts for close to $1 billion. In 1987 BCI had $2.5 billion in sales and posted $147 million in operating income.

Whenever "luck" becomes a factor in the success equation for blacks, it is usually at the point opportunity intersects with the quadrants of timing and history, social forces and preparation. The difference between a John H. Johnson, then, and a Reginald F. Lewis is the difference between segregation and integration, between a society that is closed and restrictive and one that is open and equitable, between opportunities denied yet nevertheless found, and opportunities extended and therefore seized. Reginald Lewis was to become a multimillionaire the new-fashioned way: through the tricky maneuver of a business takeover using what came to be known as the leveraged buyout, a form of transaction that would transform the nature of American business in the eighties and extend the opportunities for such acquisitions to what only a generation ago would have been America's most unlikely dealmakers.

By his own account, dealmaking is precisely what Reginald Lewis was geared and groomed to do. Like other successful blacks of his generation, he came of age in the transitional era of the civil rights sixties, a period defined by a social movement toward integration and equal opportunity. Born and raised in Baltimore, he earned his undergraduate degree from Virginia State University in 1965 and his law degree from Harvard in 1968. Following a brief stint with the New York corporate law firm of Paul, Weiss, Rifkind, Wharton & Garrison, Lewis started his own Wall Street law practice, Lewis and Clarkson, with fellow attorney Charles Clarkson in 1970. It was the height of the Nixon era, with its emphasis on "black capitalism," and Lewis's firm specialized in venture capital development for small- and medium-sized businesses, assisting a number of minority-owned businesses in structuring deals and acquiring financing. In 1983 Lewis launched the investment firm, the TLC Group, with the specific purpose of acquiring existing companies. And as it happens with timing and history, certain factors and developments in the American marketplace would provide new opportunities for a black man who was prepared and positioned to do exactly that.

If Reginald Lewis came of age in the civil rights era of the sixties, he forged his Wall Street career in the roaring bull market decade of the eighties, an era marked by a soaring stock market, colossal business expansion, and the ascendancy of debt as a factor in the margins of profit. Debt, in fact, by the early eighties literally made the economic world go round. There was national debt and consumer debt, municipal debt, corporate debt, and sovereign debt —debt so enormous, pervasive, and interconnecting that only the might of computer technology could fathom the figures or conquer the data. Debt would thus set the stage for the emergence of the leveraged buyout, and become the axis on which the Reginald Lewis deal was to turn.

Lewis had actually started the spin in 1984, when his newly formed TLC Group made its first business acquisition, the McCall's Pattern Company, for $25 million, by leveraging $1 million of

TLC's own capital with $24 million in financing underwritten by the First Boston Corporation. Though McCall's was struggling at the time of the purchase, Lewis was attracted by the fact that the company had sizable brand recognition, good cash flow, and strong management. Three years later, on the eve of his deal to acquire BCI, Lewis profitably proved the wisdom of that decision by selling McCall's for a cool $90 million, nearly quadruple the original purchase price and 90 times his own investment of $1 million. He then used the proceeds from that transaction to stake his claim for BCI Holdings. And on August 6, 1987, Lewis led the TLC Group to victory in winning the bid to acquire BCI for $985 million, beating out twenty other investor groups, among them such Goliaths as Citicorp, Nestlé, and Shearson Lehman Brothers.

For this billion-dollar transaction the TLC Group brought about $120 million of its own capital to the table—a little more than 12 percent of the price—and financed the rest through a combination of credit lines from Manufacturers Hanover Trust and junk bond issues underwritten by the investment banking firm of Drexel Burnham Lambert, Incorporated. And in a brilliant display of financial footwork, Lewis raised $426 million in financing by selling off three of Beatrice International's holdings before he became the actual owner of record.

The deal was stunning by any standards. For a black man the achievement was nothing short of revolutionary. Yet Reginald Lewis, a compact, powerfully built man whose tan brown occidental face suggests Asian and Native American roots as well as African ancestry, dislikes being either defined or limited by race. "I don't really spend a lot of time thinking about that," he responded in a magazine article shortly after the BCI acquisition when asked what he thought his accomplishment meant to black entrepreneurship. "Now, that is not to say that I haven't been very pleased with the type of response that I've received," he continued, "especially from students and young people who have written to tell me that our work has been an inspiration to them. But the TLC Group is in a very competitive business and I really try not to divert too much of my energy to considering the kind of issues [race] . . . raised."

If wealth is indeed an indicator of success, then Reginald Lewis may be the quintessential barometer of black progress in America, for he is a black man who has made his fortune in what he calls "the capital markets," that arena of free enterprise where a man's success is measured not by the color of his skin but by the daring of his vision, the capacity of his risk taking, and his natural ability, as Lewis puts it, "to analyze the fundamentals and ferret out facts and opportunities and then, through labor and effort and creativity, to bring value to those opportunities that in the end will result in superior returns."

These are the very qualities that contribute to success for anyone. Yet for African-Americans the *opportunity* to succeed has never been equitable. Like freedom, opportunity has had to be prayed for, struggled for, died for, legislated for, and even now hard won and still relative. But when opportunity *is* extended the result is often spectacular success, whether it be Reginald Lewis or any of the legion of other African-American men and women who have achieved and continue to succeed against the odds and the obstacles. For the success generation of blacks who were to come of age during the second half of the twentieth century—the generation that would begin to live out the promise of the American dream—opportunity had to first be seized before success could finally be realized.

GETTING READY

Democracy doesn't guarantee success.
It guarantees opportunity.
The Reverend Jesse Jackson

A REUNION
IN LITTLE ROCK

*O*ctober 23, 1987. The first ones to show up that day are a gang of six black girls, wearing colors: short, pleated, black kick skirts trimmed in gold at the hem; black pullover sweaters with a "mighty tiger" crested in gold across the chest; spit-smooth black-and-white saddle shoes. It is a scene as American and old-fashioned as pompoms, cast in spirit and history as primal as ju-ju. The cheerleading squad of the Little Rock, Arkansas, Central High School Tigers has arrived early, not knowing exactly what to expect, but knowing the occasion demands attention and respect.

They assemble at the top of the wide landing intersecting the double stairways that lead to the school's entrance and stand in loose position, waiting. It is an excellent vantage point from which to view the gathering crowd below: reporters, photographers, cameramen, soundmen, old-time civil rights organizers, city, state, and school officials, black parents and white. The press, politicians, and citizens of Arkansas's capital city have turned out this day to celebrate a most curious sort of reunion: the return of the nine black teenagers who put their lives on the line thirty years ago to get an equal education.

"Here they come!" says one of the cheerleaders excitedly, spotting a caravan of cars turning onto Park Street. The cars pull up to the school's entrance, delivering nine passengers—six women and three men—accompanied by respective spouses, children, friends. The nine are all grown now, graying and somewhat solemn in their middle ages. It is the first time in thirty years that they have been together again, as one of them put it, "joyous that we made it, sad that we had to." Their return to Central High was to be one of those bittersweet reunions, the kind war veterans hold to commemorate a victory, celebrate survival, and remember what was lost.

Thirty years before, on the very steps and grounds where the black cheerleaders of the Central High School Tigers now stood, over three hundred and fifty soldiers and paratroopers of the 101st Airborne Division, at a cost of $100,000 per day, had also stood—defending the right of nine black schoolchildren to integrate an American school system. It was the closest America had ever come to a second civil war. And as with the first one, race was at the heart of the conflict. But if the first American civil war was essentially about slavery and emancipating a race, the second one, which threatened to erupt in the capital city of Arkansas in the fall of 1957, was clearly about integration and assimilating a race.

Central High School seems almost naturally poised for battle. Built in 1927 in the medieval, baroque style of architecture so common to American educational institutions of the time, its sprawling gothic brick-and-stone structure rises on seven levels, standing like a citadel at the corner of Fourteenth and Park Streets, both the symbol and the guardian of a distinctly American tradition: free education. And that is precisely what made it a battleground in 1957, and nine black teenagers its formidable insurgents.

"BLOOD IN THE STREETS"

Battle lines in American education started forming almost as soon as the Supreme Court handed down its landmark ruling in *Brown vs. the Board of Education,* the 1954 decision that outlawed segregation in public schools. And wars and skirmishes over integrating black and white children in American classrooms would convulse both North and South—from Boston to Prince Edward County, from Los Angeles to Little Rock—for the second half of the twentieth century as a democracy struggled to come to terms with what it meant to integrate "with all deliberate speed." It was a struggle that brought back old notions and introduced new concepts: states' rights, busing, community control, de facto segregation. And it was a struggle that threatened to tear apart a Southern state's capital city in the fall of 1957.

Events in Little Rock in 1957, however, might never have boiled over were it not for a collusion of political and racial forces fueled by the grandstanding of then-governor Orval E. Faubus, who built a political career appealing to racist sentiments. Like many American cities in the South of early fifties, race relations between blacks and whites in Little Rock were fairly cordial—as long as blacks knew their place and kept it, leaving whites snug and smug in their superiority. It didn't appear that even the Supreme Court's decision on May 17, 1954, to order integration in the schools of the South would disturb the order of things, and certainly not constitute a racial crisis.

As early as the summer of 1954 Little Rock's superintendent of schools began to comply with the Court ruling, and drafted a plan for school integration that would begin with two high schools then under construction and scheduled to open in the fall of 1956 in middle class white neighborhoods. Little Rock's school board, however, adopted a diluted version of the plan, which came to be known as the Little Rock Phase Program. It limited integration to just one school—Central High, in a working class neighborhood of Little Rock—and specified that only a limited number of black students were to attend that first year, 1957.

Nine students, hand picked by the school board, were chosen to integrate Central High's student body of 2,000 that September. "None of the children were A students," remembers Daisy Bates thirty years later. In 1957 Bates was president of the Little Rock Chapter of the NAACP, spiritual mother to the Little Rock Nine, and with her husband, L. C. Bates, owner and publisher of the *Arkansas State Press,* a black newspaper. "The school board selected those they felt wouldn't fight back," says Bates, if opposition to their integrating were to become violent. One of the children had a heart condition, another had a mother who was a teacher in the city school system, and all of them came from two-parent working-class families. And each of them volunteered, knowing the danger in which daring to integrate with whites would place them. "There was always the possibility that someone could be killed," Bates recalls.

That possibility crystalized on Labor Day, September 2, 1957, the day before school was to open. Word flashed on Little Rock's radio stations that over 200 Arkansas National Guardsmen had surrounded Central High School, ordered by Governor Faubus to keep the nine black children from entering Central High the next day. "Under the streetlights stretched a long line of brown Army trucks with canvas tops," recounted Daisy Bates in her memoir, *The Long Shadow of Little Rock.* "Men in full battle dress—helmets, boots, and bayonets—were piling out of the trucks and lining up in the front of the school." That evening Faubus went on the radio to address Little Rock's citizens. "His words electrified Little Rock," Bates remembers. "By morning they shocked the United States. By noon the next day his message horrified the world."

Under the guise of saying he had called out the National Guard because he had heard caravans of cars filled with white supremacists were heading toward Little Rock, Faubus declared Central High School off limits to blacks. "Blood will run in the streets," he chillingly predicted, if the nine black students tried to enter the school. The address was a cheap political ploy, destined to win

Faubus a third term as governor. It also resulted in fanning the flames of hatred over the idea of blacks integrating with whites.

The idea of integration challenged the central assumption that segregation was based on: the inferiority of blacks. And it fed white racism's oldest, most irrational psychosexual fantasy: the vision of blacks as a sexual threat to white purity. At its most base, most primitive, most racist level, this is the view that casts blacks—and black men in particular—as wanton, depraved sexual beasts, given to impulse and insatiable desire, uncontrollably lusting after whites —white women in particular. Variations of this basic sexual dynamic have always fueled racial fears in white America and were at the root of the South's opposition to integration. Integration meant mixing with inferiors. More importantly, for white womanhood it meant you might be ravaged by "one of them."

But the idea of integration also had another, more troubling effect: it meant confronting the possibility that whites were really no better than the blacks they had worked so hard to make feel inferior. That possibility seemed unthinkable in Little Rock in the fall of 1957, when ordinary racism suddenly turned particularly hateful and dangerously illogical.

"THE BEAST IN US . . ."

After Faubus ordered in the National Guard to keep nine black teenagers out of one white high school, white venom exploded. On September 3, the day the nine were to start school, hundreds of angry whites descended on Central, taking up defense line positions with the National Guard. Little Rock's citizenry had shown up in force to protect the sanctity of Central High School and its white students. "We won't stand for our schools being integrated," said someone in the mob. "If we let 'em [blacks] in, next thing they'll be marrying our daughters," said someone else. A white obsession with "race mingling," "intermarriage," the "deflowering of white womanhood," or "mongrelization of the races" had been the justification for every indecency since slavery for attempts at keeping blacks a racial caste apart.

Pure hatred, however, was the only explanation for the violence that greeted one of the nine—a 15-year-old girl—who showed up at Central High the first day of school alone, not realizing that the nine were to have stayed away that day. Daisy Bates, who was in charge of the children, had been unable to inform the girl's parents of the change in plans because they had no telephone. So the teen-ager arrived unescorted and unwarned on the campus of Central High that morning of September 3, stunned to find herself in a face-off with 250 National Guardsmen and a screaming mob of white bigots. "They're here! The niggers are here!" shouted some-one in the mob when he saw the lone black girl. The girl tried to pass through the Guardsmen several times—until they put bayo-nets in front of her. "Get her! Lynch her!" the women screamed. "Go home, you bastard of a black bitch!" the men were braying. The girl made her way slowly through the mob to a bus stop. Mute, impassive, she sat gingerly on the bench, tears starting to streak down her face. A white woman who had viewed the scene with growing horror sat down next to her, put her arms around her, and said softly, "Don't let them see you cry." It was one of those low points in American history that led Eleanor Roosevelt to com-ment, "Within all of us there are two sides. One reaches for the stars, the other descends to the level of the beasts. The picture of the mobs in Little Rock . . . shows clearly that the beast in us was predominant."

And the beast was being riled by a recalcitrant governor whose position was a throwback to the old argument that had led to the South's secession from the Union nearly a hundred years before: states' rights. "By using the state's military power to defy Federal laws, Governor Faubus, in effect, proclaimed that the rights of the State superseded the rights of the Federal government," says Daisy Bates. But those "states' rights" were violating the law of the high-est court in the land by denying nine black children their right to a desegregated education. It would take the military might of the United States Army to finally secure these children that right.

The Little Rock Nine remained in limbo for most of the month of September, unable to go to Central, which by the middle of the month was barricaded by city police and still flanked by the National Guard, who had been ordered to keep them out; and refusing, at the instruction of Daisy Bates, to go to the all-black Horace Mann High School, which would have been a capitulation to the governor's defying the law against segregation. Racist sentiment was at fever pitch. Hundreds of jeering whites booed the police outside Central every day, hurling insults at the reporters who covered what had now become a national spectacle of unbridled racism. Daisy Bates' home was bombed; a cross was burned on her lawn; her life was threatened. Some of the parents of the Little Rock Nine lost their jobs, and the teenagers lost sleep and school time, but never their resolve. "I loved them," says Daisy Bates of her charges. "We had a kind of mutual understanding. I made them understand that this was something we had to do—they *had* to succeed. There was nothing they couldn't tackle."

WALKING INTO WAR

On September 24, 1957, faced with a crisis that threatened to lead to a nation once again "divided against itself," President Dwight D. Eisenhower made the decision to federalize all ten thousand men of the Arkansas National Guard units. He further authorized the Secretary of Defense to send in whatever regular United States troops he deemed necessary. The Secretary ordered a thousand paratroopers from the Screaming Eagle Division of the 101st Airborne into Little Rock from Fort Campbell, Kentucky. The regiment, along with the 10,000 soldiers of the National Guard, formed the first line of offense for the Little Rock Nine. And on September 25, at 9:22 A.M., surrounded by twenty-two airborne troops, another 350 flanking the school building, and an Army helicopter circling overhead, these nine teenagers walked through the doors of Central High School and into war.

Although the black teenagers' first few days at Central were marked by a period of fairly calm acceptance on the part of most white students, the Little Rock Nine soon enough became the Embattled Nine. A few vicious white students, taking their cue from the jeering white adults outside who still surrounded Central High, began their own reign of terror inside against the nine, all of whom were variously kicked, beaten, taunted, threatened, attacked, humiliated, and otherwise made miserable for most of the school year.

Nonviolence as a protest tactic had not yet been fashioned as the centerpiece of the movement for civil rights by blacks, which made the stoicism of the Little Rock Nine that first year of integration at Central High all the more remarkable. One of the Nine, for instance, was attacked from behind one day by two white boys and hit so hard that he fell to the floor unconscious. He nevertheless showed up for school the next day, explaining to his mother, who tried to persuade him to stay home, "If I stay out today, it will be worse tomorrow."

It was this very perseverance, this capacity to prevail in the face of relentless and often unfathomable racism that earned the nine teenagers their distinction in history and gave their homecoming thirty years later its special victory. They could indeed be considered returning veterans, soldiers who had elected not to stay out thirty years before, because "it will be worse tomorrow." As a result, tomorrow became better for a generation that followed. By 1987 Central High School's student body was 60 percent black and had accounted during the past six years for 10 percent of the state's National Merit Scholars. In 1980 it produced a black Rhodes Scholar. And from 1983 to 1986, 7 percent of Little Rock's student population transferred from private schools into Central High, which now had a faculty that was 35 percent black.

The Little Rock Nine might best be described as the youth brigade in the vanguard of a people's movement to liberate themselves through the double-edged sword of integration and education. They had helped to change not only history but the fortunes of a race. And they were their own best testament to just how great the change had been during the past three decades. Now scattered far from the cradle of the South that had given them birth and turbulent fame, each had become in his or her own way that rare but growing phenomenon in American society: a successfully integrated, successful black.

There was Ernest Green, the oldest of the Little Rock Nine and the first black to graduate from Central High School in the spring of 1958. Returning at the age of 46, he was now a senior vice president in the Washington, D.C., office of Shearson Lehman, an investment banking firm. There was pretty, dimpled Melba Patillo, now Melba Patillo Beals, 45, a writer living in Sausilito, California, and a freelance radio talk-show host. There was Minnijean Brown, 44, who lived on a farm in Ontario, Canada, with her husband and six children. She too was a writer and a conservationist, as well as an antiwar and antinuclear activist. At Central High she was the only one who had fought back—by dumping a bowl of chili on the head of a fat white boy who had kicked her in the cafeteria line. She had been promptly expelled from Central.

There was Terrance Roberts, 45, an assistant dean at the UCLA School of Social Welfare, and Jefferson Thomas, 44, an accounting technician for the Department of Defense in Los Angeles, who refused to let being knocked out by two white boys thirty years ago stop him from getting up and keeping on. And there was Carlotta Walls Lanier, 44, a real estate broker in Denver, and Gloria Ray Karlmark, 45, who became a magazine editor in the Netherlands. There was Thelma Mothershed Wair, 46, a home economics teacher in East St. Louis, Illinois. And there was Elizabeth Eckford, 45, an Army veteran and housewife and the only member of the Little Rock Nine who remains in the Little Rock area—her moody, somber silence still reflecting the horror of that fall morning thirty years ago when, at age 15, she was surrounded by a mob of whites who taunted and threatened her with death. To this day she has never given an interview or spoken on the subject of that particular trauma.

The very presence of the Little Rock Nine at a thirtieth reunion was a triumph, a victory over odds. Yet seeds for this victory and for black success had been sown long before there was a Central High or a Little Rock Nine. The seeds had first been planted in the harsh, bitter earth of slavery, then had taken root in the corrosive soil of segregation, and finally had been allowed to bloom in the yielding ground of integration. And always, at the center, at the core, at the very essence of the black will to succeed, to be affirmed, to be equal, to be free, was the primal drive to be educated. The African-American struggle for education matched the quest for liberation and began at the precise moment of black captivity—at the very moment America became this great contradiction of history: a democracy built on slavery.

Three

⚑

FROM SEPARATE
TO EQUAL

*O*ne of the more peculiar and sinister aspects of the institution of American slavery was its outlawing of education for African-American slaves. In many parts of the pre–Civil War South, the mere existence of a literate slave was considered to be a capital offense more criminal than treason. Those slaves who did learn to read and write always did so secretly, furtively, as outlaws sneaking off into the night to steal knowledge and the power it holds. And if they or their instructors (often sympathetic whites, but more often other literate blacks) were ever caught, the penalty was frequently death.

It is no wonder that education for American blacks became an almost obsessive preoccupation. Education was not only the source of knowledge and accompanying power, it came to be viewed as the skeleton key that unlocked the very gate to freedom. If Southern whites found the prospect of an educated slave so threatening, education must hold the promise of liberation.

The Reconstruction Era, then, following the South's loss of the Civil War, was marked by a dizzying startup of black schools at both the grade school and higher education levels. Such premier black institutions as Hampton College and Howard University were founded within three years following the end of the Civil War, and literally hundreds of training schools, grade schools, and high schools opened in church basements, cottonfields, woodsheds, shanty kitchens, and even along country roads and in backyards throughout the South. As Vincent Harding recounts in *There is a River: The Black Struggle for Freedom in America,* quoting a white Northern journalist who observed the zeal with which blacks pursued education immediately after the war:

> "Many of the negroes . . . common plantation negroes and day laborers in the towns and villages, were supporting little schools themselves. Everywhere, I found among them a disposition to get their children into schools, if possible. I had occasion very frequently to notice that porters in stores and laboring men about cotton warehouses, and cart drivers on the streets, had spelling books with them, and were studying them during the time they were not occupied with their work."

Harding notes that "Such black people, who not only sang but studied in the sun, were a threat to many white Southerners, and the smoldering ashes of their 'little schools' often provided mute testimony to that fact." Yet these people continued to have "a disposition" to get their children into schools, and that unyielding fact would change the fabric of American education. As Harding put it, "A people just emerging from the supposedly dehumanizing experience of slavery, a people for the most part desperately poor and materially deprived, a people assumed to be ignorant of 'civilization,' was announcing in words and deeds an agenda for the continuing movement toward freedom and new humanity in the United States."

That the agenda would always in some way be rooted in education was apparent by the turn of the twentieth century. There were now were some 43 black colleges and universities in the South, including Booker T. Washington's Tuskegee Institute in Tuskegee, Alabama. And the argument over just what kind of education was most appropriate for newly freed blacks would rage for the first decade of the new century as the practical educator Washington endlessly debated the merits of technical and vocational training with his nemesis the scholar and intellectual W. E. B. DuBois. DuBois favored the kind of abstract liberal arts education he felt would make emancipated blacks proficient in handling the nuances of their new power. Washington's focus was on the immediate, on climbing up from slavery through economic development, which he believed demanded the learning of skills in the crafts and trades. DuBois's vision was to the future, to the leadership class of blacks who would emerge and thus require a "higher education" befitting a people who are to interact not just as economic equals, but as political and social equals as well with those in the majority—white America.

The notion of "equal," however, had been narrowly defined, legally interpreted, and strictly enforced by 1900. Four years earlier, in the 1896 landmark Supreme Court decision of *Plessy vs. Ferguson,* the Court ruled that separation of the races was within the bounds of the Constitution so long as equal accommodations were made for blacks. The decision resulted from a ruling brought in the lawsuit of one Homer Plessy. Plessy, who could pass for white but was known to have had a black great-grandmother, purchased a train ticket to go from New Orleans to Covington, Louisiana, and sat in the whites-only car. When he refused to move into the black car, he was dragged, literally kicking and screaming, by policemen who removed him from the train and arrested him. Plessy promptly sued the railroad, arguing that segregation was illegal under the Fourteenth Amendment, which was ratified in 1868 to ensure equal protection under the law for newly freed slaves. The Court, however, argued that "separate-but-equal" was all that was required of the railroad under the Civil Rights Act of 1875. The law simply guaranteed all Americans the right to public accommodations; it did not outlaw segregation in these facilities.

FROM SEPARATE TO INFERIOR

The *Plessy vs. Ferguson* ruling effectively sanctioned an American brand of apartheid known as "Jim Crow" segregation, which dominated every aspect of black life in the United States South for the first half of the twentieth century. During this period, writes Juan Williams in the companion volume to the PBS television series on America's Civil Rights Movement, *Eyes on the Prize,* "There were Jim Crow schools, Jim Crow restaurants, Jim Crow water fountains, and Jim Crow customs—blacks were expected to tip their hats when they walked past whites, but whites did not have to remove their hats even when they entered a black family's home. Whites were to be called 'sir' and 'ma'am' by blacks, who in turn were called by their first names by whites. People with white skin were to be given a wide berth on the sidewalk; blacks were expected to step aside meekly."

Segregation as practiced in the American South became more pathological, institutionalizing more than simple inequality. Segregation institutionalized inferiority. It produced a people who spent nearly every waking moment of their existence being reminded in ways great and small that they were less than, not as good as, not as smart as, not as successful as, not as pretty as, not as handsome as, not as responsible as, not as valuable as—not as human as—the white race of the species. These are the kind of racist assaults that wound the spirit, brutalize the psyche, erode self-esteem. And because such assaults were so insidious, and were delivered with such ruthless force and methodical consistency over time and circumstance—more than two hundred years in slavery, and one hundred years of segregation—they had produced by the second half of the twentieth century a people whose fight for freedom would take a new turn and an added dimension. The battle was still for access, for opportunity, for inclusion and recognition as equals in American society, but the struggle would now lead to the politics of integration and an existential struggle to be "worthy" of freedom.

The invasive, collective sense of inferiority that often drives and thus debilitates the black race has been slavery's most malignant and enduring legacy. Whenever a moral justification for slavery is attempted, it is inevitably on the grounds that the enslaved are somehow better off for having had the slave experience, that they are less than human to begin with and can benefit from the civilizing influence of captivity. Twelve generations of African-Americans would not only experience that lie as their reality but would begin psychologically to accommodate the lie, to give it power and weight. And while the Civil War brought an end to slavery, it could not diminish the potency of a lie that has become internalized.

What the *Plessy vs. Ferguson* ruling essentially did was to shroud race discrimination in culture, to give it rituals and customs, expectations and mutual understandings, a visceral sense of boundaries and limits, place and rank. Segregation simply became "a way of life" in the South, its ethos rooted in slavery and sanctioned by the highest court in the land. And the overriding psychology of "separate but equal" had the desired effect of perpetuating the old notions of white superiority.

Indeed, for most blacks in the South, mere physical separation from whites was never the issue. The real issue was the conditions under which they were separated. "Separate" invariably turned out to be not just unequal, but inferior. Whether it meant drinking from a dirty sink rather than a clean water fountain because you were "colored," or standing in the "colored" waiting room of the train station because there were no chairs for Negroes, or riding at the back of the bus where "coloreds" were consigned, or sitting in the "colored" section of the movie balcony, or going into the bank through the "colored" entrance of the back door, "separate" came to define a "colored" condition, the interminable and intractable state of being forever diminished by race.

Yet if the *Plessy* decision left one scale of justice stuck in the past of slavery, the other was clearly tipped toward a future marked by the phenomenon of integration and a perpetual vision—the one America has of itself as a democracy of true equality. And it is this vision that has always given American blacks a certain moral and psychological edge, for in a democracy, a class oppressed either by slavery or its devastating aftershocks remains an inherent contradiction. The very concept of "separate but equal" spoke to an attempt to reconcile the contradiction, to affirm the tenets of equality for all of America's citizens.

THE PSYCHOLOGICAL CHARGE FOR INTEGRATION

The promise of equality has always been the black American metaphor for freedom, for success, and the guiding principle that has fueled every drive for civil rights since the abolitionist movement. "A nation divided against itself cannot stand," Abraham Lincoln told the American people at the height of the harrowing Civil War that would prove him right. And "an aggrieved class cannot remain half slave and half free," Frederick Douglass said twenty years after emancipation. The grievances of the African-American have always found expression in protest and rebellion, for the spirit of man instinctively resists a social order that would deny it its human essence. Black protest against the indignities of segregation, then, was inevitable, and not surprisingly would first be mounted against inequities in the very area of American life black Americans prized most dearly: education.

If the daily insults of segregation were an assault to the collective psyche of a people, nowhere were these indignities more glaring and damaging than in the public school system of the American South. "Separate" school accommodations typically meant wretched ones for blacks. It was not uncommon to find black schools overcrowded, housed in shanty shacks with no heat or running water, textbooks worn and outdated. In 1930 the average expenditure per school-age child was $45 per white pupil and

$14.95 per black pupil. Average Southern investment in public school property per school child amounted to $120.09 for whites and $29.62 for blacks. Figures for 1928–1929 disclosed that the average Southern white teacher's pupil load was 31 for a school term of 164 days, while the average black teacher instructed about 44 pupils for 144 days. The average white teacher's salary was $1,020, while the average black teacher earned $524.

These discrepancies became the focus of a twenty-year civil rights legal thrust for integration that made education the crucible in which assimilation would be forged. The idea of integrating public schools was not a new one in the twentieth-century South. Frederick Douglass had called for exactly that in the era immediately following the Civil War: "Educate the colored children and white children together in your day and night schools throughout the South," he said, "and they will learn to know each other better, and be better able to cooperate for mutual benefit."

Yet when the National Association for the Advancement of Colored People, which led the charge and ultimately won the battle to integrate America's classrooms, began the slow, arduous task in the 1930s of assembling an unassailable legal case that would challenge the very constitutionality of *Plessy vs. Ferguson,* "cooperation for mutual benefit" was not the impetus behind the action. What the NAACP dared to suggest and proceeded to prove constituted damages of the most vicious kind: psychological damages to a people whose esteem and sense of self were being slowly eaten away by the viper of segregation.

In 1935 Charles Houston, who was vice dean of Howard University's law school and legal consultant to the NAACP, began traveling through the South, and in particular South Carolina, documenting on film the vast disparities between black schools and white ones. The state of South Carolina spent ten times as much educating each white child as it did each black child. In Florida, Georgia, Mississippi, and Alabama, five times as much money was spent on the education of white children compared to what was spent to educate black ones. "Houston knew it would take more than statistics to convince a nation that segregation was wrong," writes Juan Williams in *Eyes on the Prize.* "His film showed what those statistics meant to the lives of some of the twelve million blacks in America, nine million of whom lived in the South. He contrasted the unheated cabins and tarpaper shacks that served as schools for black children with the tidy brick-and-stone structures where white children learned."

The NAACP's initial attack on segregation did not take aim against the notion of "separate-but-equal" per se. Rather, the strategy was to document the inferiority of black facilities and demand that *Plessy vs. Ferguson* conform to the letter of the law by making these separate black facilities truly equal to white ones. But by the time the Supreme Court heard *Brown vs. the Board of Education* in 1954, it was clear that "separate" could never mean "equal" in Southern America and that the very idea was coded in racism. The stage had in fact been set for a final and victorious assault to segregation four years earlier with two cases heard by the Court—each of them revealing the peculiar perniciousness the "separate-but-equal" doctrine could have on the black psyche.

The first involved a black mailman named Herman Sweatt who in 1946 applied to law school at the University of Texas in Austin. The school, which had no policy against admitting blacks, offered to set up a legal education program in three small basement rooms downtown, where Sweatt would be taught by part-time faculty members. The NAACP contended that Sweatt was not being offered a legal education equal to that which Texas provided for its white students.

The second case involved the matter of John McLaurin, a 68-year-old professor who had been refused admission to the doctoral program in education at the University of Oklahoma. The NAACP sued on his behalf, winning in a special district court that ordered the state of Oklahoma "to provide the plaintiff with the education he seeks as soon as it does for applicants of any other group." But when McLaurin finally entered the university, he was required to sit at a desk marked "reserved for colored." He was also forced to eat at a separate table in the cafeteria and was restricted to his own table at the library. Thurgood Marshall, then legal counsel to the NAACP, appealed the case to the Supreme Court, arguing that McLaurin was not being offered an equal education.

The Supreme Court handed down its decision on Sweatt and McLaurin at the same time, on June 5, 1950. Although it came close, the Court did not actually overturn *Plessy.* First it applied its findings only to graduate schools, not to public grade schools, but it did say that "separate but equal" had to be real—that the equality had to be genuine or the separation was unconstitutional. And this paved the way for the NAACP to prove that the consequences of segregation—the psychological, intellectual and financial damage—precluded equality.

Brown vs. the Board of Education represented not just one case but five, a broadside strike that hit segregation on several fronts. Leading off was the case of 7-year-old Linda Brown, who lived in Topeka, Kansas, and could get to the black school only by crossing the railroad tracks in a nearby switching yard and waiting for a raggedy bus. The NAACP decided to lead with this case to demonstrate that segregation's reach of inferiority extended beyond the deep South. The second case, *Briggs vs. Clarendon County,* attacked the grossly unequal conditions in the elementary school system of South Carolina's Clarendon County. Although there were three times as many black students as white students in Clarendon, white students received more than sixty percent of the educational funds. The per capita spending for white students was $179 per year, for black students, $43; and the net worth of the three black schools for 808 children was one-fourth the value of the two schools that housed white students.

The third case, *Davis vs. Prince Edward County,* challenged inequality at the high school level, specifically at Moton High School in Farmville, a town in Virginia's Prince Edward County. Moton had twice as many students as it was built for and had no cafeteria or gym. Completing the line-up was *Bolling vs. Sharpe,* an appeal challenging the effects of segregation in a Washington, D.C., junior high school; and *Gebhart v. Belton,* which challenged school segregation in the state of Delaware.

When suit was first brought against segregation in South Carolina's Clarendon County in 1950, the strategy was to prove both segregation's deleterious economic effects and its psychological ones. In a move considered highly unorthodox for a courtroom, the

NAACP's legal counsel, headed by Thurgood Marshall, invited New York black psychologist Kenneth Clark to come to Clarendon County to demonstrate through his famous "doll study" segregation's damage to children. Clark had for several years been studying the effects of segregation on children by using dolls in interviews with students. In Clarendon he tested sixteen black children, aged six to nine, using black and white dolls. Ten of the children looking at the dolls said they liked the white doll better. Eleven said the black doll looked "bad," while nine said the white doll looked "nice."

Most disturbing, however, was that when the children where asked to point to the doll "most like you," many became visibly upset when they had to identify with the doll they had just rejected. "These children saw themselves as inferior," Clark said, "and they accepted the inferiority as part of reality. Segregation was, is, the way in which a society tells a group of human beings that they are inferior to other groups of human beings in the society. It is really internalized in children, learning they cannot go to the same schools as other children, that they are required to attend clearly inferior schools than others are permitted to attend. It influences a child's view of himself."

On May 17, 1954, the United States Supreme Court agreed with this assessment and ruled in *Brown vs. the Board of Education* that "in the field of public education 'separate-but-equal' has no place." Reading the majority opinion, Chief Justice Earl Warren said: "Does segregation of children in public schools solely on the basis of race, even though the physical facilities and other tangible factors may be equal, deprive children of the minority group of equal education opportunities? We believe it does. To separate them from others of similar age and qualifications solely because of their race generates a feeling of inferiority as to their status in the community that may affect their hearts and minds in a way very unlikely ever to be undone." As a result, the opinion concluded, "Separate educational facilities are inherently unequal."

It was a sweeping, revolutionary ruling, one that overturned the ghastly *Plessy vs. Ferguson* decision of nearly sixty years before, and one that would begin to shatter all the other racist assumptions that had defined segregated black life. The victory would transform a race. During the next thirty years an African-American generation unlike any that had ever gone before would come of age and opportunities. It would defy the assumptions, exceed the expectations, and exhibit the new face of freedom. A face full of surprises and contradictions, hope and promise.

Four

THE INTEGRATION
GENERATION

*T*he pub in Little Rock's Excelsior Hotel this crisp, fall evening in 1987 recalls the sleek, hushed grandeur of antebellum glory. Its suede-smooth walls are hunter green, the color of money, trimmed in polished mahogany wainscotting that glistens in the misty dimness of Tiffany lamplight. Here waiters move quickly and silently, appearing only to accommodate, to serve, to soothe. It is the kind of place that evokes the Old South at its most powerful, most privileged—where one might expect to find gathered a state capital city's patrons of power: perhaps the mayor, or a judge, or even a state legislator.

This evening, as history and destiny would have it, the Excelsior has all three. The mayor of Little Rock is sitting in a corner at a small round table mixing a second glass of Scotch. It's been a long day and she's tired. There were the Little Rock Nine reunion activities earlier which consumed the entire day, exhausting but exhilarating. Hands to shake, a speech to make, photographs to take: with Ben Hooks of the NAACP; with Daisy Bates, still spry and beautiful at age 78, despite a stroke; with a young new liberal governor named Bill Clinton, and of course, with the celebrated

Nine themselves. There were the interviews to give—in a moment yet another one—and the questions to ponder: How has the South changed in the last thirty years? Did you ever dream you would live to see the day that you, a black woman, would become the mayor of Little Rock? How does that make you feel? What do you think it means?

Like most black women, Mayor Lottie Shackelford doesn't think of herself in the specific terms of success. At age 47, she is a dark brown, round, petite woman, both earthy and coquettish, a combination that has served her well in politics. In 1987 she is in her first term as mayor of Arkansas's capital city. It is a two-year position elected by the Little Rock City Board of Directors, on which Shackelford has served for eight years. Little Rock is one of those cities actually run by a city manager, so Shackelford's office is largely ceremonial, a figurehead spot. To earn a living she directs a program for Little Rock's Office of the Minority Purchasing Council. When she ran for mayor the first time in 1983, she lost, but since she was already on the seven-member Board of Directors—a "twofer," one of two blacks and one of two women—she bided her time, waiting to make a successful run four years later.

Tonight Her Honor is cooling out at the Excelsior, sharing some drinks and reflections with two good buddies: attorney Richard Mays, 45, a former state legislator, and attorney Perlesta (Les) Hollingsworth, 52, a former state supreme court judge. The discussion is about what it has taken for the three of them, Southern blacks born into segregation, to grow up to become successful at integrating—at becoming what King defined as the very essence of the integrated soul: "both free and destined."

The three friends, like the Little Rock Nine they grew up with, were in the vanguard of the integration generation: bred in the South, the offspring of stable, working-class two-parent families. And while there were certainly daily reminders of the blatant inequities of segregation, a secure family network kept inequality from engendering feelings of inferiority. Success among blacks is traditionally rooted in kinship—in familial ties that bind and affirm the race. The common bond is struggle. Because every black coming of age in segregated America, regardless of economic rank or class position, skin shade or family lineage, political persuasion or religious affiliation, instinctively understood the essential reality of being black in America, which was simply a recognition of the fact that "we are all in this together." The family, then, often extended beyond bloodlines. The neighbor down the street assumed the role of parent when needed, and black teachers became exacting masters demanding the best of their students, for individual black achievement represented collective black achievement.

If segregation was designed to reinforce inferiority, it also became the potent force that galvanized a race to strive, to achieve, to succeed, to prove its humanity. "Remember, you must always be a credit to the race," every striving black parent has told a black child at some time. Of course, there have always been "credits" to the race, strong black men and women who raised strong black children, instilling in them the oldest of the black lessons: race doesn't *have* to be an obstacle to success.

It is a lesson that three friends who grew up to become pillars of their community, influential and powerful despite being black, have apparently learned very well.

SUCCESS AND THE BLACK FAMILY

Richard Mays, Les Hollingsworth, and Lottie Shackelford

Richard Mays is a trim and handsome caramel-colored man who exudes the kind of confidence born of privilege. His father was always in business, owning a restaurant, a liquor store, and real estate. But Mays says it wasn't until he and his brother became teenagers and started socializing that he realized they were different from most other blacks. "We had a bigger house, for one thing. And my brother had a car." And while he did not consider his family rich, Mays never had to worry about money. It was understood, for instance, that he could go to college on financial aid supplied by his father.

Les Hollingsworth, by contrast, "knew that when I was ready to go to college, if I didn't get a scholarship, I wouldn't be able to go because there wasn't enough money." Yet the perception during Hollingsworth's growing up was that he came from "a family of means." His parents divorced in 1940, when he was 4, and he moved with his mother to her parents' house, where his grandfather ruled with tribal authority. "My grandfather was in business for himself as a housing contractor. And it was perceived that he did very well because we lived in a white neighborhood, and he got a lot of job contracts on houses in the neighborhood. But I knew the reality. I knew there was not much money because we worked on an extended-family basis. My grandfather took care of his brother and his cousins, and he sent my mother back to school after her divorce, and was also letting another daughter live with us."

What the family lacked in money, however, was more than compensated for by the legacy of a strong black patriarch. "I had a lot of self-esteem," Hollingsworth says simply. "I was encouraged to go to undergrad school, to law school, or whatever. I was told I could compete with anyone. I thought I could compete with the world."

In 1958, ten years after President Harry Truman ordered the desegregation of the military, Les Hollingsworth was drafted. "That was the first time I had ever been in a desegregated situation," he says. "I was sleeping next to white people, and I was eating with them, and we took tests together. Everything was done in alphabetical order, so what your last name was determined who you would be sitting next to or sharing a bunk with. There were also a lot of noncommissioned officers who were black and who were in charge of whites. And in basic training, they had a lot of power. When they said something you jumped, and you said 'Sir,' whether you were black or white. One of the things about the service then was that most of the whites were from a lower socioeconomic class, while blacks were from all class backgrounds. And that's because draft boards didn't draft anyone but blacks and poor whites."

Indeed, for most blacks coming of age in segregated America, there was always integration to some extent with poor whites. Recounts Lottie Shackelford, who grew up in a family of four with a father who was a truck driver and had a janitorial business on the side: "I grew up in a neighborhood that was integrated in one sense —blacks lived on one side of the street and whites lived on the other side of the street. It was really not an issue that I thought about much, but being in the South then, you didn't challenge the system that much. You used the areas that were open to you and didn't do a lot of thinking about it.

"I came along at a time when nobody talked about whether or not you were poor. We never had any financial worries, so to speak, because whatever it seemed we needed we could have. My father was in an unusual profession for a black man at that time. He was a union truck driver, a Teamster, and truck drivers made more money than teachers—they still do. If he came home in the evening after work and you told him you had to have a black skirt, the next day you would have a black skirt. You just didn't think about it. As my sister once said, 'As long as all of us had brand new bikes, I knew we were rich.' "

But even relatively prosperous black children were not immune from racism's pernicious effects. It is a subject that Shackelford does not like to discuss even now as she remembers going as a youngster to department stores in Little Rock where she and her sister could not eat at the lunch counter or try on clothes in the dressing rooms. "Somehow I knew the situation [segregation] couldn't remain like that—that it wouldn't remain like that. It just didn't make any sense. But it never did really made me feel bad, and I'll tell you why. I had a very good support system from my family. I think children of my generation, rather than being taught we were different or that life was not fair, we were taught to get a good education. It was never said that we needed to go to inte-grated schools or anything like that; we were always just told to get an education and then opportunity will be provided for you."

Unlike civil rights, education can never be taken from you; knowledge is eternal, immutable. This message was driven home in hundreds of subtle and not-so-subtle ways by black parents throughout America, many of whom had little formal schooling themselves and thus revered education with near-holy devotion. The message was certainly not lost on the mayor of Little Rock or her two friends. But what distinguishes their background is the ordinary and inordinate sense of well-being they were fortunate to have grown up with. Successful children of the "integration generation" tended to start out more often with an ancestral blessing: the love and support of the family. They were more likely to have been born into strong black households, run by strong, caring black men and women, neither rich nor perfect, but always striving to be responsible. These men and women were sometimes Mother and Father, Mom and Dad, Mama and Daddy, sometimes not. They were Auntie and Nana, Cousin and Junior, Grandpa and Mrs. Washington down the street. The were the pastor and the teacher; the ones who looked out for you, took care of you, tried to teach you, tried to save you, watched your back, and slapped your butt. If you were black and lucky enough to have been born into such a family—such a community, such a support system—you stood a better chance than most of becoming the success of your greatest dreams.

Richard Mays doesn't consider his dreams to have been particularly great, but the accomplishments are nevertheless impressive. In 1973, at age 31, he was elected to the Arkansas State Legislature. And in 1979 he was named to the Arkansas State Supreme Court. Today he and Hollingsworth do business together and have equity in downtown Little Rock's Main Building, the kind of place whites might have tried to make their daddies enter through the back door thirty years ago.

Like his daddy, Richard Mays has raised a successful family, three daughters and one son, two of the children now in college, and has remained married to the same black woman for over twenty years. As sometimes happens in midlife, he has started to think about such things as what it takes to be a man today—to be black and male and successful in integrated America; to be a force of power and influence; to be a public figure, a man of the people.

Mays specializes in cases involving personal injury law. "I do a lot of them," he says. "I think you have to in order to make money practicing law as a black. I mean, I look at it like Robin Hood.

What we do is take from the wealthy insurance companies, and we take our part and give our clients a part." Mays gave up the more visible professions of judge and politician in 1981 to pursue the more lucrative practice of private law. "I still have an interest in politics. I just don't have an interest in being a candidate. I don't particularly want to be scrutinized the way candidates are today; you have to pay too much of a price. But I still want to serve."

Like his friend, Les Hollingsworth is also in private law practice and has served: first on the Little Rock City Board of Directors, and then, like Mays, as a judge on the bench of the State Supreme Court. It is the kind of historical coincidence that helps explain his natural affinity with Mays and their inevitable partnership. Hollingsworth, large, expansive, thoughtful, and tonight typically forthright, concedes that he makes about $100,000 annually in his practice. "I have been very successful," he says without guilt or shame or even particular pride. "I had no aspirations of being rich, but I wouldn't have been able to do what I wanted to do without money. I wanted to have more of an impact on social causes. You have to have influence and power, and I think you have to have money, probably, to have both of those. Or you have to be close to people with money. And you have to show some talent that they respect in order to use any influence or power. You can be close to them and not know that you had an influence because you don't take the initiative. However, I can communicate." This last assessment helps explain why Hollingsworth has been successful interacting with who he refers to as "they" and "them"—whites.

Black success is inevitably a function of how well blacks have learned to interact with whites—with those in the majority culture, those in power. Lottie Shackelford attributes some of her political success to the fact that she "truly likes people." Yet it is her capacity for judging and gauging people, and having good instincts about issues, that have made her a successful politician. Les Hollingsworth relates an incident about his friend that is telling: he and Lottie were dining one evening in the restaurant of this very hotel when a white man who recognized Shackelford came over to the table, rudely interrupting their conversation to buttonhole Lottie about an issue. Lottie smoothly dealt with the man's concerns and quickly sent him on his way. Les, however, sat smoldering at the affront, convinced that if Lottie were the white male mayor of Little Rock, there would not have been that kind of interruption.

For her part Shackelford viewed the man as simply a constituent (not even one she relied on for a vote) who needed tending to. The interruption was minor, not terribly irritating, and not to be taken racially or personally, though race and gender certainly came into play. Most successful blacks almost instinctively understand something about the nature of whites—their tendency to insinuate their presence in the midst of blacks, to assert a superiority of rights and claims regardless of the rank, station, or existing situation of the blacks being infringed upon. Shackelford agreed with her friend: the rude white man would not have been quite so rude to a mayor who looked like him. But that was beside the point. Lottie Shackelford is neither white nor male. She is, however, the mayor of Little Rock, which is the essential point. Shackelford understands that, operates from that, and is empowered by that.

Les Hollingsworth and Richard Mays also operate out of a sense of power, but for men as a group regardless of race, power tends to become more personal, a matter of pride, ego, and honor. Hollingsworth says with a trace of satisfaction that he could never had been one of the Little Rock Nine, stoic and almost docile in the face of racist abuse. "I'm not nice like Lottie," he says. "And I wouldn't have been any good at integrating. When white folks make me mad, I tell 'em off." Yet this is a man who has been quite successful at integrating—at getting elected by both blacks and whites, at being solicited by whites, courted by them, listened to—at being viewed as a full, capable human being with the power to make a difference in people's lives. A man like his grandfather. And what seems to make Hollingsworth most angry at white folks is their thinking that he could ever be anything *less* than a man like his grandfather.

Successfully integrated black men operate out of a natural sense of power: manhood is assumed, is proven when necessary, and is never to be disrespected. Successful black men have usually been fortunate enough to have had strong black fathers or father figures —strong black patriarchs who showed little black boys through word and deed how to be strong black men: how to take care of women, provide for children, protect the family, and advance the race. Richard Mays and Les Hollingsworth came from such men, which helps to explain how and why they grew up to be such men.

But success and power still do not surrender easily to black men and are often handled with fear and guilt when finally won. Mays doesn't buy the idea that successful black men are becoming an endangered species, but he does believe that despite integration many black men are still not entirely comfortable with power. "I think that's because they never had power and they don't understand how to seize power and how to use it when they have it. And there are a few people who have it and are afraid to use it. They don't think they should utilize their power in a beneficial way for either their community or themselves. As I see it, this is what power is all about. Use it in your self-interest."

What has ultimately made Lottie Shackelford, Richard Mays, and Les Hollingsworth successful is that they operate out of a natural sense of family as well as a natural capacity to persuade and influence and serve in the best interests of their people. Integration was legislated to remove the racial barriers that historically kept blacks from developing or exhibiting this capacity, and children of the integration generation who grow up to become successful tend to be the ones who are the most psychologically girded from the beginning, with a strong and powerful sense of who they are and where they come from. They have a sense of the family as well as the race, and an affirming sense of power. And that is perhaps what makes them the most emotionally prepared to take advantage of integration's democratic aim: opportunity. The opportunity to reach your highest potential, to live out your greatest dreams, regardless of race or color; to be free. As King has said, "Freedom is the chosen fulfillment of our destined nature." Or as the mayor of Little Rock puts it, "Without integration you don't have the opportunity to learn what your true capabilities are."

By the end of the eighties America had learned that when given an opportunity, blacks had a true political capacity that was awesome. On December 31, 1989, thirty-five years after the Supreme Court ordered integration, thus paving the way for voting legislation that would politically empower a generation, there were exactly 7,370 black elected officials holding public office throughout the land: one black governor, 310 black mayors (72 of them women), 415 state legislators, 439 court judges, 24 blacks in Congress. And one successful black candidate for President, a revolutionary first for a race that began its American history in slavery. It is the kind of monumental achievement that speaks to a clear and measurable change in fortunes—in opportunities, in attitudes. It also speaks to what never seems to change: the element of the struggle.

Ernest Green: The First Black to . . .

Ernest Green finds it a bit daunting that more than thirty years after he literally stormed the barricades with the eight other Little Rock Nine and the U. S. military to integrate Central High School, America can still tick off a litany of black "firsts." Yet here he is, in 1988 at age 46, a senior vice president, and the first black to occupy that position in the country's second largest investment banking firm.

Of all the Little Rock Nine, Ernest Green is characterized by Daisy Bates as the one who most clearly and from the beginning "saw the larger picture" in the struggle to integrate Central High School. The picture hasn't changed much. In 1958 Green became the first black to graduate from Central High School. In 1986 he became the first black to be named a senior vice president in the Shearson Lehman Hutton (now Lehman Brothers, a division of American Express). Green's position is senior banker, working in the area of public finance. He's been in the job a year and a half, and his Washington, D.C., office is a small one in a small suite, housed in a downtown office building ironically numbered 1776— the year America went to war with England in a fight for freedom.

Green terms investment banking "the last bastion that we have not been able to get into." Integration may have knocked down some racial barriers, but not all. Professionally, more blacks were given corporate opportunities during the thirty years following Ernest Green's high school graduation than at any point in American business history. But even as blacks integrate into mainstream occupations and professions historically denied them, real corporate power remains elusive. It is at the pinnacle of such power that the numbers tell the story. Among the country's 250 largest law firms in 1987, for example, fewer than 2 percent of the lawyers were black and only 1 percent of the partners were black—a scant 157 out of a total of 19,610. In accounting, fewer than one-fourth of 1 percent of the partners at the nation's major accounting firms were black in 1988: 37 out of 20,000. Within the country's top ten investment banking firms, there are not even ten black managing directors. And there is currently no black running a publicly held Fortune 500 company.

More significant than this minimal presence in top echelons of power in American business, however, is the fact that blacks now have a presence at all, for these are the very elite areas of power, profits, and privilege that were most tightly closed to black men and women prior to the Civil Rights Movement. Integration led to the opportunities that made it possible for African-Americans to start entering such fields, and blacks like Ernest Green were the most well-prepared and well-primed to take advantage of the opportunities.

Green, a medium-tall, slightly stooped, graying man whose tortoiseshell eyeglasses and quick and charming smile give him a boyish youthfulness, concedes that some of the value he brings to Shearson is precisely his visibility as one of the Little Rock Nine and his status as a symbol. "I figured if I'm going to be the symbol I should let it work for me. I mean, that's what everybody does. That's what maturity does. But if all I had in life was the fact that I went to Central High School, I'd get one big yawn. I always knew that I was going to be successful doing something."

Ernest was 13 when the Supreme Court ruled on *Brown vs. the Board of Education* in 1954. "I saw from the very beginning that this was something monumental. I didn't understand all the pieces of law, and like most thirteen- or fourteen-year-olds, I hadn't read the American Constitution from cover to cover. But I knew just from the reaction of the white press, the white politicians, and the white power structure that this was something the black community ought to get excited about.

"I came out of a family and neighborhood of schoolteachers. My father was a janitor in the post office, and my mother and my aunt and my sister were all teachers. My mother taught for about forty years, stopping for six or seven years when my brother and I were born. But both she and my aunt worked in the system for a very long time. They're the people who epitomized a lot of the quiet revolution. They were never going to get out and go to the barricades, but they were the ones who always told you you were as good as anybody else, and that even though you were living in a segregated city or environment, you could compete, keep up with them [whites], and you had to work to overcome segregation. We had been drilled, taught that doing well in the classroom was an important quality. You were expected to achieve. These were silent, hardworking, quiet but proud black people."

Green recalls one Fourth of July in Little Rock as a youngster when he and his family were sitting in a park listening to a concert. "It was the kind of thing all small towns do to celebrate Independence Day. But I remember some concert officials came up and told us we couldn't sit in the park and enjoy the music. The concert was for whites only. My mother always taught us to use that incident as an example of what was wrong with the system. It was wrong. We had to change it. And that always stuck in my mind. We knew this [segregation] existed because we were black, but we also knew that it didn't make any sense.

"By the time I was five or six I already knew that my mother had what we call 'Southern coping skills.' Black folks, at least the black middle class, had lots of coping skills to get through the day. For instance, in the downtown department stores, sales clerks who would know a woman's name when she used a credit card always addressed black women by their first names, okay? Well, my mother made sure her store credit cards only read 'Mrs. Green' so the clerks would have to address her like that. She was always ready to tell clerks they didn't know her well enough to call her by her first name. My mother was also part of the black teachers' group back in the forties who had to fight for pay equity because their salaries were significantly lower than white teachers'. These experiences seem small, but they were cumulative and they made me feel if given the opportunity, I wanted to change a piece of my existence in Little Rock. To me, life was terrible."

Green's opportunity to change a piece of his existence came in 1956, the year the Little Rock school board submitted its plan for school integration. In the spring of 1957 the board requested that any blacks who lived near Central High School and who were interested in attending Central submit an application. He recalls, "Hundreds of us did. But as summer rolled around there were fewer and fewer who were part of the process—who still wanted to be considered. Part of the reason was the possibility of it being dangerous, but I think also—which was the legacy of a lot of things in the South—there were just few black people willing to be risk-takers. I mean, it was a big unknown. The worst case scenario was that you could be killed. But you could also lose your job, your house, all that you worked for. Our parents were really the heroes. I was just going to do my thing. I was going to storm the barricades.

"I didn't have any sense of the danger that occurred. I figured it would be uncomfortable, but I could deal with the discomfort in relationship to what I saw as the bigger picture. Now, my bigger picture was this: the general complaint from the white establishment was that integration was something that the federal government was forcing on the child. Those who were black in Little Rock (I don't know about blacks in the rest of the country) were happy with their lot. And that if these social scientists and cultural engineers didn't impose all this, everybody would be happy as things are. Nobody wanted to change. I said 'Bull. That's not the way I feel.' And I thought if all the blacks kids dropped out of volunteering to go to Central, maybe that would make the prophecy self-fulfilling. I thought Central was clearly a better educational facility than the black high school. Not because people worked harder, but because the Little Rock school board was putting in more money, more books, more services. More everything. It was a case in point that separate-but-equal did not exist."

By June 1957 Green's aunt, who worked as a guidance counselor at the black high school, was told that Ernie's name was high on the list of kids being considered to attend Central. He was working that summer at the Little Rock "Jewish" country club, so designated because whites in Little Rock in 1957 didn't admit Jews to their country clubs. A white youth with whom Green had worked and become friendly at the club came up to him the day it was revealed in the city newspaper that Ernest Green was among the nine black teenagers chosen to attend Central. "He was practically in tears. Enraged. 'How could you?' he said. 'How could you allow yourself to be used as one of the troublemakers, one of the integrators?' At that point I said to myself, Now, something's going on here. I don't know all that's going on, but this is about more than going to school. And if I can last out this year, two things I know. One is, they'll never be able to say Central is an all-white school, because somebody black will have graduated from it. And two, that the picture will never be the same again. I mean, some bells or something in my head went off and said, This is about more than just going to class."

That 1957–58 school year, Ernest Green's senior year, turned out to be more like going to work than going to class. "I saw it as a job from eight in the morning till three in the afternoon. It was not the most pleasant job, but I was going to this job and I was going to last out the job. You learned to live for the weekend and for holidays. My salvation was that I could put things in perspective. If I lasted until Christmas break, then I had a breather. And if I lasted until Easter there was another breather. And then from Easter on it would be clear sailing because that was the last quarter mile. All I had to do was get this diploma in May, and after that they could do whatever they wanted to. But one thing they couldn't do was say nobody black had ever graduated from Central. And I guess that's been one of the motivating things for me. Black people cannot allow whites to have any institution that remains only white. We gotta be in every nook and cranny that exists."

Ernest Green obviously brings more than status and symbolism to his job at Shearson. His career has been distinguished by a number of public service, political, and influential positions that have resulted in the kinds of contacts that are the cornerstone of modern dealmaking. After graduating from Central High School on May 18, 1958, Green attended huge, predominantly white Michigan State University on a full academic scholarship. He received a master's degree in sociology from the school in 1964, then took a job in New York with the A. Philip Randolph Institute, where he spent thirteen years working as an administrator for a youth employment program. From 1977 to 1980 he served as Assistant Secretary of Labor in the Carter Administration.

It was while a student at Michigan State and president of the campus NAACP that Green met his first wife, a white student who also belonged to the NAACP. They married while Green was in graduate school and divorced in 1973. His present wife is black. "I've gone through the forty-year cycle of two marriages," he says with a laugh.

Three of the Little Rock Nine married interracially, an incidence that could certainly be considered higher than "coincidental." Green attributes part of this to the fact that once the Little Rock Nine graduated from Central High, all went to college, and many went away to big, "white" schools where most of their interactions were with whites. Also, they were young celebrities, and unlike their experience at Central, they found themselves greeted with excitement and enthusiasm by sympathetic white college students.

But there was also another phenomenon at work, one having to do with the psychology of oppression. "We as black people seem to have less difficulty separating oppression by white groups from oppression by white individuals," Green contends. "All of us had experienced oppression by white groups, and probably when we met white individuals who didn't appear to us to be the oppressor, we were able to develop extended relationships out of that."

This was due to the tendency of an oppressed class to react more favorably when treated with kindness or respect by a member of the oppressor class. As Green says, "If all of your experiences are framed by these terrible relationships, then you meet a group of people who are not the oppressor, you find it easier. You can let go, let down your guard, and feel like you're being recognized as a human being." And that simple recognition is frequently more powerful, more potent, more seductive when it comes from a member of a group that has historically despised you.

At the time he was approached by Shearson to join the company Ernie Green had been partners for three years in a general management consulting firm with a black colleague from his Cabinet days. "By the time I left government in 1981 I had decided it was time for me to own my own business. One of the constant complaints I had heard from white men was that, you know, we [blacks] weren't risk-takers. We only wanted to live off what was safe and secure; and as long as government was providing it, it was all right."

For Green the decision to give up entrepreneurship and reenter corporate life was based on two significant factors: "One, this is obviously a major-league financial dynasty with a lot more resources to pursue the kinds of things that I thought I wanted to." Second was the fact that there were still too few blacks working in investment banking, an area that was having an increasing impact on cities and other municipalities—communities in many instances now run by black elected officials or by white elected officials put in office by the power and clout of the black vote. "What I basically do for Shearson is help develop new business for them and help in their marketing in major cities," Green says. His native Little Rock is a case in point. "The governor of Arkansas, Bill Clinton, is someone I have worked with on a number of projects. The first time he ran for office I helped get him elected, and a lot of people who are in his cabinet are people that I've known. And because of the ties at home as well as the contacts that I've kept up through business and other professions, it gets to be a network. You've got a lot of coverage, a lot of resources, and the ability to do a lot of business."

Ernest Green has managed to become in the thirty years since he graduated from Central both a business success and a political success—a black man who uses personal power, political influence, and promotor-type visibility within a vast network of professional contacts, old friendships, and patronage relationships to get things done. He grew up to become something perhaps even he never dreamed: a successful good-old-boy.

Most good-old-boys, however, are still white, and Green contends that one of the things that has made him successful interacting with white men is the fact that "I'm a quick study. I mean, I can distinguish a white who's willing to be open. I have a category I call the Larry Bird white person, which is someone who has been close enough to black people to know things like how you fix your hair—the kind of nuances that a segregated life kept at bay. He is the white person who thinks he knows you, and in some ways he does. He is perceptive, and you have to learn how to read him. The old type I grew up with you could read pretty clearly. They would reveal their feelings on their sleeves. You knew precisely where they were headed and where they weren't, and you took it from there."

Green does not necessarily view the white man today as his enemy, but as he points out, "He is certainly someone you've got to be competitive with. You've got to demonstrate at all times that you are his equal. That you can look him in the eye and not blink." The major impact of integration on men such as himself, Green believes, was that it provided opportunity, which in turn eliminated a lot of the anger blacks felt in being shut out. "People like me got pushed by other people to achieve something. We were made to feel that at any point in time there was nobody else as good as we were. And that to me may be the most important factor in integration, because the older I get the clearer it is to me that success is not all about book knowledge; it's about being confident within yourself. And about being willing to struggle."

Yet confidence and the will for the struggle are the very qualities that integration may have now diminished within the black race. "We've obviously paid an enormous price for integration," Green says slowly. "What made it possible for me to operate in a very tight, aggressive segregated system was being drilled day in and day out with what the struggle was about. Now that doesn't exist." Nor is the sense of community the same. "You get six black people over the age of 40 in any one room for longer than ten minutes who weren't born in the North, you will, before the eleventh minute, start a conversation about missing the community factor—the kind of teachers they had when they were growing up, the kind of parental authority, the neighbors, the extended family that if you ventured a half block from the neighborhood and Mrs. Jones saw you, she was on the phone calling your mother, saying, 'I saw him and he don't belong up there.'

"The second thing integration demonstrated is that as you challenge the system, it doesn't just stop with schools. I mean, it extends to include all other arrangements and relationships. Schools, housing, jobs, politics, recreation. The avid segregationists argued that integration would destroy the sum of their lives, which it did. Once you open Pandora's box and let the genie out, you can't put the genie back in."

Indeed. The genie unleased by integration broke down barriers everywhere, proving that when opportunities are presented, there is no stopping that old black magic.*

---

*In May 1991, Ernest Green was named a managing director of Lehman Brothers.

GETTING
OVER

*If you can't bear no crosses,
You can't wear no crown.*
African-American spiritual

Five

✌

TO BE YOUNG, GIFTED, AND QUALIFIED

There are two kinds of Negroes—
those who obey, and those who don't.
Carolyn Sawyer, ABC News, 1988

*S*he refers to herself as "the other Sawyer" at ABC News. Not blond, not white, not Diane. Which is fine, because by the time she was 12, Carolyn Sawyer knew exactly who she wanted to be like when she grew up—and it was Monica. *I want to do that!* Sawyer remembers shouting when she was a kid as she pointed to the television screen the first time she saw Monica Kaufman, Atlanta's first black anchorwoman, delivering the news in 1976 on Channel 2, the city's ABC affiliate.

Now, twelve years later in 1988, Carolyn Sawyer is 24, and she has done exactly that—reported the news, anchored the news, served her time, and paid her dues in the minor-league markets of Spokane, Washington; Columbia, South Carolina; and Atlanta, Georgia—and landed in the big time of New York, New York's prime time. It has been a winding, rugged route, this journey to network news and to what is considered the pinnacle of success in broadcast journalism. Sawyer, who has been in this position nearly a year, is one of 164 correspondents at ABC News, though she has the added label of being one of two "minority trainees" in ABC's new minority training program, created like others in American business during the past twenty years to harness and package black potential. Sawyer has been in training much of her life, it seems, for this shot, and as she says with the combination of good humor and wry sarcasm that gives her youth its cynical edge, its rueful wisdom, "Potential for me means if I were white, Barbara Walters might be in trouble."

By the time young blacks like Carolyn Sawyer came of age during the waning days of the Civil Rights Movement in the mid-seventies, there had developed a new class of older black professionals—spirit guides, you might say—who had pioneered the path to integration and become role models and mentors to a new generation of success-oriented, ambitious black youth. This was a very different breed of black young people—driven, confident, full of the promise and the hope engendered in a society striving to be integrated. Their dreams of achievement had not been extinguished by the degradation of slavery, nor their expectations stunted by the restrictions of segregation. Sawyer's generation grew up taking certain assumptions for granted—that opportunity, if not unlimited, would certainly be provided if one were prepared; that race would not be an obstacle to success if one could demonstrate "merit," if one were "qualified." And for this generation there were more examples of black success to draw upon than at any point in American history. Indeed, as integration pioneer Ernest Green said, the struggle to integrate did not stop with education.

By the end of the seventies there were such positive role models as black mayors, black school superintendents, blacks heading large city hospitals and running powerful labor unions. There were blacks of power, influence, and visibility in banking, advertising, law, medicine, business, and the media. You could turn on the television news in any American city and there would no doubt be an African-American anchoring the news, announcing the sports, forecasting the weather, or reporting from the field. There was Ed Bradley of CBS's "60 Minutes" and Bryant Gumbel of NBC's "Today" show, two black men earning in excess of $1 million who coanchored the two most popular news shows in America. In 1968, when Carolyn Sawyer was 5 years old, blacks made up less than 1 percent of the employees working in the media. Twenty years later blacks comprised 7.7 percent of the staff in American broadcast stations. And in 1987, 27 percent of the black women working in television were local on-air reporters. This was the gradual yet revolutionary kind of change in odds that suddenly placed a 12-year-old black girl's dream of television news anchoring within the reach of possibility.

Carolyn Sawyer: Breaking into the Business

It is lunchtime, and Carolyn Sawyer, stunning in a close-fitting white wool jersey dress and matching coat is riding down the escalator of ABC's cavernous chrome-and-glass domed headquarters building on Manhattan's West 66th Street. As she steps off the moving stairway and onto the lobby's marble floor, its sunlit brilliance evoking Emerald City in the middle of Gotham, Sawyer moves with the kind of ease and boldness that has come to characterize urban confidence—not quite a swagger, but an assured long-legged stride. At five feet nine inches tall and one hundred and thirty pounds, she is at once imposing and striking. Her short hair is brushed straight back, exposing a tawny-smooth complexion, a full, round face, and a sensual mouth that can't hide a trace of fierce determination.

As is true for most broadcasters, Carolyn Sawyer's real beauty is her voice, big and rich and confident and smooth as fine silk. It has been clearly trained to enhance its natural power and reveals no hint of accent, racial or regional. Over lunch in a noisy French café Sawyer speaks with clipped, articulate precision, punctuating her conversation with odd, old-fashioned endearments such as "honey" and "dear" to make a point. The effect is Southern—comforting, commanding, seductive—and a bit off-putting, hearing what sounds like the voice of age and reason, experience and seasoning, resonating from the mouth of a 24-year-old. Yet as Sawyer herself explains it, in that voice which is currently earning her $65,000 a year, "I may be young, but I have an old mind."

Sawyer was born in California but spent her early childhood living in Europe and Taiwan as the daughter of an Air Force pilot before moving to Atlanta in 1975, when her father retired from the service. "I've heard this before, but didn't believe it until I'd felt it," she says, explaining the early influences that were to help shape her success. "You hear people say that black youngsters need black role models who are visible when they're growing up. Well, Carol Simpson [a reporter for NBC News] was the first one for me. Growing up, I knew her name and thought she was sharp. But when I came to Atlanta—you know, *the* city in the South and the first to have a black anchorwoman—I saw Monica Kaufman. Monica was on the air Monday through Friday, which is the greatest visibility. And honey, there is just something about being somebody up there anchoring the news. I saw this woman, and I looked at her every day for five years, and I said, by gosh, I can do it.

"I loved to write, and I knew I had a good speaking voice—when I first moved to the South everyone told me how 'properly' I spoke—so I said to myself, Well, now, what if I put the writing and the speaking together and work in the communications medium, doing broadcast? One of the first things I did in high school was convince the band director to let me announce at halftime for the band. It was an experience I'll never forget; it helped me with a lot of stagefright. But there's no doubt in my mind that the visibility of just seeing black folks out there doing the news is what made me think, *I can do that too.*"

If visible role models gave Sawyer the inspiration and impetus to pursue her dream, her own drive and ambition put her in a state of readiness for success. By the time she graduated high school at age 16, Sawyer had talked to as many people "in the business" as she could, trying to figure out where they had gone to school, what they had studied, and what, if they had it to do all over again, they would do differently. Was there something they had missed? Would they do it the same way? How did they break into the business?

"I ran across a black newscaster in Atlanta who had come out of Washington, in Seattle. He had gone to Evergreen State College. However, he didn't recommend Evergreen. He recommended Washington State University, which didn't just teach communications theory but gave practical experience. So many other communicators had told me it does no good to go four years to anybody's school and sit up and read all these books, because when you get out, employers what to see what you can do."

Sawyer heeded the advice of the broadcaster from Seattle and headed for the university town of Pullman, Washington, in the fall of 1980. She pursued a double major in political science and communications. "I did everything I could get my hands on. I also kept up with whatever was going on with black journalists. There was a chapter of the National Association of Black Journalists in Spokane, seventy miles away, which I belonged to, and one of the black girls who was a reporter and a weekend anchor at station KHQ came and talked to our group. I made contact with her. As it turned out, she ended up leaving to go to Birmingham to take another job. And I knew the news director at her station was looking for somebody to fill her place. He wasn't so much concerned with qualifications— which is quite often the case, and it's sad—and I think he knew I wasn't quite ready to fill her place. But he put me on as a desk assistant, and I worked my way up to the weekend anchoring job."

Sawyer was just 19 when she became a reporter and weekend anchor at station KHQ, the NBC affiliate in Spokane, Washington state's second-largest city. "This is a business where you're supposed to start out in the wee-wee-bitty market, and then get back to Spokane," she says with a deep chuckle. Based on its population of about 300,000 people, Spokane was a 70 market, considered a decent size and certainly an above-average beginning point for a 19-year-old black girl. "You couldn't do better as a place to start," Sawyer confirms, "and I had all these wonderful co-workers. I was the only black person, the token."

Yet despite the support of co-workers, there were higher-ups at the station who thought a 19-year-old still in college should be starting out somewhere down around a 250 market. Sawyer had actually started working for station KHQ in November of 1983, during her senior year. She left school to work full time in Spokane and completed her bachelor of arts degree via correspondence school that summer, finishing college in three years. Even so, the station's executive producer didn't think she was "qualified." As Sawyer viewed it five years later, "If the executive producer had had a say in the decision [the station's news director had hired her], I probably wouldn't have been his choice. Bess, the girl I replaced, was fairer-skinned than me and from Spokane, and I think it makes a difference when you're in that environment [covering local news] to be from the area."

Carolyn Sawyer's fate, then, probably like that of anyone else caught in a web of corporate politics, personal egos, and parochial biases, was sealed before she even had a chance to prove herself. "I was getting crazy assignments because they didn't think I was qualified," she recalls. "Things like covering night meetings, car accidents—garbage. I finally went out on a story they had given me one day—a water main had broken at a roller rink. It had been snowing all winter long and I had on these black pumps because I was so tired of wearing rubber shoes. I looked at that water, the water looked at my shoes, and I said to myself, Lord, Jesus Christ, there must be someplace I can go and not be doing these kind of stories. This is not why I got into this business."

That Christmas, when Sawyer went home to Atlanta, she ran across an ad in a black magazine from a television station in Columbia, South Carolina, that was looking for a reporter. Minorities were encouraged to apply, the ad stipulated. The next day Sawyer made the three-hour drive to Columbia, walked into the news director's office, and told him simply that she was the person he needed. "It would be a lateral move, because at this point I had been anchoring the news on weekends in Spokane. But I told him I was the person he needed to hire and it would be the best move he could ever make." Sawyer then drove back to Atlanta. "I was so impatient, waiting to hear, and I didn't want to go back to Washington state without knowing. The news director had to get approval for hiring from his corporate board."

Days passed with no word, and on the day Sawyer was to fly back to Washington, she called the news director. "Listen," she told him with the forced bluntness of one attempting to make a lie sound convincing. "I've got another job offer and I need to know what's happening with you, because I'm about to get on this plane."

"Carolyn," the news director said quietly, "I haven't met with my board yet, but I'm convinced you're the right person."

"Fine," Sawyer responded. "When I get back to Washington, I'll call you and we'll work out the money." Carolyn Sawyer was then 20.

Sawyer got the job and and stayed with station WIS, the NBC affiliate in Columbia, two and a half years before leaving one day in 1986 following her breakup with "the man I thought I was going to marry" to take another job in Atlanta as a news reporter. The new job, as fate would have it, was with Channel 2, the station where Monica Kaufman still reigned on the air as the six o'clock and eleven o'clock news anchor queen. "It was a great experience," Sawyer says of becoming the colleague of an idol. Yet it was in her own hometown of Atlanta, the city that had come to epitomize the "New South" with its black-run city government, its Atlanta University complex of prestigious black institutions, and its burgeoning business opportunities for blacks, that Carolyn Sawyer would come face to face with an old bugaboo still haunting both blacks and women: salary discrimination.

Sawyer began at station WSB as a nighttime reporter, doing live shots for the six o'clock and eleven o'clock news. "When I came in they realized that this Negro had potential," she says with grim humor. "Then one day Monica decided she needed the day off for something and I filled in for her as anchor." The next thing Sawyer knew, the regular weekend anchor was fired and Sawyer was given her job—with no warning, no word, no welcoming. "The station managers sent a note to the corporate board saying I was the new weekend anchor. I found out about it in the newspaper. I never even got a courtesy note." Nor did Sawyer get a raise. Her $30,000 salary was exactly half that of the weekend anchor at the competing station across the street. Its weekend show was third in the ratings. Station WSB's, on the other hand, was number one six months after Sawyer took over as weekend anchor. "I ain't seen a dime, honey," Sawyer says of the difference a number one rating made in her paycheck. "Now, I was ready to kill these boys, so I went in and said, 'Look, I happen to know that the weekend anchor at the number three station makes $60,000 a year.' Granted, she had been there five years, but I'm sorry, number three and making $60,000. Come on!"

Management offered Sawyer another $6,000. "I pretended I didn't hear it. I went back to negotiate again, thinking I'd give them another chance. They just hemmed and hawed, saying they didn't think I had enough experience. I finally said, 'I'm not anchoring another weekend at the station'—and I was serious. 'Consider me dead on the weekends, okay?' I told them. That was probably a mistake, because my grandmother always said, 'Never tell them what you're going to do.' But I thought it was the least I could do. Anyway, they thought I was kidding."

To prove she wasn't kidding, Sawyer stayed home the following weekend. She had developed the flu, largely as a result of being tired and under pressure. When management called her at home on Monday, she threatened to quit. And when she went into the station later that day, she was offered a settlement: the station would buy out the remaining year and a half on her contract, but it wanted a stipulation added—she would agree not to work in the Atlanta market for one year. Sawyer quickly called her attorney, who told her such a restriction was illegal and advised her to threaten the station with a lawsuit. "What they were doing to me was an atrocity. Here I was, a strong enough anchor to fill in for Monica Kaufman, who I think at that time was making about $250,000 a year. So how could they consciously pay me only $30,000? That shit would have looked mighty funky in court."

Management apparently agreed, and in the end a weary and demoralized Sawyer left the station with a settlement worth $10,000. She paid off all her bills and then took off for Hawaii, where she spent a month lying on the beach, contemplating her future. "I thought, you know, for $30,000 I could run a McDonald's or a pretzel stand, or at worst sell fruit in a hula skirt. I said, I'm 23 years old, what have I got to lose?"

IN THE MATTER OF BEING QUALIFIED

What Carolyn Sawyer had clearly lost by age 23 was her youthful optimism. Her dream of success had a nightmarish underside and a psychic price. Unlike whites, for whom success is frequently a matter of contacts, connections, family combinations, and in the end simply the circumstance of being born white, black success seems always to carry certain prerequisites, chief among them the requirement that a black first prove he or she is "qualified" for achievement. The very notion of becoming qualified, of course, assumes an element of deficiency, a lacking of the skills, training, values, talent, or intellect that ordinarily renders one fit for accomplishment. But this idea of becoming qualified, of being made "fit for success," as it were, is yet another psychological assault to black aspirations, and one that has been frequently used to undermine much of the integrationist thrust for equal opportunity. It is the old notion of black inferiority updated for an era of liberal sentiment: "We'll give blacks an opportunity, if we can just find some who qualify."

This was the very idea behind many of the minority "training programs" American businesses created during the past two decades to "find" and develop black talent. Since race discrimination had historically kept blacks out of both the corporate mainstream and most professional positions, African-Americans, the thinking went, were not as well prepared as those in the majority society to succeed in these areas. They needed to be remediated, ameliorated, or otherwise "trained" for success. Young blacks in particular who showed "promise" and "potential" were especially ripe for such training and help in playing catch-up. The premise was not altogether unfounded, though it was seldom acknowledged that whites also benefitted from many of these training programs. As the decline in American productivity has proven, being white does not necessarily equate with being qualified. A generation of successful blacks would turn training programs to their own advantage, however, and actually advocate for them when it meant greater access to certain high-profile, high-paying positions.

Ironically, it turned out to be a training program that would bring Carolyn Sawyer back from Hawaii and the pit of despair— back from what she calls "that awful feeling you get when somebody is trying to kiss you and you don't want them to," that awful feeling you get when you are being exploited, misused, undervalued, underpaid. Sawyer's rescue call came from Ray Nunn, then Southeast Bureau Chief for ABC in Atlanta, who had tracked her across the country and the Pacific Ocean to the 808 area code number she had left on her answering machine when she had fled Atlanta after quitting station WSB. The two were friends, and Sawyer even considers Nunn her godfather, though the relationship was tested when Sawyer refused to heed Nunn's advice and stick it out at the station.

"Management had made me a counteroffer to leaving," Sawyer says, explaining the final assault that made her quit. "The alternative was, we could rip up the settlement and I would stay, continuing to make $30,000. And I asked, 'Doing what?' Because, you know, I would have stayed and just been a reporter, but not a reporter *and* a weekend anchor for $30,000. But they said to me, 'You'll do whatever we tell you to do.' Just like that. And I said, 'Oh, no. This is crazy.' But you know, Negroes were expected to obey. I took two days to think about it and called up all my mentors. Ray Nunn, who had helped me get the job at WSB, called Thursday morning as I was getting dressed to go in. I had already said no to management and Ray was calling to tell me to stay because questions might come up later over what really happened. I thought, Oh God . . . I couldn't even get my blouse on. I felt paralyzed. You know, that feeling you get when you become mentally paralyzed with something so awful you can't even think about it. I started crying out, *Dear God, this is everything that I worked for, but at the same time, it's nothing.*"

Now here was Ray Nunn, on the phone to Sawyer in Hawaii a month later, telling her to hurry back to Atlanta. "Listen, girl," he said. "There's been some movement on the positions we were talking about, and I want you to see the woman who will be doing the overseeing." Nunn was part of a black advisory board at ABC that fought to have the company create a minority training program that would help place blacks in network positions. ABC had consented, and Nunn was now calling to tap Sawyer for one of the four slots, a correspondent's position with ABC News.

"No matter what you hear in this business about Ray Nunn, he is a *wonderful* man," Sawyer says with rising conviction. "He's the only black bureau chief with ABC, and they're afraid of him. White people don't know how to take him, and black people probably question his motives. But it's all bullshit. I've never doubted him, and I think it's good they're afraid of him, because he is a different breed of black man. He's from Yale, so they can't say he's dumb. He was a hellacious producer in Beirut, so they can't say he can't do the job. And he's the only black man to survive the crazy maze over here and move up. We became friends because we had a mutual friend in Columbia, South Carolina, his college roommate. You know, it's just getting to the point where we have those kind of connections."

Carolyn Sawyer has always cultivated such connections and used them well, drawing upon a vast network of peers and colleagues, mentors, friends, and family for advice, reinforcement, affirmation, and support. "People say, get a mentor. I say, get several of them. And then you balance. You take all of the information you can get and then decide what's the best information you've got." This attitude has helped to shape much of Sawyer's success, for such affirmation and support has contributed to her unflinching belief in her own potential, her own abilities. As a result, whenever either her age or her supposed inexperience get used as an excuse to discriminate or to imply that she is somehow not qualified, Carolyn Sawyer calls it as she sees it: "Bullshit."

"You know, I was in television for four and a half years," she says of the qualifications that got her into the ABC training program, "and overall, I did very well in TV. Now, at network my office is two doors away from a thirty-four-year-old white male correspondent who was never in TV before coming here. He worked at a newspaper, okay? That's fine, but the point is, he's *never* been in television." Nor has he ever been in a television training program. "But it's a different ballgame with them, you know," says Sawyer.*

PEOPLE GET WORTHY

Integration as a concept has its roots in the philosophy of equal opportunity, in the idea that all Americans, regardless of race, creed, or color, are to be given equal access to the kinds of opportunities that can result in citizens becoming self-actualized—in developing their potential to its fullest. Yet race discrimination and its subsequent damage to the black psyche has resulted in a curious corollary to integration, one that both reinforces the supposition of black inferiority and reveals the depth and scope of the damage: blacks must somehow be made "worthy" of opportunity. This is an idea that blacks and whites alike have bought into and unconsciously conspire to perpetuate, for at the heart of the struggle to integrate there has always been a black existential quest to be validated, to be confirmed as human, to be proven as equal.

This existential pursuit has taken varied forms and exhibited peculiar manifestations, yet the single overriding motivation has been the desire to demonstrate that despite the handicap of race, it is possible to become a "proper Negro." To be well groomed, well behaved, well spoken, well thought of, and, well . . . just plain well accepted. At its most elementary level, integration means black access to opportunity, but at its most profound social level, integration has meant black interaction with whites on a scale never before considered: as equals. The snag is that blacks find themselves perpetually in the position of having to prove that they

---

* Carolyn Sawyer left ABC News in 1989 and went to the Lifetime Television Network to anchor a daily news update and host a half-hour weekly news show. The station cut its news division in 1990, and Sawyer is now with WBZ-TV, an NBC affiliate in Boston, working as a general assignment reporter and as host of a weekly public affairs show.

deserve to be treated as equals, that they do indeed qualify for opportunity.

Of course, African-Americans are the only ethnic group that has ever been saddled with bearing this particular burden of proof. Opportunity has been the inalienable right and exercised prerogative of every immigrant group to arrive on these shores, be it the Irish farmer seeking relief from famine in Ireland in the nineteenth century or the Vietnam refugee fleeing war-torn Southeast Asia in the 1970s. It is only the former slave class of Americans, those brought to the United States by force and in chains, who still find that equal opportunity is not a thing to be automatically assumed.

Arnold F. Roane: Ready to Go at All Times

In January of 1988 the mile-high city of Denver is caught in the grip of blizzard and Bronco fever. *"Weeee will . . . weeee will . . . rock you! Weeee will . . . weeee will . . . rock you! Go-go-go Brr-r-r-roncos!"*

The commercial blares across the airwaves of every television station in Colorado's capital, its litany the chanting war cry of a city whose football team is headed for San Diego and Super Bowl XXII. Tickets to Denver Broncos home games are reportedly sold out through the year 2015. And except for the annual cattle show held at the Denver Hyatt during Super Bowl Week, nothing else even tries to compete for attention in this city seized with football madness in the winter of 1988.

Arnold Roane may be the only man in town who hasn't caught the fever, though the very first thing his mammoth office at the Martin Marietta Corporation connotes is precisely a football field. Its carpeted expanse runs at least thirty feet, accompanied by floor-to-ceiling windows that showcase in awesome, panoramic relief a riveting view of the Colorado Rockies outside. Martin Marietta's business is aerospace, yet its corporate building has been constructed in a chunk of Colorado mountain about 25 miles outside of Denver. The result is a futuristic steel-and-glass corporate underground carved in a labyrinth of endless, intersecting hallways, sliding glass doors, and massive metal columns built beneath rock and earth. Roane's office, though, is something of a fishbowl. While one wall is made entirely of window glass exposing the Rockies, the opposite wall, also made entirely of glass, exposes the public corridor and office cubicles outside the door. The effect is somewhat unsettling, these wall-to-wall, two-way looking-glasses through which to see and be seen.

From the hallway Roane can be seen this snowy afternoon standing at the other window in his office, gazing out at the Rockies. He is a compact, muscular, light-brown-skinned man elegantly dressed for success in tailored beige pants, a pale pink-and-white pinstriped shirt trimmed with white French collar and cuffs, solid gold cufflinks, and a wide navy patterned silk tie. He seems as finely polished as the cherry wood conference table in the middle of the room —nails manicured and impeccable, "good" hair closely cropped, still black and thick in midlife. Only the smooth, pensive face is beginning to show the fine, grainy lines of age and strain.

At 50 Arnold Roane exudes the quiet confidence and comfortable strength of the successful, seasoned executive, one who has little left to prove, for his major battles are behind him and he is still standing. An engineer by training, Roane has been with Martin Marietta for eight years and is currently director of administration for the company's astronautics group. In this $100,000-a-year position he is responsible for the $100 million worth of management connection services that are provided for the group each year.

Roane is just old enough to remember when qualified black men were denied such opportunities in the professional and technical fields. He was one of them. When he graduated from Penn State with a bachelor's degree in mechanical engineering in 1959, he joined the military, and when he got out he went to work for the federal government in Philadelphia because he couldn't find work in the private sector as an engineer. "You must understand that when I got my degree from Penn State, all the guys in my engineering class were white. When they went on job interviews, they got job offers. Well, I had twenty interviews and no offers. I was the laughingstock of the crowd."

In 1961, at age 23, Roane joined the General Electric Company in its Philadelphia plant, where he would spend the next nineteen years agitating for every advancement he made. "Every now and then the company would hire a black it thought was really outstanding," says Roane, explaining how General Electric came to hire him after he submitted his résumé three times. Moreover, with America rushing headlong into a competitive "space race" with Russia in the early sixties after the Soviet Union's launch of Sputnik, "There was a big drive on at GE to hire anybody with technical expertise—black, white, green, gray."

Even so, Roane's entry into General Electric "was tough, because in 1961 whites hadn't accepted blacks in the professional workforce." Roane was one of a handful of black professionals in a total work population at GE that at the time numbered around 140,000. Having neither mentors nor the example of other blacks who had done well at the company as models for achieving, he had to chart his own rocky course. "What I saw happen over my twenty years at GE is that it no longer became a problem for blacks to get in the door. Almost any corporation in the United States, no matter what color you are, if you are qualified, you can get in. The issue is really in moving up from entry-level positions into the beginning supervisory positions. We're always told we're not ready, that we need more training."

Roane was told this nearly every time he came forward to demand that he be promoted to the next level. Although he had a degree in engineering, he was hired as a designer with GE, one grade below the engineer's level. "Maybe that's where it all started for me. Maybe I said to myself, If you guys put me down, then I'm going to pull myself up. In the beginning I had goals, and I also was very aggressive in pushing. And I realized fairly quickly that I didn't want to stay in engineering—I wanted to get into management." Roane describes how he got his first promotion.

"I went to my manager and said, 'I want to be considered for the next level because I'm ready.'

" 'Well, we don't have any openings,' the manager said.

" 'What's that got to do with it?' I asked him.

" 'We've got the best people for the jobs,' he told me. I've already got managers.'

" 'Well, I think I'm better than some of them.' My tactic was to say, You said you wanted the best person for the job, and I think I'm better than somebody you've got. Now you put up or shut up. Either say I'm not better, or stop saying you want the best. And if you don't have the best person, then take the appropriate action."

This was the first of many confrontations Roane, then 25, would have at GE concerning the course of his career track, but he scored the first down and became the first black manager in the company's aerospace division. "But now my manager thinks he's done a great thing promoting me. Turns out I got the job because the other person they had in it—somebody who was brought in from the outside—had failed and nobody else wanted it. That happened a lot. Other people would get jobs and when things got really sticky, they'd say, 'Gee, let's call Arnold. We'll give it to him.' And there I was, and I would say okay. I was aggressive and I wanted to prove something."

What Roane wanted to prove was that he was qualified. And that he was willing to be trained. "One of the things management tells people, and sometimes it's true, is that you need to be rounded. 'You've still got some rough spots. So why don't you take this course?' And my feeling was, up to a point they're correct, and I'm going to take advantage of these [company training] programs. So whenever management would say, 'Gee, Arnold, you need training,' I'd say 'Ah!' because I already knew what courses I wanted to take."

In 1974 Roane applied for a Sloan Fellowship in the Sloan School of Management at the Massachusetts Institute of Technology. The program was a prestigious sabbatical for business executives, a paid leave-of-absence for one year, "time out to think, to travel, to become rounded." No General Electric employee had ever participated in the program, however, largely because GE had its own training and management facility in Crotonville, New York. Roane had been there several times himself and now felt he had run out of courses to take in house. Yet he also knew management would never agree to pay his salary for a year for him to go off to "round" himself at MIT—unless he went to them saying he had already been accepted into the program. He had, so he did. "How could General Electric turn down MIT?" Roane says with Machia-vellian delight. He had applied to MIT *before* getting GE's ap-proval, and once he was accepted, GE was forced into a save-face position of having to go along.

Roane would become very adept over the years in leading Gen-eral Electric in the direction in which he wanted his career to go, but confrontation took its toll. "After nineteen years I just got tired of it," he says now. "That's not a healthy, growing environment. My kids were in college and that was really one of my biggest priorities, to be able to send them to school and get them started. So with that in hand, I said, I don't really need this hassle every two or three years. I gotta go up and beat on the door to get promoted. After a while you get fed up with that. And I mean, you cannot force people to adopt you. If it doesn't happen voluntarily, it just won't happen. You can't force it."

And so in 1980, at age 42, with neither a golden parachute nor a concrete game plan, Arnold Roane bailed out of General Electric. The fact that he had risen to program manager in the company's computer printer business by the time he left made him more than trained and qualified to land at Martin Marietta. He concedes that he has had a much easier time of it at the aerospace firm, where as a director he is part of senior management. "I report to the guy that runs a $1.7 billion business. He's a senior vice president of the corporation and there's only one person between him and the chair-man, and that's the president." In the hierarchy this has made Roane the highest-ranked black in the company.

Such distinctions are no longer the issue they once were, how-ever. After nineteen years at one company Roane said that he learned something very valuable: "I could leave." And now that he has raised three daughters, career advancement does not seem to have the urgency it once did. In the autumn of his work life Roane has grown philosophical: "Hell, I could pump gas if I had to; I'm not that proud. And I'm smart enough to be able to make it. I'm not trying to be a millionaire." But on other occasions the worka-holic executive emerges: "I say to myself, Arnold, you can't just sit around and play tennis for the rest of your life. You gotta have some goals."

Having goals is exactly what kept Roane focused as he charted his own personal path to the success. As he says of what it has taken for him to make it, "I always had a plan and I could always trace what I wanted to do through a logical path. You have to be determined and you have to be smart, but it takes some luck—I don't give a damn what you say. You have to be in the right place at the right time. And what you have to be able to do is go in and take advantage of the opportunity." For Roane this ultimately means being ready—trained and qualified. "It's tough, if you've been on the sidelines for fifteen games out of a sixteen-game season and suddenly you have to go in—but you have to be ready. So I've tried to keep myself over the years mentally and physically ready. It's an extra strain, but I work hard to keep myself physically and mentally alert and ready to go. I'm ready to go at all times."

Arlene Roane: On the Daddy Track

At 25, Arlene Roane is exactly half her father's age—the age he was when she was born—and like all children, she represents a generation of difference and a generation of change, as well as a continuing connection. Like the father, the daughter stays ready to go. She has driven the 25 miles from Denver to Martin Marietta this blustery winter day to pick up two magazine articles Roane has Xeroxed for her. One is a piece in *Fortune* on how black executives are doing in the American corporation, the other a feature in *Black Enterprise* listing the 50 best places for blacks to work.

"Hey, baby," Roane says delightedly as his daughter enters his office. He settles her in a seat next to his at the conference table and shows her the articles. "Read this," he orders gently, pushing the *Fortune* article in front of her. "And let's talk about it. There's some information that I think will be particularly useful to what you're going through." Roane then shows Arlene the *Black Enterprise* list. US West, the company she works for, is on it. *"Whaat?"* Arlene whoops. Father and daughter break out laughing.

Arlene Roane is actually employed by Service Link, an unregulated subsidiary of US West, which owns three Bell operating companies: Mountain Bell, Pacific Northwest Bell, and Northwestern Bell. In the old days this would have simply meant that Arlene worked for the phone company. But in this new day, following the breakup of AT&T into the vast network of local "baby bell" companies, subsidiaries, and affiliates, Arlene is a technical specialist in an industry of increasingly complex and interrelated specialities—not just telephones but telephone products and telecommunication systems; not just communication but data bases and information systems. Her title is staff manager of strategic planning.

Dressed in a navy blue suit and pink silk blouse that ties at the neck, Arlene is a physical and corporate replica of her father. Petite and pretty, she is also competitive and analytical, with a style at once strong, independent, "and like my father's, very confrontational." Yet hers is a generation that has clearly had more opportunities than her father's, more role models, more contacts, and thus seemingly less cause for confrontation. Unlike Roane, whose corporate route at General Electric might best be described as "ascent by agitation," Arlene began her career at the phone company a year and a half ago with the kinds of credentials and connections that should have made the black struggle for success, if no less inevitable than her father's, certainly less agitating.

Of course, Arlene Roane was born with connections—a father who struggled at General Electric for nineteen years to pay for her credentials, an education at MIT. She would grow up with the added advantage of having a father who was also a role model and a mentor, an influence and an inspiration for black success in corporate America.

Arlene graduated from MIT in 1983 with a degree in economics and management. The next three years were spent working in minority recruitment for two of the seven sister colleges: Vassar and Wellesley. She didn't want to stay in higher education, so in 1986 Arlene headed West, planning to join a sister who was living in Los Angeles and look for a job. She took a planned vacation detour in Denver to visit her parents for her mother's birthday and decided to use some of the time to go on practice interviews. "I thought I might as well live and learn while in I was in Denver. So I'd go on these practice interviews, you know, to try to iron out my rough edges. Well, after my first interview I was called back and offered a job. The people from the second interview called me back and made an offer. And I thought, Hey, I'd better cut this out!"

The call that would lead to Arlene Roane's position at US West, however, was first made by her father, who called somebody he knew back East, who called somebody he knew out West, who called somebody he knew in Denver who happened to be the president of Mountain Bell. It turned out that the person who called the president also knew Arlene. "He was a Sloan Fellow my senior year," she says of the connection. "He's black, so he was very easy to pick out. There weren't many blacks at MIT and at that time he was in his thirties. He was there that first day [her senior year] with his wife and daughter and some executives, and I gave them a tour."

But Arlene hadn't made the connection when her father's friend first told her about the man who could be helpful if she wanted to work at US West, Denver's largest employer. "We spoke through this third party, my father's friend, for about two weeks and then decided to meet. Well, we soon realized we knew each other." The Sloan Fellow Arlene had been gracious to the first day of her senior year at MIT was Jerry Johnson, then a corporate fast-tracker at US West, now a corporate vice president. "I showed up at his office— he was then computer director at the corporate level—and we just sat and talked." Johnson talked to Arlene about working at US West. What areas did she have an interest in? She told him analysis or research, because those were her strengths. He was frank, and recommended she consider a marketing job that was available at Mountain Bell. She would be in a bigger organization, he said, run by a president who had stated his intention of getting more minorities, minority women especially, into the company. Johnson had already set up some interviews. He told her what to expect.

"He armed me so well," Arlene remembers of Johnson's godfathering. "He took a whole afternoon—and he didn't have to do that." They spent two hours talking in his US West office, then Johnson drove Arlene to downtown Denver, where the Mountain Bell headquarters rises in the cattle town like a towering anvil of black glass and steel, its stark sleekness a glinty contrast to the rolling brilliance of the Rockies. Johnson told Arlene what the company was about—how it did business, how it made its money. Then he told her about the people he had lined up for her to see. "You're having lunch with the president of Mountain Bell, he said. Just like that." They were, in fact, that very moment en route to meet the president, Gary Ames, for a private lunch.

Arlene took the job in marketing at Mountain Bell, where she stayed a year before moving to Service Link. It helped that she was black and female, competent and credentialed. But like her father, she had to prove that she was "qualified." As the only black woman in the company's marketing division, Arlene was believed to have gotten the job because of her contacts, which was true, and not because of her abilities, which was not true. "There was a lot of resentment in the department because of the people I knew," Arlene says. "The president of the company would actually call me to talk about his son, who was applying to Dartmouth. He knew I had done recruiting for the Ivy League and would call to ask questions or get some advice."

To the old-liners in the phone company who had worked themselves up from cable cutting, cable splicing, cable laying, truck driving, or pole climbing to marketing and sales, Arlene was the great interloper who had been "hauled in off the street" (as she was repeatedly told) because of her connections. "The inference was that I couldn't handle complicated technical projects," she says, "despite the fact that I had had more math than anyone in that department." There were rumors that she was sleeping with the one white man in the department who treated her fairly. There were rumors that she was sleeping with her other connections.

Yet when MCI, a Mountain Bell customer, had trouble with a computer-based ordering system purchased from Mountain Bell, Arlene was the one who figured out what the problem was. No one else in the department had a computer background. And she was the one who took on the issue of fraud in the long-distance phone company. "MCI had a big, big problem with fraud, so I was given the case, the thinking being there wasn't much to it. Well, we found out there were thousands of dollars being lost in fraud every month. I worked with MCI and came up with a solution. It didn't cost them anything and it didn't cost us [Mountain Bell] anything. It was fixed with just a little trigger in the computer data base system. It's so ironic I was told I wasn't 'technical.' In terms of education, I had a stronger technical education in mathematics, physics, science, and basic engineering than anyone I ever met in that department."

The difference between Arnold Roane's experience in corporate America and that of his daughter's twenty-five years later is, of course, the difference of a lifetime. A lifetime shaped by another set of history and circumstances, another dimension of struggle. Yet the struggle is eternal, carried on by the sons and the daughters— the new generations who reflect a spirit past and a better future—of the mothers and the fathers. Roane sees the better future in a daughter, and knows what the struggle has been. The pressure to "prove" yourself, to be counted as qualified, as worthy, afflicts each new generation just as it has each one that has gone before.

"Parents always give advice and I give advice," Roane says, explaining the support he tries to provide his daughter. "Arlene doesn't always listen, but I didn't always listen when I was her age. I think that she probably picks up a lot of unsaid things as advice. She has seen what has happened to us over the years . . . the progress I've made, the frustration . . . and I'm sure she's learned a hell of a lot."

In the twenty-five years since Arlene was born, there have been more opportunities for black success than during any other generation in African-American history. Arlene has benefited not only from the opportunities, but from having a father who helped pave the way for the opportunities and then lived to benefit in his own lifetime from the opportunities: to become a corporate success, a godfather himself, a man of power, weight, influence and contacts.

Arnold and Arlene Roane represent the older and the younger links on a modern chain of black success. Both are of the generation that finally achieved the opportunity to cross over—to live out black possibility in freedom, in the arena of an integrated America. It was a freedom hard fought and hard won, secured by a long black line of struggle—by all the many thousands gone who agitated and demonstrated, preached and prayed, rioted, burned, fought and died, got a good education, seized black power, exerted black influence, mentored, godfathered, took affirmative action, and networked for success.

What this new black generation so well primed for achievement would ultimately learn, however, is that even when one is qualified, success is not always guaranteed, for there remain continuing obstacles—from within and without—to opportunity. For this new generation, then, as for the old ones gone before, success still means first to be trained, qualified, worthy—and then ready for the struggle.

S i x

ACTING YOUR COLOR

When the Lord said, "Let there be light," and there was light, what I want to know is, where was us colored people?

Langston Hughes, *The Best of Simple*

*I*f the undermining of black ability and black worth is a defining feature of white racism, the extent to which such undermining has impacted on the black psyche and become internalized is probably nowhere more graphically revealed than in the jokes, folk sayings, teasings, and putdowns that define much of African-American humor. Only in America, where race remains an inherent and virulent contradiction, could black humor become a double-edged razor slashing back on itself—a parody of racism reduced to signifyin' one-liners. Indeed, black American humor has always cut quick and deep, illuminating a people's insecurities, the scope of their feelings of unworthiness.

Significantly, it was the signifyin' monkey, that wily chatterbox indigenous to the African motherland, that became the emblematic griot transmitting humor in black America. Unlike his apathetic brethren who heard no evil, saw no evil, spoke no evil, the signifyin' monkey could always be expected to "signify" on the peculiar dimension of being black in white America. He signified on success: "You have to be twice as good as whites to get half as far." He signified on achievement: "You should act your age and not your

color." He signified on ambition: "Be light-skinned—or be a doctor." He signified on white women: "I like an old white woman
because she's been white so long—and I like a young white woman
because she's got so long to be white." He signified on sexuality:
"The blacker the berry, the sweeter the juice." He signified on skin
color: "If you're light, you're all right; if you're brown, stick
around; but if you're black, get back!"

The signifyin' went on and on, through twenty generations of
plaintive, comic riffs—through black men "playing the dozens"
("Yo' mama's so ugly her face has been declared a disaster area");
through the rueful wit of Langston Hughes's cautionary Jesse B.
Simple tales ("Feets, don't fail me now!"); through the urgency of
contemporary rap music, with its clever, scathing lyrics on drugs
and crime and sexuality. In the end, black American humor became
the psychocultural looking-glass through which to see all the
funny, sad, biting, wry, and tragic takes on the black condition—
the reflection a painful view of just how much white racism has led
to black racism and the creation of a people whose oppression is
perhaps most dramatically revealed in the profound ambivalence
with which it views being black.

In a society whose psychological imperative for slavery was based
on the "inferiority" of skin color, it's not surprising that color has
become the prism through which black America both sees and
defines itself. Indeed, color has become the very identity of the race:
black. And color is the very language used by the race to describe
itself: jet black, blue black, black as the ace of spades; dark brown,
brown-skinned, medium-brown, redbone, yellow, high yellow,
light-skinned, light, bright, and almost-white. Such distinctions
between dark and light tend to blur into the single image of black
when viewed by whites, but among African-Americans the distinctions not only frame one's identity but often have an impact on
success.

A particular burden of black America has been the history of
rape and miscegenation that grew out of slavery, producing a race
of people whose rainbow of colors—from ebony black to milk
white—physically resembles every other race on earth. And the
particular pathology is that success in black America is often a

measure of the degree to which blacks physically resemble any race on earth other than the black one. Only in a peculiarly racist culture where skin color has developed emotional as well as esthetic meaning—with black invariably meaning the pejoratives of dark, bad, and ugly, and white the virtues of light, good and beauty—could it be considered "better" to look brown, red, yellow, or white if one happens to be black.

The fact that attitudes about skin color remain one of the most sensitive and explosive issues in the black community underscores the depth of the ambivalence color has made on a race. Achieving blacks of any skin color have experienced such ambivalence, but a hallmark of their success is their ability to move past the conflicts of color to a point of affirming blackness in all its shades and complexities.

Maxine Waters: The Color of Power

"Psychology tells us that a rejection is permanent with little children," says former Head Start teacher and current assemblywoman Maxine Waters. "For example, if a child experiences constant rejection at an early age, they can never overcome. It manifests itself in all kinds of ways—you know, forever. Also, if you are told that you're nothing over and over again, then I think the majority of people begin to believe it. You know what I'm saying? The scars run very deep."

The assemblywoman admits she has been scarred, but she is also proof that psychology is not necessarily destiny.

Maxine Waters, who for eleven years has represented the largely poor, black, Hispanic, and Democratic 48th District of Los Angeles in the California state assembly, is considered the most influential woman, black or white, in California politics, and her success reflects the formidable political power blacks have come to wield in the state during the last thirty years. She is one of nine blacks in this year's 1987 state assembly, which is presided over by a black

speaker of the house, Willie Brown; and she represents a district in
the second-largest city in America, run by a black mayor, Tom
Bradley. Waters herself chairs the state budget and pension fund
committees, and is being touted as the most likely candidate to
replace Augustus Hawkins in the United States Congress when he
retires in 1990. It is the kind of success that could perhaps happen
only in America's last frontier of the West Coast, a region not yet
tamed or dominated by white machine politics.

Yet black political success is simply an expression of achievement, not an explanation. What makes one black succeed when
another does not—when family background and opportunities
seem equal, expectations similar, native capabilities approximate?
"What's the difference?" Waters asks thoughtfully. She smiles
gently and then answers obliquely: "I really don't know. I don't
think many people really know." The question may be one of those
eternal ones, like the riddle of how the pyramids were built. "What
can I say?" Waters asks again, trying one more time to give a
personal accounting. "I had a lot of supportive teachers, black
teachers, in grade school. I think I discovered at some point in time
—or believed—that I knew things that others didn't know, that I
had some insights."

Maxine Waters leans on the table and rests her chin on the back
of her hand as she says this, gazing at the cup of hot tea in front of
her as if it brewed the secret to her success. It is 1987 and she is
sitting in a ballroom of the Wilshire Hotel in Los Angeles, where
she has just finished hosting an enormously successful luncheon to
raise money for her political action committee. Over five hundred
black women packed the place to hear "mean Maxine" deliver the
message of black woman empowerment. Petite, dark brown, and
lovely, and filled with the features and spirit of an African warrior-
woman, Waters looked splendid in a close-fitting forest green suede
suit that showcased her stunning 49-year-old figure and brought
the women to their feet with the gospel of political organizing:
"It's important that people know who we are," she said to cheers.
"And it's important for us to not only know who we are, but to tell
people who we are. Because if we tell people who we are, they will

stop messing with us and stop speculating about what they can get away with."

Like many dark brown girls, Maxine Waters grew up hearing, in various ways, that to be black meant to "get back." "I was the first dark child born in my family," she says with an oh-Lord tone. "I was number four, and I had three sisters ahead of me who were all light-skinned with long, thick hair. I had that soft, fine hair and I always had a bald spot—and boy, they never let me live it down." Waters gives a pained laugh as she remembers, then instinctively touches the back of her head, which in adulthood reveals full, healthy hair. Born in 1938 in St. Louis, Missouri, that middle compromise region of the country which is not quite the South and clearly not the North, Waters didn't consider the city any worse than any other when it came to matters of color and opportunity. "Those were the days when it was considered a good job for a black to run an elevator—but I mean, you had to look like Lena Horne to be an elevator operator."

By the time she was 10 or 11, Waters started to notice how some blacks viewed black in their own community. "My uncle was a guy who had a lot of buddies, and my sisters and I would visit our uncle a lot because he was the favorite uncle—the one with money that he would give us on the weekends. Well, my uncle and his buddies would sit around and talk about yellow women—about how fine yellow women are; how the only beautiful black woman was a light, yellow woman.

"And you know, I discovered that it didn't really make me believe something was wrong with me. It probably made me think something was wrong with them. But it did make me work harder to prove that I was *smarter* than my sisters." Waters' mother, a pretty, light-skinned woman who had a total of thirteen children (Waters never knew her own dark-skinned father) and was inter-mittently on welfare, married an old boyfriend when Maxine was in the sixth grade. "He was a weird man," she recalls, "a real victim of these color and class distinctions in the black community. He really did put people in categories, you know. If you were light-skinned, you were all right. If you were black, you didn't know anything."

Maxine Waters' salvation and support system came from her teachers, who took a special interest in her. "I went to an all black primary school and my teachers were fabulous. They spent time with you. I was considered bright, and I think they liked me because I cared about school and I was competitive and cooperative and I did my work."

Immediately after high school, Waters married, had two children, and worked in factories and as a waitress in segregated St. Louis restaurants. Her husband was in the service, and a military transfer took the family to Los Angeles in the early sixties. She entered California State University at Los Angeles in the late sixties and majored in sociology. In 1972 she and her husband divorced, and Waters became a single mother.

Maxine Waters' political career was launched in Head Start, the early childhood development program started in the seventies as part of the nation's War on Poverty. She served as an assistant teacher as well as director of parent-training programs, positions that brought her into constant contact with elected officials, where she lobbied for Head Start funds. She saw up close the difference politics made. "I saw how I could help people," she says simply. Just as Head Start made a difference in the psychology and lives of black children, Waters recognized the difference politics could make in the lives of all people.

For California's most powerful female elected official, Waters' strength and power base have always been at the grass roots—the constituency of ordinary folks whose fears, frustrations, and needs have been a touchstone to her own. But she exercises power in the state legislature, that political cabal of predominantly white men, where she makes a difference. She introduced (and reintroduced six times) the legislation that divested California state pension funds from companies doing business in South Africa. She sponsored the legislation that resulted in Project Build, a community program that provides education and job-training services, and information about health, child care, and day care to residents of six Watts housing projects. She and the other black members of the assembly are the driving, collective force to be reckoned with in California politics, the closest any state comes to a black machine.

"We're talking about blacks being comfortable with power," Waters says of blacks and politics. "If you believe you have power, that gives you power, and if you use it, act on it, you can make things happen. You can create change. I really do believe there is a black experience. And I really do believe that culturally it's important to understand who we are so that when we interact with whites we do not automatically accept others' values or give up who we are. Because if we do, just during their normal actions whites will try to make us feel *less than we are.* You know what I'm saying? We cannot be victims. We cannot be victims forever and ever and ever. You have to act on your own behalf—on behalf of your people and on behalf of your community. You cannot be successful and continue to be a victim."

But one of the recurring success themes in the African-American community is the frequency with which being a victim actually drives ambition. How much did being a victim of growing up dark in a community that revered light drive Maxine Waters? "It may be," she concedes slowly, "that because I had three sisters in a community, a black community, that valued fair-skinned, long-haired women I had to prove that I was just as good. It *may* be. But in addition to that there were people who believed that I was just as good. You know what I mean? And I had something to reinforce that. I learned that no matter what you may or may not have, as perceived by a misguided community about what is valuable, people understand hard work and talent—and it can prevail."

Maxine Waters has also learned to turn the double negatives of white and black racism into the plus equation of success by recognizing the value of images—black images especially. Which accounts for her passion as a collector of black memorabilia, and Aunt Jemima images in particular—Aunt Jemima banks, Aunt Jemima dolls, Aunt Jemima mirrors. " 'Anything I can find,' " Waters told a reporter from the *Los Angeles Times* who interviewed her a few years ago and asked why a black woman of her stature would collect such things, and why she wasn't ashamed of the Aunt Jemima stereotype. "Aunt Jemima is very special," she answered him. "She symbolizes the strength of our people and the strength of black women. Aunt Jemima is the black woman who cooked and cleaned, struggled, brought up her own family and a white family. And if I'm ashamed of Aunt Jemima—her head rag, her hips, her color— then I'm ashamed of my people."

"What they [whites] did in creating Aunt Jemima as a stereotype," Waters now says, "was try to make fun of my people—my mother and my grandmother. And I can take what they attempted to make derogatory, to poke fun at, and see something positive. And I can say, You can't make me ashamed of my past. That tells white people something about who you are. That they don't describe the world for me—I describe it."

Waters' success stems from the fact that she defines her world from a black reference point, from a position of racial strength— even on the floor of the state assembly. "You know, there are times when Willie [Brown] and Diane [Watson, another black assemblywoman] and I will get on the floor to speak and lapse into a black idiom. We do it consciously, deliberately, just to mess with the white folks in the assembly—just to let them know we know who we are," Waters says with a power laugh.*

A continuing paradox of race in America is the extent to which color not only defines a condition or experience but also shapes behavior, points of view, and expectations. While they are growing up, blacks are often teased with such malapropisms as "act your age, not your color." The inference, of course, is that to "act colored" is to act immaturely, inappropriately—to speak inappropriately, dress inappropriately, look inappropriate, *be* inappropriate. Appropriateness is often a matter of color. The less black one looks, the more appropriate he or she is considered to be. For black women in particular, color is still often a measure of beauty, with light skin being the ideal and dark skin the least preferred. Color, if

---

* In 1989 Maxine Waters was elected to the United States House of Representatives representing the 29th district of California.

it is light, bestows power and privileges. Color, if it is dark, brings disdain and unworthiness.

In the black community, color has also become linked with class, for America's early black bourgeois class tended to be a mulatto class—those blacks whose ancestry of white blood often provided them with opportunities and benefits not available to the dark class of unmixed blacks. To be sure, the single greatest benefit of the mulatto class was that it looked white—or at least looked more white than black. The whitest-looking blacks of the class could even "pass" for white and escape the weight of being black altogether.

The truth is, few blacks of any hue ever escape the full weight of color. But a continuing truth of the black experience is that success is so very often the sum of its own contradictions. In black America, what you see is seldom what you get—or seldom even what you think you see.

Lloyd Gite: The Color of Strength

Texas Interstate 45 runs from Galveston all the way to Dallas, winding north through Houston to divide what was once the city's Fourth Ward practically in half. Everything inside the beltway is now considered the downtown Houston central business district, while everything ringing its perimeter is what remains of the Fourth Ward. Although wards haven't had any political significance in Houston since the forties, they still describe a geography and a history. And in the nation's fourth largest city the Fourth Ward describes what was once the center of black political and cultural life.

Ironically, the Jack Yates Baptist Church wound up being on the side of the freeway that constituted downtown Houston when the ward was divided. Jack Yates was Houston's pioneering black civil rights minister during the late 1800s who built and pastored the church that now stands on some of the most valuable real estate in the city. Nearly a hundred years later the church is still active, its congregation a mostly prominent middle-class representation of Houston's 28-percent-black population. Indeed, throughout Houston's black history the name Jack Yates has stood for success and achievement. The Jack Yates High School, for instance, was *the* black school middle-class black parents sent their children to before integration.

Since school integration didn't occur in Houston until the early 1970s, Lloyd Gite, 36 in 1988, Class of '69, attended Jack Yates High School, where he was the kind of in-crowd success typical of many light-skinned blacks in all-black high schools: student body president, editor of the school yearbook, cheerleader. He returned to Houston four years ago following stints in Detroit and Dallas as a news reporter, rejoined the Jack Yates Baptist Church, and went to work as a television reporter for the Fox affiliate, Channel 26. He found some things haven't changed: color still plays a major role in image, just as it did in high school. And he is candid about the difference color made back then.

Then, like now, Lloyd Gite was a tallish, medium-built man whose light skin is the color of pale gold. He wears a thick, bushy mustache that outlines a thin, determined mouth, and wire horn-rimmed glasses that frame brooding, slightly slanted eyes. The overall look is exotic, somewhat oriental. "I think I came to the attention of people first and foremost because of my color, and secondly, because I was aggressive and outgoing," Gite says of his early high school success. "If I were dark-skinned and aggressive, I probably wouldn't have had the opportunity to be known by so many people at Jack Yates."

Gite also admits there were times at Yates when skin color was probably his only qualifier for success: "I was a cheerleader during the tenth, eleventh, and twelfth grades, and I got that, certainly, because I was light-skinned. No other reason. No other reason than that. I didn't even take the cheers seriously. I mean, I could dance and I was light-skinned." Gite and his older sister, a majorette, along with her friends, sisters Debbie Allen and Phylicia Rashad— who would both grow up to be successful television actresses— formed part of an elite social circle at Jack Yates High in which the unspoken price of admission was skin coloring that could pass the "paper bag test" (was no darker than a paper bag). The phenomenon was a prevalent one throughout black American middle class high schools. As Gite said of what it meant to be a black cheerleader at Yates, "We did have some physically black cheerleaders, one in particular who was smart as a whip. She was very black but very smart, and that's one of the reasons she was a cheerleader. You either had to have long hair or be light brown or light-skinned, or be exceptional in some other way. I mean, you couldn't just be black. You just couldn't do that."

Yet even light skin is a mixed blessing in the black race, for with its privileges also come assumptions and inevitable contradictions. The contradiction in Gite's case is that his light skin led to the assumption that he came from the middle class. "Most people who meet me assume that I came from money. They always made that assumption, even when we [Gite, his sister, and his two brothers] were in elementary school, junior high, senior high. We were always in the activities that the little rich black kids were in."

The assumption was an easy one to make, for Lloyd Gite *looks* as if he comes from money. His designer suits, his hip bachelor's duplex, his natural sense of style and taste, all connote affluence and success. The last thing they suggest is a man who grew up in Houston's Third Ward in a single-parent home run by a mother who struggled to raise four children and keep an abusive, alcoholic ex-husband at bay—a home Gite terms dysfunctional. "I'm defining dysfunctional as something different from your traditional mother-father-kids, let's be happy, let's be loved, and let's all skip off to heaven," he says evenly. Gite's father, who was divorced from his mother shortly after Gite was born and never financially supported the family although he "had money," was a menacing presence during much of Gite's early childhood. His memories of that time are many and terrible and tumble out in a rush.

"One time my brother and I had pneumonia; we were very sick and my father brought us a quart of orange juice. A quart of orange juice, that was it. That has never left my mind. . . . I remember my father used to take us to his girlfriends' houses when he had visitation rights. . . . I also remember my father one time taking

my older brother and dragging him across the floor by his hair—I remember him doing that. . . . I also remember, once, my father being drunk and coming to our house, and my mother huddled all of us in the bedroom and we had all the lights out. And I remember us being in this dark room hoping and praying he would not be able to break into the house. . . . And I also remember my father coming in once with his brother and being kind of drunk. My mother was ironing and he hit at her, and she raised the iron and burned the shit out of him. Burned his hand. And I remember as he was going out the door I took a pair of scissors and stuck him in the back. . . . I was about eight or nine, but I remember that anger and the rage."

Gite leans back on the red silk and linen sofa that occupies the middle of his living room and lets out a sigh. "Real wholesome stuff, huh?" It was in fact the painful, awful stuff of real life—the very stuff that keeps successful blacks like Lloyd Gite honest about the pathological stuff of skin color. "Unlike some light-skinned blacks, we didn't take our light skin all that seriously. It opened some doors for us, sure—doors that probably wouldn't have been opened, given our socioeconomic background, if we'd been dark skinned. But my mother instilled in us that we were to never *ever* let color be a factor in terms of how we dealt with people."

Even so, color is still a factor in how people now deal with Gite. But now, as an adult, he thinks being light-skinned works against him in an industry that expects to see dark when it views black men. "I think if a station is going to hire a black male, it wants to make sure that people know the person is black," he says of television news reporting. "None of the black guys in this market are light-skinned except me. I'm one of the few light-skinned male reporters I've ever seen. Even when you look at the networks, the reporters that they have, the black male reporters, they're physically black. And there's been some discussion here in this market about me. 'What is he?' people ask. Some people think I look Puerto Rican. One person even thought I was Greek, which to me is so totally out of the box."

What Lloyd Gite really is, he says with fierce pride, is very good at his job. "If my work wasn't good, they probably would've gotten rid of me a long time ago." Like other light-skinned black men whose color congeals into an unexpected yellow badge of courage, Gite has become something of a militant, a late-twentieth-century race man. As a reporter he is both objective and an advocate: "I try very hard to use, whenever possible, blacks in my stories. Why go to a white psychiatrist when I can go to a black psychiatrist? Why go to a white economist? If there's a black economist, you'd better bet your bottom dollar I'm going to try to find that man or that woman to use in my story, because it's important for the white community and the black community to know that there are black folks just as articulate, just as professional as these white people."

Yet Lloyd Gite the race man is frustrated as an advocate: "It's a constant battle—trying to get whites to understand the importance of covering black issues. South Africa, for example. Even black issues right here on a local level. You try to sneak in a little bit of it every now and then."

Gite's color position hasn't made him popular at Channel 26, as it did in high school. "People in my office and even peers of mine in this city still cannot deal with the fact that I am first and foremost black. I am intelligent, I am rather attractive—and I can 'rag' [dress well]," he adds, laughing. "I mean, I pull it all together. Some people have problems with that, with the fact that when I do a story, I do a very good and thorough job, I'm well read and well prepared; that I'm a good writer; that I'm not afraid to call a wrong a wrong when it's wrong. That bothers some people. The thing I keep hearing is that I'm too aggressive. I've actually been told that if I was going to make it in this city I would have to tone myself down." If anything, Lloyd Gite has done quite the opposite and been quite successful.

The phone rings. It is a salesclerk at Nieman-Marcus calling. "Mr. Gite, those Perry Ellis shirts you were looking at last week are about to go on sale. Would you like me to put aside a couple for you?" Clearly, the last thing Lloyd Gite appears to need is another shirt—or another tie, or another bow tie, or another suit, or another pair of shoes, or another pair of glasses, or another set of cufflinks.

His walk-in closet, which is the size of many Manhattan studio apartments, already resembles a designer showroom, beginning with the sea of shirts impeccably starched, pressed, and draped on the padded hangers that line the stainless steel clothes bar that runs through the center of the closet. Along the back of the door are at least a hundred ties, hanging in straight formation, silk, sorted, and coordinated. Beneath them a procession of bow ties—at least twenty-five—are stringed on hooks. There is a box filled with cufflinks and a tray stocked with eyewear: glasses for reading, sunglasses for shading. There are tuxedo suits for black tie, designer suits for work, safari suits for travel to Kenya and Egypt and Japan. There are rows of boots and shoes, bins of sweaters, and racks of trousers. As he himself has said, Lloyd Gite can rag.

Dressing well has become as much a part of Lloyd Gite's success identity as the quality of his work. And, as is the case for most successful blacks, looking good is not so much a matter of superficial skin color as it is of personal style. Gite has worked hard to hone a style that denotes power, confidence, strength. He's worked even harder to project it, a fact that's often led to his being branded as one of those blacks who has an "attitude." But as he says, "I do very much have a sense of myself, and despite my background, I never really thought in terms of being inferior. I think I am somebody. Does that mean I have an attitude? That means I have a healthy dose of selfness, and I think there's everything right with that."

James Russell: The Color of Style

Black success is very much a matter of style and image, often fashioned in dress and speech to compensate for the expectation that being black means "acting colored." And there is perhaps no surer indication of "acting colored" than "speaking colored," that is, speaking in the idioms, dialect, or slang associated with the black class, the lower class. The first thing all successful blacks know and understand, then, as Franz Fanon said in *Black Skin, White Masks,* is that "To speak a language is to take on a world, a culture." And to succeed as a black in America is to take on the culture of white language, the Queen's English. Fanon continues:

> Every colonized people—in other words, every people in whose soul an inferiority complex has been created by the death and burial of its local cultural originality—finds itself face to face with the language of the civilizing nation; that is, with the culture of the mother country. The colonized is elevated above his jungle status in proportion to his adoption of the mother country's cultural standards. He becomes whiter as he renounces his blackness, his jungle.

Just as speech is the measure of a culture, so too is dress. And no group works harder to "dress for success" than the aspiring black American. Yet dressing, like music, is one area of black cultural expression in which a premium is often placed on being original, creative, different from whites. To dress for success is to dress with style and flair, to take a gray flannel suit and wear it with a red silk handkerchief. Interestingly, dressing is the one activity that affirms color in the black community, for to be fashionable is to be colorful and distinctive and noticed. In the American business community, however, this is the very quality that can be a liability. Betty Lehan Harragan points this out in her landmark book on female success in corporate America, *Games Mother Never Taught You,* which has application to the black American when it comes to dressing for business success:

> In business you are not dressing to express personal taste; you are dressing in a costume which should be designed to have an impact on your bosses and teammates. If your clothes don't convey the message that you are competent, able, ambitious, self-confident, reliable, and authoritative, nothing you can say or do will overcome the negative signals emanating from your apparel.

James Russell, 29, learned this lesson the hard way when he joined the New York Life Insurance Company seven years ago: he was all but sent home from a minority training seminar to change clothes his first week on the job. Actually, he was not specifically ordered to go home, but he got the message and did so when one of the men running the seminar came up to him and said, "That's a nice suit you have on, but not for a meeting like this." Russell was wearing a flashy walking suit, more appropriate for evening than for a buttoned-down corporate sales meeting. "It hit me like a ton of bricks just what I must have looked like in this crowd," he says. "I remember going up to the moderator of the seminar, one of the black company vice presidents, to introduce myself, and he gave me the kind of look that said *Come on!*" Russell hurried home and changed into his one conservative suit, the black one he'd worn to his mother's funeral.

Later, realizing he didn't have the proper business attire for his new job or enough money to obtain one, he took a hundred dollars and went to the one place in New York where he knew he could bargain for a wardrobe: the discount stores of Delancey Street. He came back with two pairs of pants, a sports jacket, three shirts, two belts, and three ties. "I knew then I would make it in the insurance business."

Russell was then 22, and straight from the streets of the South Bronx, where dressing for success meant "being as unconventional at being presentable as I could be. I'd wear anything that was different. In the totally black neighborhood of the South Bronx, being presentable was different than being presentable in Midtown. It was an environment where you wore knit sweaters, high-waisted pants, short leather jackets, or leather coats." It was also an environment in which speech was defined by that urban, male language of the street, a vernacular as lyrical as it is inarticulate: "Yo, my man. What it is?" "Ain't nothing to it, home."

Russell, in seven years, has been transformed, evolving from an urban street-slick youth into a natty, smooth, and polished black businessman. And his climb from the ghetto of the South Bronx to the office of district sales manager for New York Life, where he earns $75,000 a year, is the result of having a talent not just for sales, but for cultivating a proper image. He literally trained himself to lose his street accent by reading out loud, mimicking the people he saw on television, practicing with a tape recorder to perfect a sound and a style and a tone that was not distinctively black. "I wanted to be a disc jockey when I was younger, and in radio you can't have a particular accent or characteristic in your voice."

But what James Russell really wanted to be was successful in American business, which meant he listened, took advice, learned to do what was appropriate. As he says, "I was smart enough to know that I didn't know enough to do it by myself. I needed all the help I could get." He was also comfortable enough to see his limitations not as flaws of character or race, but as temporary shortcomings that could be remedied. Indeed, what most successful blacks learn is that most everything can, in fact, be learned—how to talk, how to dress, how to groom an image for success. The important thing is to recognize what is not known—and then learn it. Russell remembers the first time he saw a cucumber as a kid. "I got real excited and said, 'Oooh, a little watermelon.' Well, everybody laughed, and I couldn't understand why. They said, 'No, that's not a baby watermelon. It's a cucumber.' Well, okay, I said to myself. Now I know what a cucumber is. Now I have some perspective."

Kathleen Knight: The Color of Image

In the black middle class, as in the white middle class, a proper image extends beyond speaking and dressing well to incorporate a range of other experiences that convey taste, culture, breeding. E. Franklin Frazier's critical look at the black middle class in *The Black Bourgeoisie,* attacked much of the mimicking that blacks supposedly do of whites in attempting to emulate a lifestyle based on white values. Yet the very term "white values" is a notion which implies that values come in colors. Of course, values—the desire to excel, to achieve, succeed, to be of worth—represent universal ambitions not specific to color or race. Only in a culture that exalts one race over another, one color over another, do values get expressed as the intrinsic qualities of one group merely being aped by another group with no values of its own.

Like other working-class blacks with middle class aspirations, Kathleen Knight grew up with the kind of exposure to a larger education that resembled that of little middle class white girls in her native Milwaukee. There were piano and dance lessons, tennis lessons, and trips to see the New York City Ballet. Her parents were both strivers—her father a machinist, her mother an elevator operator at Wisconsin Bell—who sacrificed everything to provide Knight and her two older brothers with the sort of opportunities they thought would lay the foundation for success. The constant message was, "In order to be somebody, to have anything, to have a chance in life, you have to get an education," and that extended beyond the three Rs to activities that helped develop artistic expression.

Knight studied classical dance for fifteen years, and though her ambition was to be a professional dancer, it was not a practical choice for a young black woman coming of age in the Midwest during the sixties. "I figured I would starve to death, since there were very few blacks that made it in dance at that time," says Knight. "There was only one black dance company, Alvin Ailey, and it was in its infancy."

The next best thing to being a dancer, Knight felt, was to be in the profession that had the most black role models: teaching. So after completing four years at the University of Wisconsin with a major in English and speech, Knight worked for a while in retail merchandising, then went to graduate school, got her teaching certificate, and taught in the Milwaukee school system before marriage took her to Detroit.

At 40, Knight is now a human resources manager in the industrial relations department of the Ford Motor Company, where a liberal arts education and good "breeding" have contributed to her success in the area of personnel. Breeding has also helped her in coping with a uniquely female factor in the equation of success and color: beauty.

Kathleen Knight is cast in the ideal image of what is considered a pretty black woman in America—light-skinned and long-haired

—and that has caused her singular pain for most of her life. It meant enduring taunts as a child from others calling her "a yellow nigger with long hair"; it meant being passed over in beauty pageants because, as the judge of one pageant told her parents when she was a teenager, "Milwaukee is not ready for a black Junior Miss"; it means not always being taken seriously even now because she is "too pretty to really know what she's doing"; it means being too yellow and then too black and then not black enough; it means all of those ugly things it can mean to be both pretty and fair-skinned, and black and female, in communities that are intimidated by one and threatened by the other.

"It is probably one of the most painful subjects I can talk about," Knight says on the issue of color. She is sitting in the dim light of a Detroit restaurant, her long chestnut hair pulled back, her perfectly chiseled gold face unadorned by makeup, her loose pants suit covering a slender, perfectly proportioned dancer's body. Even in the dark light and despite obvious efforts to play it down, Knight's natural and startling beauty comes through.

Beauty in women can be as much a curse as a blessing, and for black women who are more vulnerable to being double victims of both race and gender, beauty carries its own particular set of burdens. Literature is filled with images of the "tragic mulatto," that light-skinned black beauty caught betwixt and between, often resented and despised in her own community for the status her good looks confer and exploited in the larger community for the exotic sexuality her mixed look represents. It is an old, conflicting theme which still casts pain and hurt on the fragile image of black female success.

Yet success for black women, like success for black men, means learning to move beyond the pain of stereotypes to affirm the power of the spirit. Knight's success in doing this stems in large measure to her family grounding, to being provided with opportunities at an early age that allowed her to develop her talents and aspirations —to develop her mind and not just focus on her looks. She credits a loving mother with giving her the no-nonsense facts of life when it came to color and beauty. "There are certain things in life you have to understand," her mother said the day she came home from the seventh grade crying over another insult having to do with her looks. "You are yellow, you have long hair, and that will bother some people—either because of envy or jealousy or insecurity. There are a lot of reasons people mistreat others, but don't let that impact on your ability to deal with people. You are what you are. And it's something you're going to have to face all of your life." As her mother added, and Knight now recognizes, "You can't come home crying everyday."

Indeed, those blacks who succeed have learned exactly that: You can't come home crying everyday. You cannot, as Maxine Waters said, be successful and continue to be a victim.

In the end, color, like beauty, talent, or intellect, simply represents how the toss of the genetic dice get rolled. It is a circumstance of life, but not an arbiter of destiny. To be sure, luck still favors the color of white in America, but success tends to favor blacks who act out of the power of their color—who embrace the strength of the race in all of its rich shades of darkness and light, in all of its rich, mixed possibilities. Successful blacks know that a particular skin color is neither a prerequisite for achievement nor an excuse for failure. It is very often simply a catalyst. What all achieving blacks successfully do is turn the color of black into the color of victory. This is no small achievement. For if color has been the source of much humor in the African-American community, humor only masks the fact that the color of black is often a condition mostly angry and blue.

Seven

GETTING MAD, GETTING EVEN

Of the things that need knowing, none is more important than that all blacks are angry.
William H. Grier and
Price M. Cobbs, *Black Rage*

*T*he year was 1966. The two black California doctors, Ronald Brown, a psychologist, and Price M. Cobbs, a psychiatrist, had been invited by the management of Procter & Gamble to company headquarters in Cincinnati to do a workshop with black and white employees. The idea was to get the old corporate staffers (mainly white men) to interact with the new P & G employees (mainly blacks and women) around the two major issues confronting the races: black rage and white fear.

The idea was novel, even revolutionary: blacks and whites confronting each other over a gulf of three hundred years, over an unremitting history of hard feelings and ill will, over the memory of slavery and segregation, lynchings and cross burnings, discrimination and racism. The gulf stretched to a chasm, and corporations that took on the task of trying to mend the rift through "confrontation" were not only ahead of their time but a sign of the times. Because what was most clear by the middle of the sixties was just how mad blacks really were. Watts had burned in 1965. Newark and Detroit would go next. There would be riots in Chicago and

Washington, Black Panther killings in Oakland, campus takeovers in San Francisco.

The nonviolent movement for civil rights begun in the South in the fifties had turned physical in the North by the mid-sixties, exploding with spasms of violent, collective black rage that would rock the nation well into the next decade. The result: whites got scared and moved toward change. And perhaps nothing more dramatically illustrated the nature of the change than the idea of Fortune 500 companies running racial confrontation workshops.

In the beginning, says Dr. Ron Brown, now a partner with Banks Brown Management Systems in San Francisco, the workshops were little more than group encounter sessions, with blacks doing most of the venting ("You're a racist!") and whites doing all of the race encountering ("Yes, I'm a racist, but I don't want to be —help me, help me"). "After about our third workshop we realized that our slam-bang style—coming in kicking over the table, electrifying them—wasn't working," Brown says. "What racial confrontation had to really do was help blacks to be heard, to let them tell white people what they really thought, which was difficult in those days. The big issue was for whites to hear what blacks were saying."

The times demanded that an oppressed class be heard, be dealt with. And the cataclysms of the sixties that ushered in an era of new opportunities also ordered a new psychology. As Brown says, "People were going to bed Negro and waking up black. There were major psychological changes going on."

A constant through all the changes has been the degree to which anger has molded the African-American mindset. It has variously been both a driving force for motivation and a continuing source of anguish. Sometimes it is anger low grade and smoldering—an old festering wound, buried deep in the trauma of black childhood. Sometimes it is fleeting anger—the flash memory of that one, singular time when an insult was made so quickly, so brutally, so unexpectedly that its force jolted the psyche with a velocity that is reexperienced anytime the memory is conjured up. And sometimes it is the worst anger of all, that free-floating, nonspecific anger, vague in definition, crushing in weight. The kind of anger that rolls through collective spirit and memory, gathering in its wake all of the assorted racial hurts and slights and injuries of a people before settling in as a dull ache and then knotting into a tight, searing ball of fury.

Anger is of course an emotion universally human. Yet if there is a reality called the black experience, there is just as surely an accompanying condition called black anger, black rage. Beyond the intensity of an emotion, black anger is the pathology of an affliction, of a certain scourge endemic to the spirit of a race. The riots that erupted during the sixties were simply the symptoms of the affliction, of the enraging conditions that continued to stunt black life throughout America. The reality is, any African-American living the black experience will suffer at some point and in some way from consuming, debilitating black anger. No matter the class or skin color, the personal circumstances or particular successes, to be black is to live with anger as the defining emotion of a racial experience. To be successful is to learn how to keep the emotion from consuming or debilitating black ambition.

Ellis Gordon: The Angriest Black Man in America

In 1976, Los Angeles banker Ellis Gordon was diagnosed by Drs. Ron Brown and Price Cobbs as "a powder keg about to blow." He had just joined the United California Bank after spending five years self-employed. Despite having an MBA from the University of Illinois, the Houston native had been unable to get work when he moved to Los Angeles in 1971. Those first five years were difficult, unsuccessful ones. His marriage broke up; he declared bankruptcy. He wore a huge, threatening Afro and a narrow, defiant goatee. He occasionally stuttered and too often wore his red and blue zig-zag sports jacket, navy-blue bell-bottom slacks, or platform shoes to banking interviews. He was, he thought, simply making a point about being black and proud. He was, in reality, just feeling insecure—angry.

The anger boiled to the surface his first year at United California, where Gordon was the only black in the bank's training program for MBA graduates. He felt uncomfortable, even hostile around whites—exactly the kind of trainee psychologists Ron Brown and Price Cobbs were conducting their workshops for: the new black professional who would learn how to successfully integrate corporate America by first learning to control his anger.

The workshops had been modified by the time Gordon registered for the Pacific Management Systems series of seminars in 1976. The emphasis ten years later was not so much on black and white race confrontations but on black-on-black confrontation: facing up to anger, identifying its source, and developing skills to cope. Gordon was told he was "the angriest black man" the consultants had encountered in a decade. He didn't agree. "I was traumatized," he says now, though by what is not clear—the assessment of him or the circumstances which led to his anger.

What kept the circumstances surrounding Ellis Gordon's anger from being less than typical was the era in which he came of age. Born in 1947, Gordon was in the first wave riding the crest of the black baby boom. His was the class of boomers born immediately after the second war that was to make the world safe for democracy. This was the generation that would be old enough to remember the struggles to overcome and young enough to benefit from the new opportunities that were the fruits of that struggle. And it was the generation that would cross over from Negro to black, from segregation to integration, in one great leap of history and trauma.

GETTING OVER

Ellis Gordon grew up with five sisters in what was considered Houston's poor Fifth Ward. Although his father is a minister and a college graduate, he never had his own church, nor did he make a lot of money running a small grocery store or peddling Fuller black beauty products as an itinerant salesman. The family struggled in poverty. By the age of eight Ellis was working to contribute to the household, earning 30 cents an hour distributing grocery flyers door to door. He was quick, smart, and ambitious, and he carried the hopes of a community. There was never any doubt that he would go to college. It was expected, not just by his parents, but by the entire neighborhood. "My success was the neighborhood's success," he says. "Everybody bought into my success. I mean, the neighbors would be proud to say that they had a kid on their block that went to college." Economics limited his choice of undergraduate schools to Texas Southern University, a black school which had a tuition of fifty dollars per semester in 1965, the year he graduated from high school. But fear kept him from taking a shot at the Ivy League.

In his junior year of high school Gordon was offered a scholarship to Dartmouth which he declined. "I met with the white preppy kids the school had sent in to recruit blacks. Dartmouth was in Hanover [New Hampshire] and it seemed like a whole other world to me—to go from Houston all the way to Hanover. I didn't see myself being able to cope with going from an all-black environment to an all-white environment."

Indeed, making the crossing from a black environment to a white one has always been a tricky maneuver in America, for it usually means wading through the troubled waters of racism, climbing the slimy banks of discrimination, and getting past the border patrols who still demand proof of worth. For a southern black 18-year-old coming of age in the sixties in a poor though tightly knit African-American community, segregation had its strengths and comforts, its reinforcing higher ground. "Going to a black undergraduate college turned out to be better for me," Gordon says. "That's basically where I learned people skills."

Yet by the time he graduated from Texas Southern in 1969 and decided to go to graduate school, Gordon was ready to take advantage of his privileged position as a marketable commodity in a new crossover era that would be marked not just by integration but also by the ascendancy of corporate business as an elite, new professional arena for blacks. He finished college in the top 10 percent of his class with a major in economics. The MBA had not yet been transformed from sheepskin to a gold pass, but in the late sixties, it was where the smart money was going in graduate school. Although

Gordon decided to pursue a master's degree in business administration, he initially accepted a scholarship from Northern Illinois University to work on a Ph.D. in economics. "They had come through first with a scholarship and money to pay for everything, and I said, what the heck, they're paying," Gordon says matter-of-factly. But a week after hearing from Northern Illinois, he was accepted to Stanford's MBA program and offered $20,000. The money was in loans, however, not scholarships, so Gordon turned it down. Then he got a call from the University of Illinois. They definitely wanted him, and to prove it, they were offering a fellowship, a teaching assistantship, and guaranteed admission for Gordon's new wife, who was a drama major.

Like other promising blacks of his generation who were born into poverty, Gordon represented the mind that was a terrible thing to waste: the talent and potential that white America hurried to recruit in the rush of a decade, to ply with "minority" scholarships, to woo with affirmative action, to seduce with new opportunities in an effort to cool all the old black rage that was firing up America in the sixties. He was in the vanguard of a new generation of booming black "firsts"—the first in the family to finish college and professional graduate school, the first to get hired in this white company or promoted to that vice presidency; the first to get elected to public office, to be voted onto a board of directors, to get financing for a black business, to get support for black ambition. The first to succeed in white America on integrated terms.

Ellis Gordon was not the first black to attend the University of Illinois at Champaign-Urbana, but he was the only American black in its 1969 freshman MBA class—and the only black American in the university's entire graduate business school of 500. As he understates it, "I went from being a big fish in a little pond to a little fish in a huge ocean." The little pond that was Texas Southern University had a total predominantly black enrollment of 5500, compared with Illinois's huge ocean of 40,000 students, 2000 of them black, 9000 of them foreign.

Gordon was never sure who was more foreign—the students from other countries, or the whites from middle America. "It was fairly traumatic," he says of integrating Illinois's business school that first year. "I found that most of the whites I was dealing with had never had a lot of interaction with blacks. I'm talking about guys from the cornfields of Nebraska and Iowa and Indiana and Illinois. So there was apprehension on their part—and mine—because we came from different worlds." The differences isolated Gordon. He was always the last asked to join a study group or work on a project, the last asked to integrate. As a result, "I became a group of one. I would end up doing things on my own, which made the transition from an all-black school to an all-white one even more difficult."

The rigors of business school were more demanding than anything Texas Southern had ever been, yet there was less support at the University of Illinois for anything Ellis Gordon ever did. The school was not only huge and impersonal; it was almost malignant in its neglect for the Southern black it had pursued with such liberal passion. "There was a lot less personal attention given to you," Gordon says of being in a school with large class sizes and vague course outlines. Without the critical camraderie, the academic reinforcements a buddy system provides first-year graduate students, Gordon's grades suffered. That first semester he got Cs for the first time in his school life, with some grades close to being Ds. He was used to getting As and Bs in black schools without trying too hard, and now here he was in a white school for the first time, finding it hard just to stay average. Was it him? Was he really only barely average after all, not up to standards? Or was it them—whites and their benign racism?

The question of what came first, racism, which has the impact of making blacks feel inferior, or inferiority, which has the impact of making whites feel justified in racism, is the great existential dilemma that has troubled blacks in America since slavery. It is the final psychic result of insidious oppression: to remain in the flickering shadow of doubt regarding self-worth despite all the realities that indicate clear proof of worth.

Ellis Gordon, for one, turned out to be clear proof. He graduated from the University of Illinois in 1971 with a 4.3 grade-point average out of a perfect 5. Once he made it past his first semester, whites felt "this guy is okay," so he was more often asked to join study groups. But by then he had also begun networking with other blacks on campus. His first regular study partner was the second black admitted to the business school that year, an African transfer student from French-speaking Ivory Coast: "He could barely speak English and I could barely speak French, but we learned to communicate." Gordon also joined study groups with blacks who were in related fields such as mathematics. He joined the black student union that was active on campus.

For the first line of black baby boomers integrating American higher education in the late sixties, such support groups—black study groups, black student unions, black dormitories, black studies programs—became the critical emotional reference points needed to help successfully navigate a turbulent crossing. Students like Ellis Gordon had spent a lifetime in the protective, supportive environment of black institutions—their schools, their churches, their neighborhoods—and now suddenly found themselves isolated on alien white college campuses. The passage, as Gordon kept repeating, was traumatic.

What was more traumatic was being unable to find a job once he graduated. The MBA, Gordon figured, was his ticket to success. He had chosen the University of Illinois because it was the one school he applied to that didn't have a special program for blacks. He didn't have to take "catch-up" courses or minority "orientation" sessions. He was being admitted as an equal. He thus expected his new MBA to give him an edge that would not only result in a job after graduation but prove that he could integrate. "I felt in a naive kind of way that because I was able to make it through a white school, that would show I had the ability to assimilate to some degree." Gordon turned down several offers in New York and Chicago to move to his wife's hometown, Los Angeles, where there were more opportunities in her profession, acting.

Still, Gordon says, "I just knew some company in Los Angeles was going to be more than happy to provide me with a job." He was, after all, a talented young black MBA during an era when that was in great demand. But he also looked like an angry black man every time he appeared for a job interview. Looking back on it, Gordon acknowledges he contributed to his own failure to get work. "I thought I was so good that I didn't have to cut my hair," he says of the large though now receding Afro he continued to wear once he left campus. "You know, I just felt it really didn't matter because I wore a suit and tie and I had all of the qualifications they needed. Plus, affirmative action was on the rise and qualified blacks were in." But not angry, defiant ones. In addition to the Afro, Gordon wore a goatee and Ben Franklin horn-rimmed glasses, and he frequently wore a loud red and blue sportcoat to interviews, or bell-bottom pants, or platform shoes. The total package was deliberate. "I consciously decided that the way I was going to show I was proud of being black was to maintain those physical attributes —you know, the hair, the goatee."

The look, however, was masking insecurity and anger. Ellis Gordon was qualified yet unemployed. He interviewed everywhere. One contact led to an interview at ABC. He was offered a job as a clerk and told this was where everyone started, including Reuben Cannon, who had gone on from being a clerk to become Hollywood's most successful black casting director. Gordon was not impressed, only outraged. "Now, what's wrong with you?" he said to the interviewer. "You don't seem to understand—I have a master's degree from a white school."

That didn't get Gordon a position in corporate white America for five years. From 1971 to 1972 he was vice president of operations for a black California real estate firm. In 1972 he talked the company into letting him take over its construction division, which he ran as a managing partner until 1976. Once again, it was the support of a black community that sustained him. But he had mixed feelings. He had been trained for integration, yet he could find work only in segregated black corporate America. And while he liked the freedom "being my own man" brought in black entrepenuership, it also brought economic uncertainty. He filed bankruptcy during this time and he and his wife divorced.

In 1976 Gordon renewed the search for corporate employment and this time got a bite. The United California Bank (now First Interstate Bank of California) offered him a spot in its Multi-National Account Offices training program, a fast-track program for MBA graduates. Again, as he had been at the University of Illinois,

Gordon was the only black in a training class of thirteen. But by now he was also just mostly angry. Angry that it had taken so long to get hired in a field for which he had so arduously trained. Angry that he felt compelled to show up for work by six-thirty every morning and work until eight or nine every night just to prove he could do the job. Angry that when he finally cut his Afro and his goatee, nobody noticed. Angry that any critical evaluations made him bristle, made him defensive, made him start calling white colleagues "racists." Angry enough to recognize finally that he needed help in getting his rage under control before he ended up sabotaging his own career.

What Ellis Gordon essentially learned to do in the workshops for corporate blacks run by Ron Brown and Price Cobbs was diffuse enraging situations and raise the "comfort level" of whites. He learned that everybody, for instance, not just whites, admired the work ethic. "Everybody automatically assumes that if you work long hours, that you're a good person," he says, and since he was naturally an early riser, he learned to view getting to the office early as something valuable that was probably respected, which it was. He also learned to be less confrontational, not to jump so quickly. "Now I get involved with mental confrontation rather than the physical side of things the way I did before, yelling at folks to do this and that, telling them to get out of my way. I have found you have to learn something about the people you are dealing with. You have to try to get inside of their personality, find out what they like, what their needs and wants are, and then you can make life much easier for you."

Perhaps most important, Gordon learned to face himself. "When you come into a work environment you bring a lot of background noise. You know, feelings about yourself, what you've been taught in reference to black/white relationships." It turned out the noisiest sound Gordon was hearing was the nagging buzz of doubt—"self-doubt, doubting my own worth, doubting my own abilities."

Black doubt is often precisely what resides at the center of black rage. "What happened when I started at the bank," says Gordon without a trace of doubt, "is that I was five or six years older than everybody else in the program because they had just come out of school and I had been out of school for five years. I had not had any banking training, period, whereas a lot of the other trainees had worked at the bank maybe one or two summers during undergraduate or graduate school. So here I was starting the race five or ten yards behind everybody else, just trying to catch up. And I guess I perceived that maybe I could not do as well." It is a common perception of a people arriving at the gate of competition several generations after the starting shot has been fired.

Yet Ellis Gordon closed the gap. Today he is the vice president and manager of the Capital Bank of California, a white independent bank where his prime responsibility is commercial lending. The angry young militant of fifteen years ago learned how to turn rage into corporate success. He's become sensitive enough to be reflective, comfortable enough to wear dental braces at age 40, and shrewd enough to keep the white comfort level up by driving a nonthreatening, stylish Peugeot. He lives in View Park, an exclusive Los Angeles neighborhood of successful, upper middle class blacks and is married to his second wife, the successful writer Bebe Moore Campbell.

Gordon still has a black temper and a black consciousness—which means he has learned from his mistakes and learned from history the limitations of integrated success. To be black and integrated may always be awkward for him, for he is a man who grew up in the strength and reality of "separate"—in being with his own. And while he may have pioneered integration in his youth, he found the experience painful, traumatic. Integration, he says now, may be the "the worst thing that ever happened to blacks, because of the false idea it presented that assimilation, equality, is really possible." It is not, Gordon declares simply. Not now, not in his lifetime, his generation. That, however, no longer makes him angry —or even keeps him from being a success.*

---

* In January 1991 Ellis Gordon became senior vice president and chief credit officer of the Founders National Bank of Los Angeles, the largest black-owned bank on the West Coast.

SUCCEEDING BEYOND ANGER

Like the American baby boom generation of which it constitutes 12 percent, the black baby boom generation defined an epoch. It was the generation born Negro into segregation that grew up black expecting to integrate. It represented conflict in an age of change and contradiction in the face of progress. It was protesting, angry, riotous. It was also a generation whose movement for civil rights became a journey of discovery in self-confidence.

What the real value of integration has been to today's black success generation is that it provided more equitable opportunities for interaction with a group sometimes considered superior: whites. For access to integrated competition in what had been the rarefied arena of the American corporation gave blacks a new kind of exposure to whites—"up close and personal." And what they saw was not at all superior. "Blacks entering corporate America realized that not everybody in the system had an IQ of 150," says Ron Brown. "People weren't really all that smart; the system had its benefits, but you didn't have to be a mental genius to participate. There was no longer a veil over what 'they' do—whoever 'they' are—or what the system is. We have a more refined understanding of what American business really is, and a stronger sense of what we can accomplish. Our experiences have taught us that we're as smart as anybody else; we're as competent, we can pretty much do whatever there is in a corporate arena. People like us can do that."

It turned out that successful blacks bring some natural strengths to the corporate workplace. Anger can be one of them, when used as a motivator and not an excuse. African-Americans, Ron Brown has observed during his twenty-five years of monitoring corporate black advancement, also have a certain capacity for handling ambiguity, for the art of improvising, for being able to read systems, for being flexible. Traditionally, their survival depended on it. Today, business does.

Those blacks who succeed have also found, in the words of Brown, "the appropriate level of effective relationships with whites." This remains the area of greatest ambiguity, conflict, and confusion. Yet the great truth of integration is that for blacks to succeed in America, there must be a network of relationships beyond black; there must be working, effective relationships with whites. It has become a tricky act, striking this psychic balance between being black and being comfortable and effective working with the people ". . . who are born into a culture which contains the hatred of blacks as an integral part," as William Grier and Price Cobbs said of white Americans in *Black Rage*.

This racial hatred has been the historical source of black anger, but it is also this very history that successful blacks develop a facility to move beyond in order to move forward. "Successful black people are very rooted, they know where they came from, and they're not confused by the trappings of the system," says Ron Brown. "But they have also developed a world view as well as a race view. They have a broader view of what's out there, how big things really are, which allows them to elevate a racial view beyond a point of anger. They have good instincts for determining what's racial, and what they will deal with even when it is racial, because they've learned there are bigger issues than whether you're black or not."

Gerald B. Smith: Taking the Larger View

It seemed strictly racial when a vice president of Hibbard, O'Connor and Weeks, a Houston investment banking firm, walked by Gerald Smith's desk his first day on the job and muttered under his breath, though deliberately loud enough for Smith to hear, "Black motherfucker." That was in 1974. It is now 1988. Smith says he will never forget it. He was sitting in the bullpen of the trading floor making cold calls to potential customers. He was the first black in Texas trading back then, a dark, wiry Houston maverick who had gotten the job at Hibbard, O'Connor and Weeks after several interviews by finally saying straight out to the manager of sales and training, "Listen, the only reason you won't hire me is because I'm black, and if I'm lying, you look me in the eye and you just tell me I'm wrong and you'll never hear from me again. But if I'm right, I expect you to hire me."

He was right. He was hired, and his first day on the trading floor he was called out of his name—a black motherfucker—by a company vice president. *Jesus,* was his first stunned thought. It was one of those harrowing moments in a black experience that required making in an instant one life-altering choice: either give in to race and rage and risk ending a new career, or take the larger view and focus on all the rich possibilities of that new career, on what it meant to integrate in the lucrative field of Texas investment banking in the early seventies. Smith took the larger view and did a slow, simmering count to ten.

Looking back on it, Smith is confident he made the right choice. Looking at him now, it is clear he did. He is leaning cowboy style against a counter in the kitchen of his Texas-sized Houston home, a sprawling prairie mansion built by a lumber baron at the turn of the twentieth century. Wearing a loose Italian silk shirt and tailored linen pants, Smith has the relaxed and confident, elegant casualness of a baron himself. He is a Houston native by birth, though his original ancestry looks pure Ashanti—African aristocrat, handsome and regal, a warrior spirit in the old wild west.

At 37, Gerald B. Smith is first senior vice president in charge of marketing and financial services for the Westcap Corporation, a Houston-based investment banking firm that traded $20 billion in securities in 1988. He oversees an area that generated $36 million in revenues and is one of the company's four key principals—the equivalent of partner. It is estimated he made $350,000 in salary, commissions, and bonuses in 1987 and that his personal net worth exceeds $1 million. He sits on the board of the Houston Arts Council, is married, and is the father of a teenage son born when he himself was a teenager and not married. His son lives with him now, as does his grandmother. In the roaring bull market of the eighties, Gerald Smith got rich—and then got even.

Typical of the mergers that dominated the age in the eighties, the Westcap Corporation was the new entity formed when the

National Western Insurance Corporation merged with the Capital Bank of Texas, which had taken over Hibbard, O'Connor and Weeks, which was where Gerald Smith began his investment banking career, where he was called out of his name his first day on the job by a white vice president. Ten years later, after a stint with the Dillon Read investment firm in New York, where he had bought a seat on the New York Futures Exchange, Smith was back in Houston, now a senior vice president at Westcap. The white vice president was still with the merged company—and Smith had the opportunity to fire him because he wasn't producing. Some things are worth waiting for. Smith, however, insists it was only business.

Indeed, this is the position Gerald Smith learned to take in most of his interactions with whites. When he started in investment banking as a broker pitching clients over the phone, race was seldom even an issue, for customers rarely saw his face. "My telephone voice is not a black voice per se," he says with clear, even inflections that reveal no accent of any kind. Yet he knew that meeting clients at some point was inevitable. He admits it made him apprehensive and recalls the time one of his best clients, an officer from the Savings Bank of Massachusetts in his northeastern territory, invited him to a conference in Bermuda. "I guess I was a little paranoid because I had never met him face to face. We'd done all of our business by phone." Smith, however, didn't want to wait until he showed up in Bermuda to surprise and possibly shock his client, so he took the plunge and gave warning over the phone: "Bill, I really appreciate you inviting me to Bermuda, but there's one thing I thought I should let you know."

"Well, what's that, Gerald?" Bill asked expectantly.

"I'm black," Smith said.

"What?"

"I'm black," Smith repeated.

"So? Gerald, I don't care what color you are. I don't give a damn if you're green, white, pink, or purple. As long as you've done a good job for me, it doesn't matter to me. Why are you concerned about that?"

"Well, I just thought I should let you know," Smith said, feeling the great yoke of race suddenly being lifted.

"Fine. Okay," said the white man who had just set him free.

Smith admits this was in fact the moment of his liberation, the moment he understood that not everybody, including whites, views the world through the narrow dimensions of race and color; that in business, frequently the only real dimension is the bottom line. "After that it was never a problem," he says of race. In fact, his turned out to be an asset. Clients who met him after months of doing business on the phone were usually pleasantly surprised to see an African-American. The typical reaction was, "God, the guy is black—and good, too."

And that *was* the bottom line. Gerald Smith was good. By the end of his first year, he was the top seller among the thirty-five new brokers who had started with him at Hibbard. He admits that getting hit with a racial insult his first day had a driving, motivating effect: "It was a rude awakening; it told me what I was going to have to put up with in order to make it. Until I'd proven myself as a producer or an asset, I knew I had to take a lot of shit."

The key to Smith's success is that he never took it personally. "I took it personally at the time," he says of the vice president's racist remark. "I knew it was against me because I was sitting there, but it could've been any other black that was sitting there." Remarkably, instead of feeling angry, Smith had the capacity to feel pity for the racist who had insulted him. "Here was a guy who was probably used to seeing blacks in very subservient roles instead of trying to do the same thing he was doing. I guess he felt resentful, so I felt sorry for him in a sense—but that also made me much more determined to make it."

Critical to success for blacks is a facility to first understand and then accommodate the dynamics of race in their interactions with whites. In Gerald Smith's case, he understood that race could be an issue with a white client who had never met him, so he diffused it beforehand by simply telling him, "I'm black." The client said it didn't matter, and even if it had, both men had grace time to recover before meeting face to face. Indeed, racism's very perversity is its physical focus. Smith's color, his race, was not an issue as long as he was not *seen.* With the potentially more explosive situation of being called an ugly name by a clearly racist and more powerful white, Smith struck a psychic bargain: he would remain cool and get even by doing well. That is still the best revenge. He also took the moral high ground by "feeling sorry" for a "poor racist," which had the psychic benefit of relieving him of some of his anger.

This is the psychology of adapting that has always given African-Americans their spiritual force when faced with the viper of racism. And it is this spiritual force that ultimately transcends the black anger of racist aggressions. It is the quality that gives blacks a certain superiority in the face of white oppression—the might of right wronged.

Yet blacks have spent all of their history in America anticipating, understanding, reacting to, reacting against, or manipulating the behavior of whites. Over time, that has taken a certain psychic toll, frequently exhibited as anger or doubt. But it has also produced enormous psychic strength, manifested as new confidence in the corporate workplace. A place where success still calls for some old skills: an ability to handle whites, a capacity to diffuse anger, the facility to see beyond race. The new confidence, however, is the result of important new insights illuminated by integration: that when given an equal opportunity, African-Americans prove to be good—good at what they do, good at competing, good at succeeding. To be good and know it may be the only real thing worth knowing, for it is this knowledge that will always set you free.*

* In July 1990 Gerald Smith left the Westcap Corporation to start his own asset managing business, Smith, Graham and Company, which manages money for institutional investors.

¥

A CREDIT
TO THE RACE

Race, like power, blinds before it corrupts.
Taylor Branch,
Parting the Waters

*T*he August air was hot and sticky, the kind of pressing, drippy Southern humidity that feels like "the inside of a dawg's mouth," as folks in Memphis like to say. Clarence Alvin Daniel Gasby was expecting rednecks but not the heat when he stepped off the plane that sweltering summer evening. He was dressed for neither. He had gotten a call just that morning in New York asking if he was interested in applying for a sales position with a new UHF station being built in Memphis—a startup, the kind of wildcat operation in which he knew he would be expected to hit the ground running, to make the rules as he went along because there were no systems yet, to be the underdog, to be ready and able to make a name for himself—in short, as he saw it, "to be wild and crazy."

Which is exactly how Dan Gasby must have looked to John Bailey, the general sales manager who picked him up at the airport and would be interviewing him for the job. At six feet four inches and 220 pounds, bearded and black as evening velvet, Gasby loomed in the airport, casting the taut, lean figure of an elegant shadow. On this particular 95-degree night the shadow looked very cool in his best Madison Avenue salmon-colored Geoffrey Beene suit. "John kept saying it was pink," Gasby remembers. "I had to keep telling him it was salmon."

For his part, John Bailey struck Dan Gasby as a typical good-old-boy—a "yuppie redneck"—whose style and appearance fell somewhere between Kris Kristofferson's and Bobby Ewing's. Gasby and Bailey had met five months before when Bailey and a colleague had gone to New York for a crash course in television sales with a company representing local TV stations. Gasby, who was doing grunt-level research at the company and looking to break into broadcast sales, had been helpful to the two Southerners, and Bailey promised to keep him in mind should a sales position open up at the station in Memphis.

Bailey kept his word, and now here they were on Southern turf —the black Yankee who wore salmon-colored designer suits and the Southern redneck who wore Jefferson Davis buttons on King's birthday—facing off in the Memphis heat.

"So, you think you can sell?" Bailey fired at Gasby almost as soon as they had climbed into the rental car. There was another guy from the station seated in the back, arms folded, a thin smile of amusement crossing his face as he observed the two men in front.

"I been selling all my life," Gasby fired back.

"What are you gonna do if they call you a nigger down here? Because, you know, they will call you a nigger."

"If it's a matter of placing a sales order, they can call me nigger all they want as long as I get the money. But if it's on my time and I'm in a bad mood, and if I don't feel like it—I'll probably beat the shit out of 'em. It all depends. I'll decide when I'm going to get angry, because business is business."

"You can't get sick," Bailey pressed on. "You've got to work. You may have to do everything I have to do. You may have to sweep. You may have to throw garbage in a dumpster."

"John," Gasby said with a long, patient sigh, "I'm here to learn."

With that, Bailey reached under the car seat and pulled out a bottle of Rebel Yell, Tennessee's finest rotgut whiskey. He opened the bottle, took a long swig, and passed the moonshine to Gasby, who took a swig without missing a beat. Bailey then gave Gasby a long, thoughtful look, and finally said, "You're hired."

The guy in the backseat roared with laughter.

The next thing Gasby knew, Bailey had pulled up in front of Silky Sullivan's tavern to celebrate. But no sooner had Gasby stepped into the bar than he came up against what Bailey had warned him about just minutes before: "What's that nigger doing in here?" one of the customers demanded.

"That was my introduction to Memphis," Gasby says, chuckling. "It was about 10:30 that night. I hadn't even gotten to the hotel from the airport yet. And here's this redneck calling me a nigger. I looked at him. The guy broke a bottle. And I went after him. We got into a fight right there in Overton Square."

And in the middle of the fight, Clarence Alvin Daniel Gasby, then 24, suddenly knew it, suddenly felt it as surely as he felt the punches on that hot Tennessee night. This was exactly where he was meant to be—in the middle of the action, where men go toe-to-toe, whether they're slugging it out in barroom brawls or passing rotgut whiskey in speeding cars or cutting deals in marble conference halls. The action is wherever men dare to be wild and crazy, to have courage and heart, to put it all on the line and take no prisoners. The action is in sales. And so it was, right in the middle of the fight on his first night in the South, that Dan Gasby thought to himself in a glorious moment of revelation and exhilaration, *This is for me.*

It has been nearly ten years since Dan Gasby threw down with the Memphis redneck, yet he tells the story with fresh relish, the details as vivid today as the night he lived them in the summer of 1979. Sales is still for him. And like most successful salesmen, Gasby is a natural at it, combining charm and wit with the raconteur's gift of gab, the daredevil's thrill in risk-taking, and the promoter's power to persuade. He spent four years in Memphis, where he cut his teeth in broadcast sales and got into a few more fights before taking a job at age 28 as general sales manager for a station in Jacksonville, Florida.

Now at 33 in 1988 and back home in New York City, Gasby is an account executive for Camelot Entertainment, a division of King World Syndicates, selling national bartered syndication time to advertisers for such blockbuster King World television shows as "Wheel of Fortune," "Jeopardy" and the "Oprah Winfrey Show." He was the first and only black male selling bartered time in 1988 and made $133,000 the previous year in salary and commissions. His $300,000 two-bedroom penthouse apartment on Manhattan's West Side, where he lives with his wife and daughter, is just over the bridge from his native Brooklyn, yet about as far away from the tenements of the Bedford-Stuyvesant ghetto where he grew up as any black American is expected to get. But then Dan Gasby has always defied both the odds and the assumptions, for success among African-Americans is invariably a function of having risen above the expectations.

Dan Gasby: Exceptions and the Expectations

Like most black Americans, Dan Gasby grew up with mixed messages as motivators for success. He grew up being told by his father, who was a janitor: "No matter what you are I'll always love you. Just be the best and give the most that you can." He grew up being told by his mother, who was a domestic worker: "I just want you to be able to take care of yourself. If you can feed and clothe yourself, you'll do a whole lot better than a lot of people." He became a success in sales after being told by whites, who were racist: "You'll never make it." The messages always made the same subtle and powerful point: "Not very much is required or open to you. Just be the best you can be." Yet one of the great burdens of black success has been this very contradiction: not much is expected, therefore everything is demanded. "Be the best you can be," even if you don't turn out to be very much. "Be a credit to the race," for race is at a debit. "Be successful," and prove you are as good as anybody else.

To be black and a success in America is largely to be viewed as an exception—a departure from the rule, an aberration. It is a view that skews black ambition and blinds white perception, for it is a vision still clouded in the pathology of race. As Taylor Branch said in the very first line of *Parting the Waters,* his prize-winning book on the Civil Rights Movement, "Almost as color defines vision itself, race shapes the cultural eye—what we do and do not notice, the reach of empathy and the alignment of response." Race perhaps more significantly also shapes expectations and assumptions—what we think we can and cannot be. And it is very often low expectations—for black ability, for black possibility—that both limits and drives black ambition.

Dan Gasby says that while his parents put little pressure on him to succeed, he put pressure on himself. He came to his parents late, an only child born when his mother was 38 and his father 50. He was a bright child, though by the third grade he was reading at only a second-grade level in Bedford-Stuyvesant's Public School 289. "I knew I could read better, and I told my mother I wanted to be transferred. P.S. 289 was like a zoo—I mean, the teachers may as well have just thrown meat in the class and closed the door. They let everybody run around and bounce off the wall."

Gasby transferred to P.S. 269 in 1964—bused into what was then the predominantly Jewish section of Flatbush. He was 9, the only black, and the biggest kid in his integrated fourth-grade classroom. "The interesting thing about it," he remembers, "is that when I was in the black school in Bed-Stuy, I ranked 3–2, and when I got to the white school they immediately put me in 4–9. [the first number is the grade level, the second is the ranking within a grade, with 1 being the highest]. And within seven or eight weeks, I took the standardized test and I went from 4–9 to 4–3, and subsequently I went into 5–IGC [intellectually gifted class]. People couldn't understand how I went from being behind in reading to reading on a junior-high level. It's just that I wasn't challenged, and I wasn't tested properly."

The real difference, Gasby says, is that the teachers in P.S. 269 were interested in their largely Jewish students: pushed them, encouraged them, rewarded competition and academic excellence. It was very different from the school in Bedford-Stuyvesant, which put primary value on just being tough. "Being around a lot of Jews really made a big difference. They were striving, and because I was around them I started thinking the way they thought in terms of why it was important to study, why it was important to compete. I got into some statistical things like baseball cards. Memorizing averages and knowing the minute details about players may seem trivial, but it teaches you to be analytical. It made a difference."

Gasby would benefit from both the toughness he acquired in Bed-Stuy and the academic preparation he got in Flatbush. And the combination gained him admission into prestigious Brooklyn Technical High School, where he proved to be both athletic and smart—smart enough that by his junior year he figured he could skip his senior year of high school altogether and go directly to college. He had heard there were some colleges that admitted high school juniors under an early admissions program, but when he approached his guidance counselors about this, he was predictably told, "You're not ready." He then went to a man named Al Vann, who was head of the Afro-American Teachers Association and had established a program to help black students gain early admissions to college. Gasby pored over hundreds of college catalogs, targeted twenty schools, applied to all, was accepted by most, and finally settled on Colgate, a small elite college in upstate New York "on the periphery of the Ivy League."

Since Gasby had met all the course requirements and did well on the Scholastic Aptitude Tests, scoring a combined 1388 out of a possible perfect score of 1600, he was not only admitted to Colgate's early admissions program after his junior year of high school, but he secured a full academic scholarship. He graduated in three and a half years at age 20 and to this day remains proud of a distinctive achievement: to be a college graduate who doesn't have a high school diploma.

A large part of Dan Gasby's success is due to his sheer competitive drive to succeed. Long before he knew exactly what he wanted to do, he knew he wanted to be successful. "I was eager to get into the world, to make money," he says, explaining his impatience with staying in school longer than necessary. For Gasby, early exposure to whites gave him a sense of what was possible—what to reach for. He admits experiencing a certain amount of shame in being black as a youngster because it highlighted just how different his world was from that of his white classmates. "I became good friends with a Jewish dude named Peter Smith whose dad owned a department store in Brooklyn. He had a lovely house, a lovely attached house. I remember sitting in his dad's den and being in the wonderful kitchen and the great bathroom, and then I'd go back to my house. We lived on the first floor of a tenement that had a hole in the bathroom floor. You could look down and see into the basement, where mice would come up. So you're sitting there on the toilet and here come four or five of Mickey's brothers up through the hole." To this day Gasby says he has a fixation about bathrooms and kitchens, which explains why the two bathrooms in his penthouse are lavishly styled with pristine white marble on the floor and walls, and brass fixtures on the sinks, bidets, and jacuzzis.

Gasby's early integration with whites primed him for doing business successfully in the competitive arena of sales. His first job was in the New York garment district, "one of the toughest places in the world to sell. It's very incestuous, very cannibalistic; you've got to be tough. You can't be a buttoned-down corporate guy. You've got to be able to go in and say [here Gasby lapses into an exaggerated Yiddish accent], 'Hey, Morty! Whataya think—I got a pointy hat on my head or something? I got these pieces here that are worth two dollars a yard. You wanna buy 'em from me, or what?' " Gasby breaks into laughter at his own routine, then becomes serious as he explains what it takes to be a success selling in the garment district—or anywhere else, for that matter: "You've got to know how to talk, how to say what you've got to say and when to say it, when to use inflections, and at the same time know when to back off. I learned how not to be corporate, but to get the job done. And I learned how to articulate things in a clear sell, how to get gritty—and how to be a character, and at the same time be effective.

These were the lessons Gasby used to good effect in Memphis, where he succeeded on his own terms in the hostile environment of Southern racism. But he also found that as he became successful, he became something very curious: he became non-black in the eyes of whites. He became what is known as the "exceptional" black, different from "those other" blacks who don't perform, who don't succeed. This ceasing to be black is a phenomenon most successful blacks have experienced at some point in their interaction with whites. Black failure is such an internalized, invidious expectation among whites that any exception has the result of taking black success out of the loop of race.

Dan Gasby knew he was out of the loop the day a Memphis businessman invited him to his home for dinner, showed him his gun collection, and then took him into the study to show family photographs of his slaveholding ancestors. "He wasn't a bad person, per se," Gasby says of the Southerner. "He was simply born into a system—a system that was totally irrational—but a system in which he was on top. And I was now a monkey wrench in that system because he had a perception of blacks that I just didn't fit." As the Southerner told Gasby: "I don't think of you as black."

I don't think of you as black. It is an admission that reveals white racism's peculiar schizophrenia. For if I don't think of you as black, then what do I think of you as . . . white? Hardly. Human? Maybe. An exception? Indeed. And if I think of you as black, how then do I see you? Always limited, for the view is forever dimmed by the color of race. Yet whenever whites confess, *I don't think of you as black,* it is almost always meant as a compliment—as though the idea that it is flattering to be black but not viewed as black is not *itself* a racist assumption. This arrogance of racism, however, is precisely what successful blacks manage to overcome. "My comeback to this Southerner telling me he didn't see me as black," says Gasby, "was to say, 'Hey, you're my friend. I mean, you eat with me, you hang out with me. But you don't think of me as black? Well, I *am* black.' Discounting my blackness was the same as discounting me."

It is the ability to affirm blackness as the basis of a positive identity, a source of ego strength and self-esteem, that roots black success. In the case of Dan Gasby, who turned all of the usual black male liabilities into assets—his size, his dark color, his fierce pride and quick temper, even his beard—success has been a function of comfortably integrating who he is with where he is. And it doesn't matter much where he is—the South, the garment district, a West

Side Manhattan penthouse. Gasby maintains a certain level of consistency and awareness that usually gives him an edge that makes
success inevitable. "I do two things. I have a good read about
people—I can size up a situation the same way a bat can run to a
hole to see the daylight, and I've always had good instincts. I mean,
a sales relationship is like a love affair—you know in fifteen seconds
whether this is someone you can sleep with."

Dan Gasby, after all is said and done, is simply very confident.
Race is not an issue, though it is an identity. What matters is that
he knows he is good. "I learned way back in junior high school that
I've got nothing to worry about," he says with complete assurance.
"I'm just going to be me. I am comfortable with myself." He also
learned a valuable lesson early on—how to view expectations and
possibilities: "My father always said there's a difference between
being poor and being po'. Poor has an 'or' in it, which means you
always have a choice. Po', on the other hand, means you got no mo'
—no more choice. I never believed I was po'."*

THE GROOMING PROCESS

A belief in choices has always fueled black ambition, for even in the
face of limited opportunities, one remains free to choose—to choose
excellence over mediocrity, for instance, or character over vanity, or
work and struggle over idle irresponsibility. These are the choices
to that go against stereotype and make for one being "a credit to
the race." Yet it is this very notion of being a credit to the race that
reveals just how much racist assumptions have served to undermine
black self-perception.

Much of the social grooming successful blacks learn both for-

* In September 1989 Dan Gasby left Camelot Entertainment to start his own
business. He is co-creator and executive producer of "Big Break," a syndicated
television show hosted by Natalie Cole. John Bailey of Memphis remains one of
his best friends.

mally and informally, consciously and subconsciously, is intended to instill in them such middle-class values as hard work, sacrifice, discipline, ambition—values typically associated with being white. The aim is always to be, whether in manner, speech, dress, education, or aspirations, a "cut above" the low expectations of the black class. The aim is to be an exception. But to be an exception means that a stereotype has been accepted as the standard of measure, and it is this acceptance of the stereotype that both propels black success and dislocates it. Writer Shelby Steele, in his collection of essays on race, *The Content of Our Character,* reveals how his own value system for success was shaped:

> . . . it is fundamentally true that my middle-class identity involved a disassociation from images of lower-class black life and a corresponding identification with values and patterns of responsibility. . . . Whether I live up to these values or not, I know that my acceptance of them is the result of lifelong conditioning. . . . Whether all this got started because the black middle class modeled itself on the white middle class is no longer relevant. For the middle-class black, conditioned by these values from birth, the sense of meaning they provide is as immutable as the color of his skin.

Yet this conditioning, this grooming, as it were, is essentially from a negative reference point, for it accepts "lower-class black life" as the stereotype to react against. Indeed, black success is not so much a consequence of becoming middle class as it is an ability to escape being lower class—to become an exception to the expectations. But if a distinguishing feature of black success is the capacity to be more than the sum of racist stereotypes, an exceptional feature is having the wherewithal to achieve even when a stereotype seems to fit.

Ramona Tascoe Burris: Playing by the Rules

Ernest Tascoe was determined that none of his three girls would fall into any of the stereotypes he felt were often associated with "common" black women: loud, loose, bodacious, careless. It was one of the reasons he moved his family north in the early fifties from Baton Rouge, Louisiana, to northern California, the land of opportunity, with its better jobs, better education, better social experiences. For a Louisiana Creole, Catholic school represented the best education for blacks, and Ernest Tascoe's basic take on the matter was that if you had the right attitude and the right education, you could do anything you wanted to do. For his girls, though, this meant "Finish college, so you can get a job, so if your husband doesn't work out right, you have something to fall back on and you can take care of yourself. You won't end up on welfare."

If the dreams and expectations seemed limited, they had been stunted by the special fear many black fathers hold for their daughters: that to be black and female in a society that values neither is to be perpetually at risk for being "messed up," as Tascoe always put it. The best Tascoe figured he could do was to make his daughters prepared—and also keep them pure. The girls, then, grew up learning to speak properly, to be refined, and of course, expected to go to college. Each was told she would not be allowed to date until her second year of college—and then only if she made the Dean's List. Not surprisingly, such expectations and restrictions did not apply to the two boys in the family, whom Tascoe believed had a better chance at life simply by virtue of being male.

"God rest his soul! My father was a good man, but a classic chauvinist," laughs Ramona Tascoe Burris, M.D., one of Ernest Tascoe's three girls. "He was really just so scared for his daughters." The irony, as Ramona Tascoe sees it, is that the daughter who is today the most successful in terms of education and income is the very one who was also the most outspoken growing up, who gave Daddy the hardest time.

This daughter was the middle child in a family of five siblings, younger than her two sisters, older than her two brothers. Fiery and independent, she was more like her father in spirit and temperament than the others—she was the one who sat with him in front of the television set, watching "Meet the Press" or Eric Sevareid, discussing the heavy issues just like a son. Her sisters were scared and passive around Daddy, while she was aggressive, assertive, and determined. The rule was that you dated only after your second year of college, and only if you made the Dean's List. Okay, she thought—I'll do better. I'm going to finish college in two years and I'm going to make more than Dean's List. I'm going to make *cum laude,* okay? Because I really want you off my back, Daddy.

So the daughter finished college in two and a half years, with a triple major in political science, sociology, and psychology, and a 3.8 grade-point average. But Daddy still wouldn't give her permission to date. No, wait, I didn't expect all of this, he said when confronted with the reality of her success. Father and daughter had it out then, and she moved out. Daddy said it was sinful, a 20-year-old girl leaving home, unmarried and unprotected. But she felt free at last, free at last, even as she found herself in a relationship with a married man—a doctor, no less—with whom she would live for ten years and have his child, ironically becoming one of the common statistics Daddy had always feared: an unwed mother. But she also became much, much more. She became a doctor, and thus the exceptional success in the family, for Dr. Ramona Tascoe Burris, Ernest Tascoe's middle child, his headstrong youngest daughter, the one who chose to get pregnant without being married, is the one who beat a stereotype, and then beat a system.

Northern California's black physicians in 1987 numbered over 300, with a preponderance clustered in private practice along doctors' row in a black middle-class community of Oakland known as Pill Hill. "California dreaming" of a good life is what traditionally attracted blacks in the medical profession to the Bay Area, to Oakland in particular, with its stunning hills, proximity to San Francisco, affordable cost of good living, nearly 50 percent black population, and its civil rights legacy of northern revolution. The Black Panther Party founders lived here: Huey Newton, Bobby Seale, Eldridge Cleaver, Elaine Brown. The names became household words in the sixties, synonymous with a new generation of black activists—urban guerrillas of the north—who helped transform the hills of Oakland into the West Coast's seat of black political power and consciousness.

Ramona Tascoe, who grew up in San Francisco, started her medical career on a well-known hill in Oakland—at Highland General Hospital, the Alameda County facility sprawled on a knoll near Highway 580 and the urban decay that is much of East Oakland. Like many county hospitals in the inner city, Highland is a first-rate teaching facility with a first-rate surgery department. And Ramona Tascoe had once been Highland's most promising resident, with a career as a surgeon destined to be "brilliant." That was the very word the chief of surgery himself had used in his evaluation of Tascoe, just before he set out to ruin her career.

Of course, just looking at her, the last thing one would expect Ramona Tascoe to be is a surgeon. She is too pretty, too dainty and elegant. She has inherited from her Creole dark-skinned father and her light-skinned Creole mother that perfect combination of dark and light: a glowing, honey-colored complexion that highlights an oval porcelain-smooth face, high, luminous cheekbones, and piercing almond eyes. The eyes are the givaway: steady, direct, intense, reflecting the quick thinking and natural precision of a surgeon. It was, in fact, surgery's almost militaristic regimentation, its demand for details, rules, meticulous attention, that attracted Ramona Tascoe to the profession. Growing up in her father's home, she had become used to the military style and good at manipulating it. "Just tell me what the rules are and I will follow them to the letter," she says, speaking with deep-voiced, clear precision. "In any of my training all you had to do was tell me what the rules are. The hardest part will be for me to learn them all, memorize them all, get them all. But once I get it—you will get perfection."

Despite perfection, Ramona Tascoe did not get to be a surgeon. She instead has a private practice on Pill Hill, where she specializes in legal medicine—testifying as an expert witness in court cases ranging from malpractice suits to felony charges, organizing around black women's health issues, lobbying as a health activist. She considers herself "a natural advocate," a medical crusader fighting for the patient rights of the poor, the powerless, the uninformed. Given her own story and the circumstances leading to her career switch from surgery to medical law, this is perhaps the only thing about Ramona Tascoe Burris that could have been expected.

In 1983, when she was 33, Ramona Tascoe won a discrimination suit against Highland General Hospital, its chief of surgery, its administrators, and the County of Alameda. Not only were the defendants found liable on all counts—defamation of character, breach of the covenant of good faith and fair dealing, violation of the discrimination retaliation standards of the federal Fair Employment and Housing Act, violation of constitutional due process, and intentional infliction of emotional distress—but Tascoe was awarded the largest settlement in the history of California discrimination cases. She received $75,000 for emotional harm, $150,000 for damage to her reputation, and $225,000 in legal fees, for a total of $500,000. It was the kind of unprecedented case that made the news and made Ramona Tascoe a most ironic success.

An article appearing in *San Francisco* magazine detailing the story noted, "At the outset, the case seemed to be just another one of those that turn up all too often: A young woman had accused her boss of making sexual advances and of discriminating against her when she refused them. This case was a little different because the woman was a doctor, a surgical resident in training, and her boss was the chief of surgery. But it all seemed relatively clear-cut until the extent of the chief's campaign to destroy the young doctor's career was dramatically made clear."

LEARNING TO "EAT IT"

Just as she had in undergraduate school at San Francisco State, Ramona Tascoe distinguished herself as a medical student at the University of California at San Francisco, graduating with honors in 1979. But she applied three times before she was accepted and took another six years to graduate. She believes she was denied admission under the University of California at San Francisco's affirmative action program in fact because of her undergraduate campus activism. Tascoe had not only participated in the 1968 student strike at San Francisco State calling for the tenure of black professors, but had been one of the more outspoken leaders in the school's black student union. "I had this huge Afro and would march on the picket line in my combat boots and camouflage fatigues and stand in front of the police, stare them down, and read the fifteen demands for a black studies department. The whole cultural and political revolution for black people was happening at this time."

Such activism seemed more suited to a career in law, which is where Tascoe was headed until the black doctor she worked for during the summer told her one day, "You don't belong in law. You belong in medicine." Tascoe rolled her eyes at him. "Me?" She had thought of medicine vaguely, intangibly, as a child, but never thought of it as something she could actually accomplish, even though she had always been an exceptional student in science and math, was the class valedictorian, and attended private Catholic schools. "I never had the kind of high school counselors who encouraged me in that type of career direction [medicine]."

Flattered by the black doctor's belief in her, Tascoe went back to school at night to study pre-med while she continued to work for him during the day. The University of California at San Francisco medical school admitted her in 1973. "It was strictly on merit that I got in," Tascoe says dryly, "but that first year of medical school kicked my bottom righteously."

It was in medical school that Ramona Tascoe learned just what the white expectations were for black achievement. "The whole thinking, it seemed, regarding black students was that we came in by the exception, not by the rule, that we really didn't belong in medical school. But the thinking was, 'Let's go on and let through a token number of M.D.s.' Enough said that it took me six years to finish medical school. There was one course that I just could not pass. It was physiology. This was the bust-out course for blacks. Out of the eighteen black students admitted in my class, you could count on close to 50 percent of them failing because of physiology."

What the blacks in Tascoe's class learned was that the white students had assembled files of previous physiology exams which they circulated among themselves to study. "It took us a while to realize that we could accomplish success academically if we followed their tactics—and set up our own files too."

The frustration for Tascoe was that she didn't consider physiology a particularly difficult subject. "It was the professors," she explains simply. "It was their attitude, which was absolutely racist. They weren't there to help you make it, but to prove that you couldn't." Tascoe felt her outspokenness also got her into trouble. "It seemed that I was watched closer than anybody else. I couldn't pass physiology and I knew they weren't treating me fairly." Tascoe took the course three times. Although a grade of 60 on the final exam was passing for everybody else, Tascoe was told—*after* she took the course a second time and had gotten a passing grade on the final—that she had to pass at a grade of 80 since she was repeating the course. "I screamed 'You can't do that! This is not legal!' Well, you better believe that when I took the exam again, I got a fair shake. I knew that if I could pass everything else and do well, no one was going to tell me that physiology was going to stand in the way of my finishing medical school."

It didn't, nor did the birth of Ramona Tascoe's daughter, born the year before she graduated. By then Tascoe was living with the doctor she had once worked for—the one who had urged her to go into medicine—who was now the father of her child. While motherhood may have slowed her down, it didn't place her among the 10 percent of the black students who washed out of her class. "When we get into medical school we just try like hell and high water to keep from being put out. If you get that far, you're pretty determined, which means that the more determined you are, the harder they work on you to get you to quit or leave or to realize that you don't have what it really takes, that 'We accidentally mischose you.' But the lesson I learned is that you don't quit. They can't make you quit, okay? They can't *make* you quit."

Sheer persistence in the face of racist opposition is typically the critical quality that makes the difference between success and failure in the black experience. Persistence came somewhat naturally to Tascoe, a woman whose strong will had been shaped in childhood by the demands of a father who, like the whites she would encounter later, actually had low expectations for the success potential of black women. Her father's low expectations were the result of his knowing how society regarded black women; whites' low expectations were the result of racist thinking. Yet low expectations are exactly what drove Tascoe to excel, and once she proved to be of exceptional talent and ability, confidence is what propelled her to succeed.

It was during her junior year of medical school that Ramona Tascoe discovered she had a love and a talent for surgery. "All of the myths that I had regarding surgery, women in surgery, were dispelled because number one, I enjoyed surgery, and number two, I was doing well in it. And all of the preconceived notions I had about how impossible it would be for a woman to make it in surgery became dissipated once I started doing well in it. I also got some good, positive reinforcements from my professors, who I think probably never expected that I would be interested in surgery as a career, so they felt safe being honest in their assessment. They knew I had a child, so they didn't feel threatened. They treated me well in surgery."

Tascoe did her internship at Highland Hospital, where her skills as a surgeon were quickly recognized by Dr. Buford Burch, the hospital's chief of surgery. Buford offered her a five-year surgical residency following her internship if she wanted it. Tascoe had been thinking about combining surgery with a specialty in obstetrics and gynecology, but after her internship she was convinced that she wanted to make a full-time and total commitment to surgery. She told Burch as much and said she would accept his offer.

"Oh, great, Tascoe, glad to have you aboard," Burch said, in his typical jock manner. Yet Tascoe noticed he seemed somewhat reserved. "Immediately after I joined the surgical resident staff in October of 1980, he began to take a more personal interest in me. At first I thought that he was giving me additional time because I was the new kid on the block—you know, that he was giving me welcome-into-the-club kind of time."

It soon became apparent, however, that Burch was not thinking of Tascoe in a professional sense.

"Tascoe, you know I find you very charming. You know you are just a lovely woman. It's difficult for me to be objective with you," he told her one day after she'd been summoned to his office. He summoned her often.

Is Dr. Burch getting senile? Tascoe wondered.

And then he said it: "You know, Tascoe, I haven't finished a woman in the program yet. You'll be my first chief resident that I will finish in my own program, although when I was at the VA hospital, I remember . . . her name was Jean, and you know, she had a baby in her senior year; boy, she had some big balls, too. I found her very charming and delightful, as well, if you know what I mean. She had my wife's namesake, and my wife didn't like that relationship either, if you know what I mean."

Tascoe knew exactly what he meant, and she was so shaken by the implications that she blurted out, "Dr. Burch, I know you don't mean any harm, but you really make me uneasy. You've been paging me to your office an awful lot and the guys are beginning to tease me about it."

"I don't care what they like or don't like!" Burch bellowed. "I'm the chief of surgery, and I can page you to my office when I want— and they don't have to like it!"

"Dr. Burch, you're not hearing me. *I* don't like it. I think you like my work. You told me that I'm a damn good resident, and I'd like to think that you welcomed me into the program because of my surgical competence."

"Oh yes, Tascoe, you're sharp," Buford acknowledged quickly. "You're one of the sharpest we've had in quite some time, and I'm glad to have you aboard."

"In that case, Dr. Burch, *you know* I'm glad to be here. I'm looking forward to this. But I just want to be treated like one of the guys; I just want to be one of the residents, okay? I don't want to be offensive to you, and I know you are the chief of sur-gery. . . ."

Buford interrupted Tascoe with a curt nod, one of those nods that says *uh-oh*. "I knew when I said it I shouldn't have said it," Tascoe says now, remembering the words she came to regret. "I knew I shouldn't have said 'I just want you to treat me like one of the guys.' I've regretted that to this day."

Overnight, it seemed, although it was actually two days later, on

November 21, 1980, Ramona Tascoe's thirtieth birthday, the chief of surgery demoted her from resident to intern. The sexual harassment continued. The hospital staff looked the other way. Buford told Tascoe if she wanted to make it in surgery she would have "to don a pair of ten-ton balls," and "learn to eat shit and ask for seconds."

Dr. Ramona Tascoe never did learn to eat it, nor did she ever don a pair of ten-ton balls. Instead, on February 7, 1981, she filed a Title VII complaint with the Equal Employment Opportunity Commission charging sexual, racial, and marital status discrimination by Dr. Buford Burch and the administration at Highland Hospital.

Ramona Tascoe's surgical residency at Highland then became a nine-month nightmare, escalating from sexual innuendo by her boss to psychological and emotional harassment. She found a note slipped under the door of her call room one morning that read, "Nigger Bitch." Her staff photo was defaced with the words "A real bitch" scrawled across it. She received a number of anonymous phone calls in her hospital call room, with a male voice on the line warning her to "look over your shoulder at all times," to "avoid sleeping in your call room at night because fires burn," and "to be careful when you leave the hospital at night." Her car was tampered with in the hospital parking lot.

The most vicious abuse, however, was the attempt to undermine Tascoe's ability—her talent as a doctor. On January 2, 1981, she received her first negative evaluation. It was from Michael Cummins, the chief resident, who said that while her first two and a half months of working with him had been "outstanding," her "entire behavior and attitude changed radically" after she was demoted to an intern.

On January 5, when Tascoe asked Buford about her contract for the following year, Buford said, "If you didn't have a child and a family, I'd train you in cardiothracic or vascular surgery, because you have all it takes. But you have a serious problem—motherhood, family. The guys are different—they may have families, but at any time they can tell them, forget it; you can't."

On January 28, the chief of surgery informed Tascoe she would not be selected for the second year's surgical residency program. "Let's just say you're technically inferior," Buford told her.

On June 5, 1981, without a contract for a second year's surgical residency, Dr. Ramona Tascoe resigned from Highland General Hospital. In November she filed suit in San Francisco Federal Court. It would take two years—from the initial filing of the Title VII complaint to hearings and finally a six-person jury trial—for the case, tried by John Burris, California's famed discrimination attorney, to wind its way through the slow, exacting wheels of justice. In reporting the trial, *San Francisco* magazine said: "As the court proceedings made clear . . . Burch intimidated other residents by suggesting that their careers would be in danger unless they cooperated with him in blackballing Tascoe. And residents were afraid that their board accreditation might be jeopardized if the Tascoe situation erupted."

The suit charged gender-based discrimination, Tascoe explains in the precise language of the law, which is not unlike the precision of medicine. "Gender-based discrimination is the broad term under the California law, and within that rubric come the two subcategories of sexual harassment and sexual discrimination. Sexual discrimination was the primary issue we claimed, and under that, retaliatory conduct. We didn't claim sexual harassment for two reasons. One is that as a practical matter, harassment happens. You can't go into battle each time it happens. You have to pick your battles. And two, you have to prove damages. Harassment hurts your feelings, but we get our feelings hurt all the time. Can you claim damages?"

What Tascoe's attorney John Burris proved was that Dr. Burch discriminated against Dr. Tascoe on the basis of her sex, first promising her a full five-year residency in surgery and then telling her: "You have a serious problem—motherhood. The guys are different." Such discrimination ruined her livelihood as a surgeon at Highland General Hospital.

When the all-white jury of four women and two men ruled in

Ramona Tascoe's favor, awarding her a settlement of $250,000 in damages, it was not only a clear vindication of a black woman's honor and reputation but a testament to the difference civil rights legislation in the past thirty years has made on the success aspirations of black Americans. It was the Civil Rights Act of 1964 that made it illegal to discriminate on the basis of race, color, creed, age, or sex, thus empowering for the first time in history a generation of African-Americans who could legally challenge a discriminatory system. This was the generation that would successfully seek relief and remedy in the courts—from racism and sexism, and from the professional and psychological damages inflicted on a people whose race and/or sex are viewed as a debit, as a diminished expectation.

The tragic irony in the case of Dr. Ramona Tascoe is that while she got sizable relief and remedy, it was not enough to salvage her career in surgery. Three weeks after she resigned from Highland Hospital she was rushed to the emergency room suffering from Toxic Shock Syndrome, possibly the result of debilitating stress. She was the first doctor in the country ever to contract the disease, and it effectively ended her profession as a surgeon, for it left her fingers with a trace of numbness.

Her victory, then, like so many black success stories, was a bittersweet one. She has lost all faith in the medical profession, for it closed ranks to protect its own when faced with a choice between siding with a white male chief of surgery or protecting the rights of a young black female resident. The mistake she made, Tascoe says, was that "I really believed the world was all mine—that all I had to do was earn it. I thought when I finished medical school I had achieved a level of success that would allow me into an elite club of achievers that saw no color. But at Highland I realized I really wasn't in the club—not just because of my gender, but also because of my race. I viewed myself as an equal to Buford—as a human equal in the same profession. I really expected him to treat me like one of the guys—like the other residents. But I didn't know he was viewing me as an exception who he was allowing to come across into his world."

The real mistake Ramona Tascoe made, then—the one that cost her her career as a surgeon, the one that makes black success so tenuous, such a paradox—is that she failed to be a stereotype; she failed to succumb to low expectations, as a woman, as a black. Instead she became a credit to her race.

If there is a final irony, it is this personal footnote, this happy ending that makes for a modern twist on what is often the odd theme of African-American success: Ramona Tascoe's relationship with the black doctor who was the father of her child did not survive the court proceedings. Her relationship with her black attorney, John Burris, did. During the course of the trial the celebrated lawyer fell in love with her. And after the trial he married her.

Now, high in the hills of Oakland in her gracious split-level home overlooking the cliffs and the bay, and surrounded by the requisite trappings of the California good life—a swimming pool in the back, a Mercedes and a Porsche in the front—Ramona Tascoe Burris has this last laugh: "We got all the money—and yet the struggle continues," she says with an elusive smile. The settlement and the legal fees brought half a million dollars into the household of the doctor and the lawyer she married.

Her father would be proud.

SUCCESS AND THE BLACK WOMAN

*I*t is a quarter to dawn, that sepulchral dimension in time and space most susceptible to visitations from the spirit world, to the incantations of ancestors and the talking of the drums. Julianne Malveaux's restless, nervous energy and ancestral Haitian roots perhaps explain why this night-into-morning witching hour is her favorite time to work. To rattle the serpent; throw the bones.

She has been up for over an hour at the modern altar of industrial technology—one of the three computers in her San Francisco apartment—working Western juju: running the data, crunching the numbers, extrapolating, forecasting, constructing statistical paradigms, hypothetical projections, historical comparatives. Wizardlike, she summons black economic reality at the flick of a keystroke, casting it back in time, projecting it into the year 2007, freeze-framing it in the instant of the present. She is the conjure woman for our times: an economist whose magic and scholarship is in econometrics—in taking the numbers, any numbers, depositing them in the vast reservoir of economic possibility, and then transforming the numbers through computer sleight-of-hand into data bases that provide a clear, crystal-ball view into the fortunes of black Americans.

What is clearly most telling about the changing fortunes of African-Americans during the past thirty years is the presence of black women in the equation of American success. Prior to the Civil Rights Movement and the women's movement it spawned, black women and success did not ordinarily compute into a statistical measure of either psychology or history. Historically, the reality of black women had been one of long suffering and double oppression. Their status as members of two powerless and exploited classes—the black race and the female gender—made them two times a victim, and thus considered the least likely to succeed. Psychologically, then, black women rarely thought of themselves in the ego-driven terms of success. Success was often a matter of simply surviving, of accepting responsibility, of having the capacity for struggle and the wherewithal for sacrifice. As author Toni Morrison once said, describing the traditional prospects of black women, ". . . She had nothing to fall back on; not maleness, not whiteness, not ladyhood, not anything. And out of the profound desolation of her reality she may well have invented herself."

It was out of the fire and smoke of the Civil Rights Movement and the dust and foment of the women's movement that the black woman would become empowered to *reinvent* herself—to be recast, reincarnated. To emerge in this lifetime a success, resembling something at once very old and also very new.

Julianne Malveaux: Feeling Fulfilled

Julianne Malveaux is considered one of those "evil" black women typically thought to be "too smart for her own good." Brash and belligerent, angry and outspoken, intense and defiant, she grew up a "problem child," the oldest of five children in San Francisco's Mission District, where she gave her mother both fever and grief. A large part of the problem was being black and female with an IQ of 140. This made her too aware, too sensitive, too frustrated. She was a rabble-rouser in high school, an activist, political. She is still those things, though now as an adult they all contribute to a certain uneasy success.

Julianne Malveaux, Ph.D., 37 in 1990, is an economist, a professor, and a writer—occupations that were not exactly traditional for black women a generation ago. Today such occupations not only represent new opportunities, new possibilities, they provide an outlet for Malveaux's activist passions, making those passions acceptable, respectable, even successful. Malveaux, however, like most black women, is not entirely comfortable with the notion called success. "I'm still struggling," she says by way of explanation and also history. "I haven't reached all my goals yet."

So far the résumé includes a Ph.D. in economics from the Massachusetts Institute of Technology, earned in 1980 at age 26 (she was the second black woman in MIT's history to be awarded the doctorate in economics); an associate visiting professorship at the University of California at Berkeley, teaching economics and Afro-American studies; a syndicated column for King Features; a contributing editor position at *Essence* magazine; books and articles on the subject of black women and work; an impressive run for San Francisco City Board of Supervisors (she lost); an effective campaign to get San Francisco to divest city pension funds from companies doing business in South Africa (she won); an annual income of about $65,000 as a freelancer and her own woman, militant and independent. Yet Julianne Malveaux doesn't think of her herself in the specific terms of success.

What keeps Malveaux on edge and feeling like less than an unqualified success is the continuing war she says is being waged against black people. Unemployment, drugs, crime, police brutality, AIDS, welfare, single-headed households—Malveaux can spew figures on any indices of black life with nearly the same speed and accuracy as her Apple Macintosh. The findings tell her that the African-American community is under siege, and that as long as there is war there can be no real victory in individual black success. "Anytime you hear someone like Bill Moyers say some stupid shit like the black family is vanishing, you know there's a war on black people," she grumbles in the rapid-fire staccato that always infuses her words with a sense of urgency, a streak of anger.

Malveaux takes up battle position from the command post of her San Francisco duplex. The apartment looks like an intellectual's war zone, littered with paper of every imaginable description covering nearly every inch of carpeted floor space on both levels: newspapers stacked, magazines scattered, notes scribbled, articles Xeroxed, printouts computerized, data sheets spread, cards unfiled, letters read and written, books marked and researched. The exterior mess, however, belies the orderly, disciplined mind of the prodigious thinker who resides here. So, too, does the appearance and the style. Julianne Malveaux is a light-skinned, buxom woman with carrot-red hair, the swagger of a brothel madam, and the orneriness of a root worker, given to invectives and expletives. "Hussy" and "bitch" are the terms of endearment she uses for women she likes. "Motherfucker" is what she frequently calls the men of her race; "shit" is how she most often characterizes racism, white folks, and the general state of black life in America.

Like beauty, a keen intellect in black women has often been its own curse, its own source of anguish and frustration, for to be a thinker frequently means to have both the gift and the weight of insight without the outlet for healthy expression. Malveaux finds release and expression in the numbers—in running the data and doing the tallies that give an exact accounting. Yet numbers alone, she knows, tell very little; alone they are only relative, inconclusive, without shape or spirit, untouched by the reckonings of time. It is only when they are *read*—placed in a context that illuminates struggle or marks progress—do the numbers become meaningful, a useful way to interpret reality, an instructive way to tell the fortunes of a people. And what Julianne Malveaux, the economist, the teacher, and the writer perhaps does best is read fortunes.

"In 1954 about half of the black population was poor, having family-of-four household incomes of under $3000 a year," says Malveaux, giving a read on black economic progress since the Supreme Court ruling of 1954 that outlawed segregation in American education. "In 1974 only 28 percent of the black population was poor. In 1989 about a third were poor, with family-of-four incomes under $12,000 annually. So it's been a mixed history." Malveaux herself, with a 1990 income of $65,000, is in the top 1 percent of black women's earnings. Her Ph.D. makes her one of .03 percent of black women in America who have doctorates, with less than fifty in all having a doctorate in economics. If the numbers are not sizable, the significance is. "You cannot deny there has been significant progress in the aspirations of black women, [their] expectations and clear achievements," says Malveaux. "For anyone to say there has been no progress is to totally negate the Civil Rights Movement—people dying in the streets—and the women's movement, and you just can't do that."

Yet progress for Malveaux personally is not defined by a label tagged "success." The term she prefers is "fulfilled." As she puts it, "I feel fulfilled because I like what I do. I like my life—being an advocate. I like being a writer. I like the fact that my work has visibility and that it makes a difference in relation to public policy."

Such fulfillment, such astonishing affirmation of power in the simple act of declaring "I like what I do," is perhaps the most telling indicator of what achievement has come to mean for the successful black woman: the freedom to do work that *means something personally,* that has value in being fulfilling; the freedom to have options and shots to call, power to exercise; the freedom to be the sum of her own definitions, the arbiter of her own good fortunes. This is new. This is revolutionary. This is liberated success.

UP OFF HER KNEES

Work has always been the common denominator in the history of black women in America, and the fortunes of the black woman have always improved in direct proportion to the opportunities she has had to get up off her knees. Emancipation freed her to get off her knees in the fields of slavery and off the floor of the master's bedroom; education freed her to get up from scrubbing Miss Anne's kitchen and raising little white children. The Civil Rights Movement and the women's movement freed her to raise both her income and her expectations.

If work defines the reality of the black woman's experience, the nature of that work has helped shape her psychology. In the beginning, work simply meant slavery—hard labor without payment, choice, or respect for gender differences. Under the peculiar institution, black men and women were enslaved equally and thus labored equally. The enslaved abolitionist Sojourner Truth vividly pointed out what it meant to be a woman equal to a man under slavery when she made this now famous, anguished oration at a women's conference in Akron, Ohio, in 1851:

> I plowed and planted and gathered into barns and no man could head me! And ain't I a woman? I could work as much and eat as much as a man—when I could get it—and bear the lash as well! And ain't I a woman? I have borne thirteen children and seen them all sold off to slavery, and when I cried out with my mother's grief none but Jesus heard me! And ain't I a woman?

Being a woman did not exempt the black female from hard, menial work even after slavery—work, for the most part, that was neither satisfying nor high paying; work that brought no power or privilege, little status or position. The image of the black working woman is aptly summed up by Julianne Malveaux in her introduction to *Slipping Through the Cracks: The Status of Black Women,* a volume of essays on black female labor issues which she coedited with economist Margaret C. Simms: "Work has been so major a part of black women's legacy that it is frequently jested that black women are born with a broom in hand." The broom is the telling image. By the late nineteenth century, 20 percent of all school-age black girls worked full-time, and the majority of black women worked either in private households as maids or on farms as sharecroppers.

One hundred years later, following two back-to-back social movements, the black female's work prospects have improved dramatically. "Work remains as much a part of the history of black women as it was in 1890," Malveaux says in *Slipping Through the Cracks.* "But the work that black women now do is very different from the work we have done in the past." Indeed, by the last decade of the twentieth century, the majority of black women had moved from the fields and kitchens of hard labor into the cleaner, more prestigious, and better-paying ranks of the white-collar clerical class.

Nevertheless, the black woman is still on the bottom economically, compared to the rest of America's workers. In 1990 the median annual individual income of black women was $7,800 a year (meaning half earned above this amount and half earned below it), compared to a median annual income of $9,800 for white women, $12,600 for black men, and $20,800 for white men. Yet more black women could also now be found working in every modern high-paying profession from advertising executive and magazine editor to television scriptwriter and district attorney than ever before in their history. Unlike the black professional middle class of earlier generations, whose women tended to be confined to traditional women's jobs such as teaching, nursing, and social work, today's black female could become a professional in just about any field she had the aspiration and the aptitude for—and be a success.

What was different was not just the nature of these occupations, but also how black women now tended to view work: as a career and a profession, and an enterprise that brought not only personal fulfillment but also economic rewards. As Karen Fulbright explains in another essay from *Slipping Through the Cracks:* "The civil rights movement changed those conditions [for black women]. In a very concrete way it changed the opportunity structure for black people in this country. On a less tangible but no less important level it raised black people's expectations about what they could seek to achieve."

OF RACE AND GENDER

If the aims and results of the sixties Civil Rights Movement seemed concrete, clear, as resolute as the might and right of God, the women's movement, by contrast, threw an existential snare into the civil rights struggle of black women by raising the sticky cosmic question: What is more oppressive—racism or sexism? Which is worse? Being black? Or being a woman? Pick one.

By the early seventies, as the women's movement started bearing down upon the Civil Rights Movement, the hot breath of feminism threatening to overtake and extinguish the black cry for freedom, black women felt the pressure to choose. Did civil rights and the grievances of a race take precedence over gender rights and the grievances of women? Women wanted freedom too. They wanted the freedom to be independent. To work, like men, if they chose to and be equitably paid. To be more than the sum of a marriage and children. To express their sexuality without the consequence of pregnancy. To be unchained from roles, let down from pedestals, in control of their own bodies, recognized and respected as equals.

The issues, though real and legitimate, were typically perceived by black women to be the preoccupations of a bourgeois sensibility —the concerns of the "haves," of the women who have the time and have the luxury to agitate for freedom from the comfort of their affluence. The women's movement initially, then, turned out to be a largely white and middle class march for equality. Most black women never embraced feminism with conviction, for as it turned out, black women and middle class white women had very different ideas about what constituted freedom. Freedom for white women seemed essentially to mean exchanging privilege for power. Since the black woman had neither, freedom for her meant acquiring both. The conflict, not surprisingly, was most glaring around the issue of work. As the black feminist writer Michele Wallace pointed out in her own significant work *Black Macho and the Myth of the Superwoman*, the book and controversy that launched the eighties and introduced race into the politics of the women's movement:

> Before black women or white women said a word, there was a basic communication gap between them on this subject of work. When the middle-class woman said, "I want to work," in her head was a desk in the executive suite, while the black woman saw a bin of dirty clothes, someone else's dirty clothes . . . Women's Liberation, the black woman reasoned, would chain her to Ms. Anne's

stove forever. None of that for her. She wanted, she said, to stay home and have her man take care of her. A movement offering her that would be the only one in which she could be interested.

A civil rights movement offering freedom was the one movement in which black women were primarily interested. Freedom from unremitting hard labor, freedom from *having* to work; the freedom that comes with privilege, with power, with options. Middle class white women already had that. Now they wanted what black women had in slavery: equality. Understandably, black women found it hard to identify. That, however, didn't preclude an opportunity to benefit.

Like the Civil Rights Movement, which successfully made the race case for equal opportunity, the women's movement successfully made the gender case. Consequently, for the first time in history there was now some perceived advantage to being black and female. Whether they identified with one movement or two, black women clearly had the benefit of both civil rights and women's rights as dual driving social forces to propel them toward success. They became the "twofers" considered to be privileged inheritors of double opportunities.

The results of those opportunities were apparent by the dawn of the eighties, most significantly in the arena of work. In the ten years between 1970 and 1980—considered the epoch decade in the rising power of women—the number of black women working as household domestics at the low-paying, menial end of the labor market dropped by more than half, from 590,000 in 1970 to 233,000 ten years later. Moreover, the number of black women now working in white-collar administrative support services such as clerical work virtually doubled during the same period, going from 634,000 in 1970 to 1,201,000 in 1980. And at the upper class professional end, in 1970 only 56,000 of the 3,309,000 black women in the American workforce held executive, administrative, or managerial positions. By 1980, 219,000 out of 4,659,000 black women held such posts.

The women's movement had helped to empower one gender within two races. And in the hard labor of a decade, it gave birth to a politicized generation that would take the sexism explicit in the idea that "You've come a long way, baby" and turn it into the sound-off battle cry of brave new women boldly marching into new territories and storming new hills in a successful charge for liberation.

Of course, what the generations coming of age during both the Civil Rights Movement and the women's movement discovered once they had reached the mountaintop is that freedom isn't free. Like the old war song says, "You've got to pay the price, you've got to sacrifice, for your liberty." No one knows better than black women the nature of sacrifice or the price of struggle. And no one has experienced more acutely the painful conflicts new opportunities have wrought, or the exacting, unexpected cost that success has brought.

Jennifer Lawson: The Life and Times of the Movement People

When Jennifer Lawson, 44, speaks of the Movement, there can be but one: the one in which she was on the front lines, skipping class in high school to march with King in Birmingham; spending college weekends at demonstrations in Montgomery; volunteering after the summer of Mississippi burning to register blacks for the vote; loving a revolutionary, then losing him to the revolution in the burst of a bomb explosion. When Jennifer Lawson speaks of the Movement, it is the one to which she bore witness, personal sacrifice and the passions of her youth: the one for civil rights.

Civil rights activists of Lawson's age and generation refer to themselves with fondness and a certain wistful pride as Movement People. It is the recognition of a special kinship. Movement People were all of the activists—mainly young, black and white, male and female—who made up the ranks of the volunteer foot soldiers in the struggle for civil rights in the sixties. They were the ones who showed up for the marches, sat in at the demonstrations, organized the boycotts, rode the freedom buses, registered the people to vote, passed out the petitions, typed the letters, stuffed the envelopes, and put their lives on the line. Fired by the optimism of youth and the hope they carried as the next generation, Movement people were as indispensable to the success of the Civil Rights Movement as the strategic tactic of nonviolence. It was their energy, their youth, their passion, and their faith fueling the engine that would drive a nation head-on into social change.

Collective success in the black community—the kind that moves a race forward and not just its individuals—has always been dependent on having an element of Movement People, "race people," within its midst, people who are driven by a certain spirit of activism, a sense of mission, a racial consciousness that promotes a racial militancy. Every black generation has had such people, working and organizing, giving back, reaching back, speaking out. Like old soldiers, black activists never die. If they are successful, they simply come of age.

HAVING IT ALL

Jennifer Lawson hasn't been on a march in over twenty years. She is grown now, a busy wife and mother, a successful working woman. In these middle age days she no longer defines herself in the particular rhetoric of an activist, though she does indeed represent a revolution. Lawson is executive vice president of national programming and promotional services for the Public Broadcasting Service (PBS), overseeing a staff of 74, a budget of $105 million and a constituency of 344 public broadcast stations throughout the country. She earned $108,000 in 1990, which placed her in the top 1 percent of all American wage earners that year.

The historic success here is that Jennifer Lawson the revolutionary helped to change the system, then grew up to join it. The personal success here is that Jennifer Lawson Gittens, wife and mother, has managed to combine a happy marriage and family with a career of meaningful, creative, and lucrative work. Lawson has become one of those rare, successful women in contemporary black and white America—one of those modern women who "have it all."

"Have it all?" Lawson repeats rhetorically, giving a deep, low chuckle as she slowly turns in the gray swivel chair in her Alexandria, Virginia, office. She finds it amusing that what women of her mother's generation did with almost natural instinct and reflex—get married, stay married, have children, work, be active in the community—should be viewed as a major achievement among the new, successfully liberated women of her generation. Yet this is the very generation whose march for civil rights and women's rights ran into an unexpected, disturbing detour on the road to freedom, swerving off into a spiraling divorce rate, a precarious leap in female-headed households, an increase in professional women opting for single motherhood.

During the seventies, the same decade that marked the economic advance of black women, the number of divorced black women in 26 reporting states rose from 27,320 to 46,757. By 1987 it was 49,124. Black female-headed households grew from 716,000 in 1967 to 1,524,000 in 1989, with 46.5 percent of these families below the poverty line. The price of the black female's liberation, it seemed, were deteriorating relationships with her men and economic uncertainty for her children.

Among her friends, Lawson, then, is considered one of the successful, lucky ones. She is married to a loving, supportive man, Anthony Gittens, executive director of the Washington, D.C., International Film Festival, who was a good friend before he became a good husband. She has a bright, healthy 7-year-old son and a satisfying, well-paying job that has empowered her to reach America with some of the finest moments in television programming, including *Eyes on the Prize,* the two-part award-winning series documenting the Civil Rights Movement, and *The Civil War,* the acclaimed, evocative series that masterfully employed photographs and narration to tell the harrowing saga of the War Between the States and became the highest-rated documentary in the history of PBS. This is perhaps the best success: being recognized for documenting the struggle, telling the story, carrying on the movement.

Jennifer Lawson is a warm brown, elegant, and instantly likable woman, her manner as engaging and easy as Southern comfort. She speaks in the husky, rolling cadence of the black South, her Southern middle-class upbringing reflecting a certain charm. But there is also confidence, authority, and the kind of wisdom that comes with having lived an active, integrated, and committed life: a life that has known tragedy but also triumph, a life that has grown, changed, and found its balance. Jennifer Lawson's good fortune in combining a successful marriage with a successful working life perhaps says as much about class and background as it does about the changing opportunities for blacks and women. "It doesn't say anything so much about me as it does about an odd psychology that I think we as a group share—by that I mean a group of middle-class black women—who have come from backgrounds where we had healthy role models. It gave me this priceless sense that I could have a good relationship." There was also a priceless sense of what was possible, and thus a priceless sense of successful change.

Jennifer Lawson grew up with two brothers in Birmingham, Alabama, in a family headed by a father who ran his own auto-repair business. Her mother was a teacher, though "one of the things that showed how well off we were was that my mother didn't have to work after she married my father." Lawson considers her father, Willie D. Lawson, one of the great influences of her life. "My father was a very gifted, self-taught person—first-generation urban from rural Bullock County, Alabama—who migrated to Birmingham at age 16 to work in the steel mills. He bought a car, took it apart, put it back together, and started an auto-repair business. He just sort of repaired everything, but he also became an inventor, a tinkerer."

The elder Lawson was also considered something of a character—odd, eccentric. In the workshop behind the family house he'd mix concoctions that occasionally blew up. The Lawson house was on a corner, and one year Willie painted it—but only the two sides that faced the street, reasoning that he didn't have to paint the entire house every year just because the neighbors did. Yet Willie Lawson was also a man greatly respected in the community, even if he didn't bother to wear socks the day he accepted the Man of the Year award from a local men's organization. Older members of the Lawson family always talked with special pride about the issue of *Life* that ran an item on Willie the time he drove from Birmingham to Canada and back on just one gallon of gasoline. It was during the gas-rationing era of World War II, and he had developed a low-cost alternative fuel that required gasoline only for starting the engine.

"My father used to tell me that I was going to be absolutely useless unless I could do a transmission job," Lawson recalls with a rich laugh, adding that she does indeed know how to do one. "He really made you feel that the world was your oyster, and he encouraged travel. We always traveled. We'd just pack up the car and head out to California. Or go north, up to Canada. We'd go to Mexico. Anywhere you could drive we would go. He was a naturally curious person, and he'd take us to museums to stimulate us, encouraging us to learn. I got a tremendous education and also self-confidence from my father."

Jennifer was 13 when her mother, 51, died of a heart attack, leaving her father a single parent at age 63. The loss influenced her desire to go to medical school and become a doctor. But a movement was brewing that would escalate right in the streets of Birmingham and spiritually claim the hearts and minds of a young generation of blacks.

Like other black children growing up in the South under segregation, Jennifer had experienced the stings of racism. And Birmingham's were particularly pernicious: sitting behind the sign on the bus marked "colored," allowed to use only the "colored" gas stations and laundromats, told before you entered kindergarten that black children were not allowed to play with white children. It was in Birmingham that a black church was bombed one Sunday morning, killing four little black girls.

The struggle for civil rights, then, in the mind of a young, black Southern girl who had become a Catholic as a teenager, took on the mission of a crusade. She believed that those who were fighting against segregation "had the same nobleness of purpose as the saints." Lawson says that while much of the passion black youth felt at the time was certainly "naive," it was fired by a belief in the "possibility that things really could be changed."

In 1963, her senior year, Jennifer was part of a group of students who were expelled from Fairfield Industrial High School for defying the principal and joining Dr. Martin Luther King, Jr.'s historic civil rights march through the streets of Birmingham, facing down firehoses and police dogs. The students became instant local heros and were promptly reinstated at the school.

By the time Jennifer Lawson graduated from high school and left for Tuskegee Institute on a full scholarship with a major in biology and chemistry, the course of her activism had been set. She spent nearly every weekend in nearby Montgomery, demonstrating, organizing. In the summer of 1964 Jennifer took advantage of an opportunity to work in New York City at the Sloan-Kettering Institute for Cancer Research. She enjoyed the work but missed the Movement, felt almost guilty for not being on the front lines of revolution.

When she returned home, Jennifer took a two-week leave from Tuskegee to work on an election campaign. She knew she had to make a decision. More volunteers were needed to work in Mississippi following the murder of three civil rights workers in the summer of 1964. Jennifer wanted to go, but what would her father say? His daughter dropping out of college to go work in the racist, dangerous Delta state? "He was wonderful," Lawson remembers. Willie Lawson told his daughter to go ahead. "Whatever you do, it's important to have victory in life," he simply said. "I want you to have victory."

Jennifer Lawson would have victory, though not without struggle. She would end up successfully working a lifetime in some aspect of civil rights or the "nonprofit" service sector: as a project coordinator in the Student Nonviolent Coordinating Committee (SNCC) working with black power activists Stokely Carmichael, Ruby Doris Robinson, and Ivanhoe Donaldson; as a teacher at Brooklyn College; as a fundraiser for the New York Film Fund; as an executive in public television. She would encounter along the way not just racism but sexism, often from other comrades-in-arms in the Movement—black men.

She would experience her first love with the formidable activist Ralph Featherstone, then leave him before he was killed in a bomb explosion, and flee the country after the FBI subpoenaed her to testify. She would live for three years in the Motherland, recovering in Tanzania from the pain and the cost of revolution. She would marry the first time in her youth for all the wrong reasons, and marry again as she entered her thirties for all the right ones. She would have her first child at 37 and help raise the stepchild that came with the father of her son. She would have it all.

Loretta Johnson: A Success in Her Own Time

By the eighties, America had come full blown into the "transitional" age of changing roles, rising expectations, and revealing labels. It was the era of the superwoman and the liberated man, of women who could have it all and men who could share the housekeeping. The movement for women's rights, perhaps more than expanding opportunities, had irrevocably redefined the nature of relationships between men and women.

It used to be that most women automatically married and had children. This was assumed, expected, as immutable as natural law. Women either worked or didn't, but they invariably married and had children. It defined them, reportedly fulfilled them. The women's movement, of course, challenged much of that. Women were more than the sum of their relationship to men and children. Women could be just as fulfilled by interesting, satisfying work outside the home, work that paid, work that would free them from economic dependence on men, on husbands, work that would lead to independence, liberation, success.

While the women's movement shattered many of the assumptions that had defined and limited the female gender, it never quite succeeded in completely dispelling the old, primal notion: women are somehow less than a real success without a husband and children. It is an idea as deeply rooted in the psyche of black women as white women, and one that threw a snag into the politics of women's liberation, for when the majority of women said they wanted freedom, they didn't mean freedom from men and children. Women could not only have it all, they wanted it all, and that often started with both a good man and a good job. For black women, it appeared, however, that gaining one was too often at the price of losing the other.

Like most women, Loretta Johnson had a basic life plan that included a good man, a husband. "Basically my plan was to go on and finish college, work, and possibly be married by 25, have my first kid at 26, 27. Hopefully I would marry someone [with enough economic resources] that I would not have to work full time, but work nonetheless." Work was important to Johnson. She didn't want to suffer the fate of her mother: be a housewife married to a mailman for ten years, bear six children and then one day at age 30 have your husband die, leaving you pregnant with the seventh child and little marketable skills. "When my father died, all my mother knew how to do was babysit. She had to work as a maid."

Loretta Johnson, on the other hand, is one of 175 assistant district attorneys in the Harris County prosecutor's office in Houston, Texas. She finished college, graduated from law school, became a prosecutor, and turned 30 still single. For Johnson, a tall, strikingly sensual deep brown woman, that has ruled out pregnancy, though not necessarily motherhood. "I might adopt, but I made a conscious decision that I was not going to become pregnant after age 30," she said at age 33 in 1987. "I saw what it did to my sister's body—she had a child at 32." Besides, these days Johnson works too hard prosecuting cases, and she hasn't met anyone she's attracted to.

It has become a blues note on the success refrain of the new professional black woman. Attractive, smart, educated, she is often also unattached, too busy to meet a potential mate, too successful to have to be economically dependent on one. For many, this has been the down side of the revolution. The fact that the number of single, never-married black women between the ages of 18 and 39 had grown to 3,073,000, or 51 percent of all black women in this age group by 1990, compared to 1,061,000, which represented 30 percent of black women in this age group in 1970, has reconfigured the black American family and underscored a devastating slide that has resulted in more female-headed households and more single mothers than at any point in black American history since slavery.

Yet for educated black professionals like Loretta Johnson who benefited most from the women's movement, liberation has brought more than economic independence. It has brought transforming, revolutionary personal freedom. The freedom of choice. The freedom to marry or not, to get pregnant or not, to have children or not, to adopt as a single parent or not. Women, both black and white, have never had more freedom to exercise more choice and more control—over their own bodies, their own lives.

Most women, to be sure, still want to marry and have children. And this is still certainly one measure of a woman's success. But among successfully liberated, integrated black women, marriage and children are simply that—a measure, not a definition. Real success comes with the freedom of discovery: finding out who you are, what affirms you, what makes you happy. As Johnson says, explaining the two times she had the opportunity but passed on marriage: "It was before I went to law school. I was working for Southwestern Bell. I could have stayed at the phone company and been married. But it was a question of suddenly just being a housewife and not going further. I would have died.

"When my mother married, I'm sure she married because she loved my father. But I also think she married because that's what they did then." When one of her seven uncles raised the inevitable question on Loretta Johnson's thirtieth birthday, asking her mother, his sister, "Well, when is she going to get married?" her mother responded, "She will do it in her own time." It was the highest vote of confidence: "That's when I realized that my mother was really quite happy with me the way I am."

Women like Loretta Johnson's mother, who came of age in another, less revolutionary time, understood the value of a black woman having choices. Men like Loretta Johnson's uncle, on the other hand, frequently did not. Men, not unexpectedly, often found the prospect (to say nothing of the actual reality) of successful, independent women unsettling, disturbing, threatening. Successful black women typically, then, have had to battle not just expected racism from whites, but often rampant sexism from black men— oppression from their very own "brothers" in the struggle.

Barbara Britton: Dealing with the Brothers in the Struggle

To many professional black men who by the seventies were just as new to the corporate arena as women, the black female professional represented a particular threat, a historic conflict. In the black man's mind she had the advantage of being a "twofer" in the era of affirmative action. Her double status as a member of two disadvantaged minorities gave her a double advantage in terms of getting jobs, being promoted, in short, doing better than black men in the ongoing struggle for freedom.

Every black man knew that a black woman has historically been less of a threat to white men than a black man. She has had an easier time of it. Even a white man, Daniel Patrick Moynihan, said as much when he wrote the controversial "Moynihan Report" in 1965, which not only blamed a "black matriarchy" for the problems of the African-American community but concluded that black men had suffered more from racism than black women. "It was the Negro male who was the most humiliated" by racism and discrimination, Moynihan said. "Segregation and the submissiveness it exacts is surely more destructive to the male than the female personality," for "the very essence of the male animal, from the bantam rooster to the four-star general, is to strut."

Ultimately, what the women's movement would most seriously challenge was traditional male power. If women had power, what did that leave men? Apparently, with less power, according to men. Among African-American men and women, the issue exploded with conflict. Black women may never have become active feminists, but the women's movement raised female consciousness just the same. Black women soon enough realized that they, too, like all women, were often victims of sexism, and not just racism. Black men could be just as sexist as any white man, just as oppressive, demanding, controlling, and macho in their thinking. It seemed to be the nature of all men; this need to have power and dominion over all women—this need to strut.

Barbara Britton remembers the brother well. He was the only other black in the sales department with her at Petry Communications in 1978. They were selling television advertising time. And he was the one who made a point of showing her his commission statement, his paycheck, every week. He was the one who made the snide comments and public insults about her in sales meetings in front of his white male colleagues. He was the one who told an outright, vicious lie about her one day: "She's selling reefer up on 125th Street."

"It was a trip," Britton recalls. "He wanted to be the only black in the corporation and saw me as a threat. He thought we had to compete. It got to the point where even the whites in the company started to notice." White men, in fact, were the ones who came to Britton's defense when the brother accused her of selling marijuana in Harlem. "These were white boys I had bonded with; they knew me, respected me," Britton explains. "They called me the 'black bitch' and the 'black princess' because in their minds I was tough enough to do the job to become one of the gang. I had paid my dues."

At the time she joined Petry Communications, Barbara Britton was the unwed mother of two daughters by two different fathers. An only child of working-class parents, she became pregnant the first time during her sophomore year at Hampton Institute, dropped out of college, and had the baby. The second time was five years later. She was living with the father and had even bought a house with him but didn't want to marry him. The one thing she knew for sure she had known as far back as the sixth grade when she had looked down on the New York skyline from the streets of Harlem one day and thought to herself, I want to be a businesswoman. "I didn't know what it was, but I knew that's what I wanted to be."

Britton, who had her two children by age 25, also knew for sure that she didn't want to end up like Miss Josie, the single mother down the block who epitomized the old nursery rhyme that is every woman's nightmare: "She had so many children she didn't know what to do." Nor did Britton want to end up like the men she ran with as a delinquent though straight-A teenager growing up in Spanish Harlem—men with names like Brother and Freddy and Fatty Rat, the hustlers and the gamblers who drove the Cadillacs and the fast, pretty women like Britton and her two best girl-friends; men who lived fast and died a statistic—black, male, and most likely murdered between the ages of 15 and 24. After all was said and done, after she had the kids, Barbara Britton knew she really just wanted to make money. As she said, she wanted to be a businesswoman.

In 1970 Britton gave birth to her first daughter and managed to hustle about $9,500 in income that year by "proceeding to take advantage of the things that were available"—welfare, a work/ study job, and a Model Cities scholarship. Less than twenty years later in 1988 at age 38, she was earning exactly ten times that, $95,000 in salary and commissions, selling advertising time for Music Television (MTV). By then she had her second daughter and a master's degree in economics. She had continued to benefit from the particular opportunities available to young, bright black women in those two decades: scholarships, training programs, positions in "nontraditional" fields.

But Britton, like many successful blacks who have learned to integrate black and white cultural experiences, also had the advantage of possessing survivor instincts that had been honed in the streets of a community where the most successful businesspeople were often the outlaws. She had the benefit of street smarts. "I realize now that I glamorized the life of the street, growing up," she says, "but there were things I learned from the street that have been absolutely invaluable to me." The sales business, Britton discovered, is basically the game of the con, the art of the hustle, wherever it's played. "They [white business] are not doing anything different downtown than they [black illegal business] are doing uptown," she says. "The only difference is, downtown they carry a briefcase and the streets are clean. But in terms of the mechanics of business, I find it very dirty, lowdown, backstabbing, and just plain old evil sometimes."

Yet Britton also found that she has a certain capacity for "being able to handle myself in any situation, no matter what goes down, to be cool, to be able to assess a situation quickly, manipulate it, and hold under pressure, to be able to see the advantage and take it, no matter how rough the situation, no matter how bleak it looks," all essential qualities she developed to survive the streets of Harlem that now give her a winning edge in the game of business.

And if the game turns foul and sexist, as it did when the brother she worked with accused her of selling drugs, Britton simply deals —coolly, pragmatically, honestly. "Hey," she finally told him. "You know, I'm not here to take your spot and you're not here to take my spot. So let's stop this." The two eventually became friends, though Britton continued to be tested in big and small ways as a black and a woman in business. There were the racist jokes—"Hey, Barbara, lights out. We know you by your eyes and your teeth." There were the sexist innuendos, the blatant propositions, occasionally from white women and not just black or white men. "Anything is possible in this business," says Britton the businesswoman, now 40, in her deep, smoky voice, still tinged with a trace of the outlaw. "It's all a mind game, all about asserting power. You cannot get crazy."

Anne Ashmore: Woman Power

If black women have had more successes than ever before, more power, it has invariably been at the cost of greater uncertainty. The kind of uncertainty that can lead to life crises even in the face of liberating life changes. Dr. Anne Ashmore, a psychologist in private practice in Brookline, Massachusetts, confronts such crises everyday in work that brings her face-to-face with some of the new questions that now try women's souls: "Do I do what's been done traditionally, or do I do what's in my best interest? And how do I know if it's going to be in my best interest?"

These are the very questions Ashmore is now asking herself. She is in session, sitting at the dining room table in the new condominium she moved into three months ago. It is the spring of 1988, she is 46, and she has just left her husband of fourteen years, the renowned psychiatrist Dr. Alvin Poussaint. It was the kind of bold, shocking move that still reverberates with conflict, uncertainty, fear. "Who wants to start over again?" Ashmore asks in the high, plaintive voice of the Atlanta southern belle she grew up be. "Who wants to take the kind of risks you take—financial, emotional, psychological? What you stand to gain is a maybe. What you have is clear. What you give up is clear. What you gain is possible."

What Anne Ashmore Poussaint gave up when she left her husband was fame, fortune, and the Poussaint name, which has been seen on countless talk shows, in articles, and on every Bill Cosby enterprise from the television show to his books. She gave up the glitter and the glamour that go with being the wife of a celebrity: the parties, the trips, the entrée to elite circles. She gave up being married to power.

What Anne Ashmore gained when she left her husband was a sense of her own power. She had changed, grown, become a successful professional woman in her own field, in her own name. Being identified through marriage and another's success was no longer affirming, if it ever had been. But was leaving the right thing to do? There was a 9-year-old son to consider. "I really don't know," Ashmore says, filled with an angst new to the American black woman. "I want somebody to tell me whether it's right. In our generation they've changed the rules—there are no rules anymore. It's considered admirable and good if you do things for the right reason. But that doesn't mean you survive. The bottom line is to ensure survival, and the best way to do that is to use your head. Use your head before your heart uses you."

Anne Ashmore has always used her head, even when she could just as easily have simply used her looks. Tall and light-skinned, with the classic, chiseled features of the European, Ashmore epitomizes what many consider the pretty black woman in America, the kind of aristocratic-looking beauty who becomes Morehouse College Homecoming Queen or grows up to marry a successful, famous black doctor. Yet successful black women know that beauty is not only fleeting, skin deep, but in the black community a matter of relative perceptions. "I don't care how attractive you are, how pretty, how anything else, you also need to just *be,*" Ashmore insists. "You need to use your head." Besides, she adds, growing up, "I was just cute. I wouldn't say I was gorgeous. And I wasn't considered as intriguing as a whole bunch of other kids who *were* cute."

Growing up in Atlanta, Anne Ashmore lived in the shadow of another male: a brother who was thirteen months younger, blond, and blue-eyed. He was the one considered gorgeous. He was the one who got all the attention. "He commanded attention just by walking the earth, looking the way he looked," Ashmore says. "So I didn't grow up thinking I was cute. I grew up feeling that if I wanted any positive attention, I was going to have to do something to earn it." Ashmore, then, learned to develop personality and style; she learned to think. "I remember consciously and deliberately thinking that I wanted to develop my brain to be smart. I wanted to be intelligent. I wanted to develop that, and then I wanted to be attractive. It seemed to me this is just what you had to do to be special."

Ashmore's family was middle class, various shades of light-skinned—from Anne's pale yellow to her brother's milk white—and emotionally troubled. She had a half-sister who had "problems" and a mother who was consumed with her sister's problems. The conditions led to Ashmore's interest in psychology. "I went into social work first. I wanted to help. I wanted to give back something to my people."

As a psychologist, Ashmore says her role now is "to take people to places they cannot go alone." To emotional, frightening, painful places where images may have been distorted, ambitions stunted, the spirit bruised. It is a brand new field of work for the black woman, leading many times to a very new exploration into the terrain of the black female psyche, a mind field where, as for all women, looks still matter, beauty confers a certain power, if not certain success, image is still fragile, and new roles have yet to be clearly defined.

Anne Ashmore, who finds the territory both personally and professionally challenging, has turned out to be quite successful in a field where the whole point is to use your head. She is "an excellent clinician," she says, a sympathetic therapist. She can empathize, identify. But what's most important professionally, Ashmore adds, "is that I have integrity, that I feel good about myself." What makes a difference personally is that she takes responsibility and is also willing to take risks. "I'm not done yet," Ashmore says with an excitement about her new life that could just as accurately characterize the new lives of today's successful black women. "But I feel empowered."

Susan L. Taylor: The Essence of Success

If any one phenomenon could be said to be a harbinger of the liberated success of black women during the past 20 years, it is the emergence of *Essence* magazine, "the publication for today's black woman." When *Essence* debuted in May of 1970, the African-American woman had rarely ever seen her beauty reflected in any of America's images. The magazine thus became the affirming new mirror mirror on the wall: *You are the most spectacular of them all,* it told black women every month. *Essence* did the usual women's service magazine things: run recipes, give career and health advice, discuss men and children. But it also covered tough social and political issues and reveled in the simple glory and majesty of the black woman, passionately documenting her struggles and triumphs, applauding her achievements, showcasing her splendor in fashion and beauty. *Essence* was also bottom-line proof in the seventies of just how far the black woman had come: she now constituted a profitable advertising market.

By 1990 *Essence* readers numbered 850,000, with a pass-along readership of four million. They ranged in age from 18 to 49 and had an average household income of $37,300. A third were married, over half had children under the age of 18, and 81 percent had attended college. In marketing parlance the reader became known as the *Essence* Woman: smart and curious, striving, ambitious, and in the vanguard of change, a position that makes her at times uncertain, vulnerable, but no less enduring.

The *Essence* Woman is a woman not unlike Susan L. Taylor, 44, *Essence* editor-in-chief. Taylor recognizes that hers is the first gener-

ation of African-American women with the freedom and the ability
to *choose,* and the hard-won respect to be valued for her mind and
not just her labor. "When I think of being out in the cottonfield,
pregnant, picking cotton, I know the hardest work has been done,"
Taylor says of the black women who have gone before and the
legacy they have left. "I can use my mind—I have the freedom to
think. I can order my time and I can order my life. I don't forget
that."

It is indeed a great psychic distance from the cottonfields of
slavery to a chief editor's corner office overlooking Times Square, a
six-figure annual income, and the constituency of 850,000 black
women who look to you for inspiration, guidance, leadership. Susan
Taylor's understanding and respect for what it took to empower her
to make the journey is what roots her success.

Taylor started at *Essence* in 1971 as a freelance beauty writer
earning $500 a month. She was a former actress who had the long,
lean elegance and natural grace of a timeless beauty. She was also a
new mother who had recently reconciled with her husband, a hair-
dresser who owned a beauty salon in the Bronx. "He was making a
great deal of money," says Taylor, explaining that for her marriage
at the time meant "for the first time in my life I didn't have to
worry about finances." Yet the marriage was stormy: her husband
was unfaithful, abusive. She took their 6-week-old daughter, Shana,
and "ran to my mother's house" in Queens. But returning home at
age 23 with an infant wasn't the answer either. Taylor's mother, a
proud, stern Trinidadian, tried to run her grown daughter's life, so
Taylor went back to her husband five months after leaving him.

The marriage fell apart and Taylor left a second time for good.
By then, "My freedom was the most important thing to me,"
though Taylor soon learned it is young single mothers who usually
pay the highest price for freedom. Suddenly, money was a problem.
She was making $500 a month and living in a Manhattan apart-
ment that cost $368 a month. There were the consuming expenses
of raising a child: food to buy, clothes, child care costs.

Then one day Taylor woke up with "this incredible pain in my
chest." She rushed to Columbia-Presbyterian Hospital, where she
sat waiting in the emergency room most of the day, feeling she had

hit rock bottom. "I was actually suicidal at that point. I had two or three dollars to my name, my car was broken, and I had these chest pains that doctors couldn't find any physical explanation for."

As she was leaving the hospital, walking along Broadway in upper Manhattan, Susan Taylor experienced her own "miracle on the road"—a force of compelling, inexplicable power suddenly drew her into the United Palace Church on Broadway, the church of the evangelist Reverend Ike, a man Taylor "had once laughed at." Reverend Ike was not preaching the sermon that day at the three o'clock service, however. It was a minister named Alfred Miller, whose message on the power of positive thinking would transform Taylor's life. "He was talking about what our thoughts had the power to accomplish. I had never heard this before." Taylor, who was brought up Catholic, sat in the back of the church, riveted. Here was a man of God suggesting that God is within, that each soul is imbued with its own godpower, its own capacity to be a life force that can direct and shape its own destiny.

The pain in Susan Taylor's chest started to subside.

Taylor refers to the day she found herself in the United Palace Church as the day she "came to faith." It was the day she recognized that real power lies within the human spirit ready to be tapped with the act of faith. She did not have to be a victim, for victimization often begins with negative thinking. "I started refocusing. Instead of focusing on this new baby I had to worry about feeding, I said, Thank God, she's healthy. Instead of worrying about a broken car, I said, Thank God I have limbs and can walk."

Faith has been as critical to black success as personal ability or opportunity, for it is the force of faith that has always given blacks, and black women in particular, their spiritual power in the face of adversity. Susan Taylor found faith—and "things began to turn around." In 1972 she was hired at *Essence* full time as fashion and beauty editor, and more than doubled her salary to $13,500 a year. Rent was no longer a problem. Neither was child care. Taylor now frequently brought her daughter to work, took her along on business trips. "I changed my mind and changed my attitude," says the woman whose faith today remains "unwavering."

That faith is what sustained her when she was named editor-in-chief of *Essence* in 1981 and found herself under pressure "to now know everything," not just fashion and beauty. That faith is what sustained her to take a freelance beauty writing job in the first place twenty years ago with no experience other than having developed a line of black cosmetics that were distributed in her husband's beauty salon. "Nobody had trained you to do the job," she says of those early days at *Essence.* "You just had to do it." Taylor had faith that she could.

Much of Taylor's belief in the power of her own possibilities stems from the example of her West Indian parents, especially her father, a hard-driving man who owned a ladies' clothing store in East Harlem. "Watching my father work six days a week in that store and open it even on Christmas because he was determined he wasn't going to work for white people was my inspiration. My parents never said *you can't.*"

It is her incredible energy, however, that empowers Susan Taylor to give inspiration to others. She continues to personally write her monthly motivational column "In the Spirit," which for ten years has been the magazine's most popular feature. She is in constant demand as a lecturer and accepts about twenty speaking engagements a year. In 1984 she went to college for the first time at age 38 and earned a degree seven years later at age 45. And in 1989 she married a man five years younger for what she calls "all the right reasons—love and respect."

There is perhaps no better role model representing the changing, growing, self-actualized, empowered possibilities of black women than Susan Taylor herself. It is her own life that represents both an identification and an inspiration for the four million black women she reaches. Her story may be set in the era of new opportunities, but it is rooted in the tradition of African-American values, for she has achieved success the old-fashioned way: she's earned it—worked hard, pulled herself up by her own bootstraps, remained loyal to the same company for twenty years, been rewarded on merit—and kept the faith.

Susan Taylor knows as well as any black woman that real success is most often marked by struggle, tenacity, and great acts of not just faith, but also will. As she wrote in her "In the Spirit" column in the twentieth-anniversary issue of the magazine, which best sums up the essential success of the black woman:

"We are the founders of civilization, the keepers of the culture, the matrix. We sisters have endured. Through the dispersion of our people, the carving up of the Motherland, through the Middle Passage and slavery. Through the denigration of our bodies, our beauty, our culture. We have survived. We are here."

T e n

SUCCESS AND THE
BLACK MAN

*H*earing room 227 of the Rayburn Building is packed. The removable wall dividing the huge room in half has been removed to double the space, and still, it is standing room only. Hundreds of black men and women, young, middle-aged, urban, rural, and from all across America crowd into the overflow, standing in the aisles, crammed in the back, pressed at the door trying to get in. The seats filled up an hour ago. There are lights, cameras, action.

The scene is Washington, D.C., in September 1987, on the occasion of the seventeenth annual Legislative Weekend of the Congressional Black Caucus. Once a year the Caucus holds political workshops and hearings on the Hill—and parties and fundraisers at the Hilton—during what's been called the annual reunion of Black America, the largest black political event in the country. The weekend draws some of the most influential blacks from not just political circles, but from academia, business, media, state and local governments, and civil rights groups. The idea is to give the black representatives in Congress who represent their own varied constituencies but also seek to act as a caucus in representing the interests of 30 million African-Americans an opportunity to assess the state of the race, to address the critical issues facing the people, to meet the voters and take the pulse and temperature of its black American citizens.

On this third Friday in September the noise level in hearing room 227 tells the Caucus that the hottest issue raising the temperatures of both black men and women is precisely the explosive nature of current relationships between black men and women. It is the subject that has drawn over 2,000 of them to the workshop "Black Male/Female Relationships," chaired by Representative Kweisi Mfume, the freshman congressman from Maryland. The workshop topic was his idea. And it has clearly drawn the biggest crowd of any hearing of the weekend. It is the kind of successful event that marks a new congressman as a comer to watch. It also underscores the extent to which personal relationships between black men and women have come to influence racial politics in America.

If the seventies defined the decade of women, the eighties had the decidedly masculine cast of a roaring bull market, business takeovers, greed, and Donald Trump. It was also in a very singular and odd way the decade of the black man—one very odd indication being the evening in 1989 Donald Trump appeared on the NBC television special, "R.A.C.E.," saying "If I were starting off today, I would love to be a well-educated black man because I really believe they do have an actual advantage. . . ." Exactly which educated black men Trump was referring to is not clear, since by 1987, according to a 1990 Carnegie-Mellon report on higher education, 33 percent of African-American males with college degrees were still earning poverty-level wages.

By the end of the eighties, black men constituted 6 percent of the nation's population, yet accounted for 11.5 percent of America's unemployment. They were imprisoned at a rate four times that of the black men imprisoned in South Africa, with one quarter of the African-American men between the ages of 20 and 29 either in jail, on parole, or on probation. Among black men aged 15 to 24, homicide was the leading cause of death, with the murder rate for black men overall jumping 67 percent between 1986 and 1990.

The fortunes of the black American male during the decade of the eighties turned harrowing, declining in direct proportion to the rising fortunes of black women. And what resulted was the kind of "crisis" in male/female relationships that could be expected within any group said to be distinguished by female success and male failure. It was in fact the various reported failures of black men— from his addictions to his crime rates, his joblessness, his abandonment of the family, his womanizing, his violence—that became the focus of media, literature, and politics for much of the eighties. Maligned, beleaguered, and beset upon, the black man became a study in pathology, regarded as a species apart, thought to be at once dangerous and endangered.

"It's about power!" a well-dressed woman in her early thirties shouts from the back of the room as the video camera pans in her direction. "If I'm going out working every day, making maybe even more money than he is, I'll be damned if I'm going to let some man tell me what to do!" Room 227 erupts with roars of approval from the women, and grunts and grumbles from the men. A crisis seems evident right here on Capitol Hill as the workshop on black male/female relationships fires up the heat and the passions. There are the accusations hurled, the old wounds laid bare. Black women want too much, demand too much, accuse the men. Black men don't want to accept responsibility, yet want to call the shots, charge the women. It is a new round in the old war between the sexes, and black men seem under particular fire.

Yet the one black man most likely to have been a casualty, given the odds and the circumstances, is now standing before the public body of yelling men and women, restoring order. He is dressed in the pinstripe power suit of the natty politician: conservative yet stylish, subtle yet arresting. Of medium height and lean weight, with thin, faint worry lines that etch his brow like old, faded tribal marks, Kweisi Mfume at this particular moment has the intense, guarded look of a wary boxer. He is standing slightly wide legged, rolling casually on the balls of his feet, gesturing with both hands as he tells the audience that while these are indeed painful issues, painful times, it is important for black men and women to have dialogue, to speak what's in their hearts and minds, to try to hear each other through the confusion and the hurt.

Then he offers this personal revelation: "I've run the streets, fathered five children out of wedlock, been one of those irresponsible black men," he confesses in a rush. It is a startling, stunning admission that brings a hush to the audience and makes the crucial point: Representative Kweisi Mfume is proof that the black man can not only beat the odds, rise above the circumstances, be more than the sum of bad press and terminal pathology; he can succeed on his own terms and come into his own power. "I stand before you," Mfume says in the vulnerable, yet soothing tones of the natural politician, "as a living testament to the possibility of change."

Kweisi Mfume: Against the Odds

Kweisi Mfume's five children are all boys, though by 1988 they have grown into big, strapping, handsome teenagers and young men. In the photograph they sit posed on a couch flanking another strapping, handsome black man born out of wedlock, the Reverend Jesse Jackson. It is the only photograph in an otherwise unadorned and unofficial looking Washington, D.C., office occupied by the man who took Parren Mitchell's seat as representative of the Seventh District in Baltimore when the 100th Congress convened in January 1987.

Mfume arrived in Congress with twenty-three other African-American representatives that year; he was 38 and the only bachelor. He had beaten out ten candidates crowding the field during the primary in Baltimore to win by a hefty 47 percent of the vote, and quickly made it clear he would continue along the trail blazed by his mentor and predecessor Parren Mitchell, who had been the formidable champion of minority business development in Congress for sixteen years. Just eight years before, as a maverick starting out on the Baltimore City Council in 1979, Mfume had been the quintessential black politician—a long shot, the kind of successful outsider who gets inside and then learns the rules, the formal and informal procedures, the structures, the parliamentary lessons, "how things get done," as he puts it.

Like politics, success among black men typically involves not just the art of compromise or the instinctive exercise of power, but the triumph over odds. In the case of Kweisi Mfume, success has also been shaped by pain and loss and tragedy, and consequently, by early, life-altering responsibility.

Tragedy is known to be both defining and transcendent, to paralyze, galvanize, to elicit great faith or shatter all faith. Kweisi Mfume was defined—and transcended—at age 16, the evening his mother keeled over in his arms and died. They were sitting on the couch in their Baltimore living room, talking as they usually did about his responsibilities as the manchild in the family.

"My mother had been diagnosed with having cancer six months before. This was 1965, and in those days it was just assumed that when you got cancer you were going to die, period. So it was a matter of time. After the diagnosis my mother didn't share it with anybody. But she told me. I'd come home every night after school and we would talk about it. What she expected of me. How she wanted me to keep the family together." Mfume was the oldest of five children and the only male, groomed to "become a man" even while still a boy, to assume the weight of great responsibility under great, trying circumstances.

It was during one of her usual lectures to her son that Mfume's mother suddenly in midsentence let out a rattling sound that sears his memory to this day—"A sound I had never heard before," he says slowly. "It was a deep, eerie, terrible kind of sound halfway through her sentence. She fell over into my arms, and I held her. I got scared because I could see the great pain she was in. She was looking at me and her mouth just kind of opened. And then she closed her eyes and died."

Mfume didn't immediately comprehend, so he did the responsible things. He called one of his uncles—his mother's brother—who lived nearby. He called an ambulance. He called his mother's priest. He accompanied his mother as she was carried out on a stretcher, rode with her in the back of the ambulance, numbly watching as the medics beat her chest, gave her oxygen; he followed her into the hospital emergency room, growing ill at the thought of her being gone, becoming transfixed as he watched the attendant pull the sheet on the stretcher up over her face, performing the rite of passing that pronounced it, confirmed it, made him finally comprehend it.

For Kweisi Mfume, the loss of his mother led not just to an early assumption of responsibility, but to the early loss of faith. He dropped out of school in order to work two full-time jobs and one part-time job to provide for his sisters, who went to live with their grandmother while he went to live with two uncles. He became "rebellious," "wild." He gave up the Catholic faith, unable to understand how a just God "that my mother worshipped over and over could allow something like this to happen." He questioned other injustices: why he and his family were poor and other families were not; why he had only one parent, a mother, he felt close to, a stepfather he never got along with, and a real father who didn't make himself known to Mfume until after his mother's death.

The Church wasn't answering any of these questions, "so me and Catholicism fell out." Like many young black men who find that America's institutions offer neither answers to their terrifying questions nor hope for their troubled spirits, Mfume "hit the streets," finding there no answers or hope either, but a certain escape and relief, in clothes, music, and finally in girls. "I just went crazy," Mfume says of the period between the ages of 17 and 21. Indeed, these are the very teenage-into-manhood years that have become the most vulnerable for the black man: the ages 15 to 24, during which time he is most likely to drop out of school, get a girl pregnant, be unemployed, run into trouble with the law, or get killed. "That was the only period of my life where I did not have a sense of control about myself. My children were born out of wedlock then,"—five sons born to three different mothers. There were minor brushes with the law. Hanging out on the corner. Speeding in rented cars. Disturbing the peace. Raising a little hell.

Such extenuating circumstances have historically narrowed the odds for black men in America. Yet there have always been black men who defy the odds, who go against the odds to succeed, and thereby beat the odds. Men like Kweisi Mfume. Men who are successful because they ultimately take responsibility; they are accountable and thus develop a natural sense of power, becoming a force that can change the odds.

"Responsibility was something that I grew up with, so I was always taught to be responsible for my actions," says Mfume of what would finally define his own success. "Even when my sons were born, I could not bring myself to suggest to any of their mothers that they ought to abort them." His children, whom he helped to support financially, stayed with him every weekend. "And if we were lucky during the week, once or twice we'd get a chance to do something together. I got me an old beat-up jalopy to get around in. It was big enough to carry them all, and we just hung out together. I was determined we were going to be a family. I explained to them early on how things developed with me and them, and what the situation was. I've always been kind of frank and honest with my boys, probably because they are boys. I figured if I could deal with all this at an early age, they could deal with it."

Just as his mother's death led to a loss of faith and a certain loss of control, her memory led to Mfume regaining control. "I was hanging out at the liquor store not far from where I had lived when my mother was alive, shooting crap with the guys, talking trash. Something just came over me that night. Something told me that how I was living was probably hurting my mother. So I stopped. I went back to my room and sat up all night thinking. I realized that although I couldn't explain why things had happened to me, I apparently was going to live a while, and I sure didn't want to end up like the old-timers in the neighborhood—the ones who would always come up to you and say 'Ah, you young buck. You don't know. If I had it to do all over again, I'd do it this way.' It started making sense, and I knew that it was really up to me to set my own direction. Not the guys I ran with in the neighborhood. Not the people I worked for. Not the Man. It was up to me—to take advantage of the things I'd learned from my mother, to make sure that I took care of my responsibilities."

It was from his mother that Mfume developed his social activism, his racial consciousness, his politics. "She was always dragging me to meetings and organizing activities. I learned about jazz and black writers from my mother, who always had books and albums in the house. She'd read to me and my sisters, explaining to us that we didn't just happen in the world, but that the world was made up of different people and we [blacks] had a legacy to be proud of."

It is a legacy the Congressman honored when he dropped his given "slave" name, Frizzell Gray (a.k.a. Pee Wee), in 1971 and took an African name—Kweisi Mfume, which in Swahili means "conquering son of kings." He made the name change legal when he declared himself a candidate for the Baltimore City Council in 1979. By then he had gone back to school and received his graduate equivalency diploma (GED); graduated *magna cum laude* from Morgan State University at age 28 with a degree in urban studies and a minor in fiscal management; gotten a master's degree from Johns Hopkins with a concentration in international studies and foreign relations; worked on both the presidential campaign of Hubert Humphrey and the congressional campaign of Parren Mitchell in 1968; and developed a public following as a radio talk-show host, which enabled him to put together a political organizing team when he was ready to run for office himself that would blitz Baltimore and, against all odds, land him in the city council by the minuscule margin of three votes.

"I never think about odds," says the conquering son of kings, who has found that hope and perhaps some of the answers lie in the institution of American politics. He knows that while survival for black men is precisely a matter of odds, success is invariably a matter of power.

Power, that is, the ability to provide for and get things done, is to men what marriage and children are said to be to women: the force that defines them, the very measure of what it means to succeed as a man. Men, however, tend to think of power in the terms by which they define their politics, their sports, their commerce—in terms of contests and competitions, positioning and ranking, in terms of winning against all odds and winning the only thing; in terms of being superior, having advantage, taking control, being number one. It is the ego-driven psychology of the patriarchy, the classically male quest for omnipotence.

In the end, "Black Power!" became the battle cry on which the Civil Rights Movement would finally turn, head north, grow urban, militant, and distinctly male, and become a threatening euphemism not just for freedom, revolution, but black manhood and black male prerogative. It was perhaps inevitable that the struggle for civil rights would get down to a struggle for power, a charge for manhood. As Michele Wallace wrote in *Black Macho and the Myth of the Superwoman,* "The black man of the 1960s found himself wondering why it had taken him so long to realize that he had an old score to settle. Yes, yes, he wanted freedom, equality, all of that. But what he really wanted was to be a man." Like all men, the black man wanted power. Like all men, he wanted to win.

BLACK MEN, BLACK POWER

In the pantheon of black male heroes that came to characterize black male success in the last third of the American twentieth century, Martin, Malcolm and Jesse rose as the exalted, triumphant trinity. Martin Luther King gave black men their moral force. Malcolm X gave black men their manhood. Jesse Jackson gave black men their victory. And all three gave black America its voice.

King's Southern movement for civil rights in the sixties became the moral crusade of the century, its ethos rooted in the theology of liberation and the sacrament of nonviolence. It was a combination that would give black men decisive, winning spiritual power.

In the North, where the sixties politics of nonviolence was replaced by the politics of confrontation, Malcolm X came to represent black man at his emerging best: strong, uncompromising, clear, committed to securing power "by any means necessary." He was the former convict, the pimp, the gambler and the hustler who had successfully turned the odds around to emerge a leader, a thinker, a man of revolutionary power.

Jesse Jackson became the success metaphor for black manhood and power in the eighties, the crossover ambition of both Northern and Southern black male sensibilities and competing yet appealing contradictions. He was the renegade and the avenger, the outlaw and the reverend, the civil rights veteran who defied politics and conventional wisdom, the southern/urban preacher/rapper signifyin' hard. When he first ran for President in 1984, it was largely on inspiration and symbolism; when he ran again in 1988, it was on divine mandate. He had successfully united Americans as diverse as a rainbow from sea to shining sea, across class and color lines, from the ghetto to the bourgeoisie, in a stunning show of black male power.

Power, of course, is historically and exactly what the black man has been denied. If racism and discrimination seem particularly debilitating to the black male psyche, it is because such oppression relentlessly strips black men of their ability to do what men are supposed to do—work, earn money, take care of their women and children, run their communities, rule their destinies—have power. The idea of black men having power, however, has long been a threat—ever since Nat Turner, ever since Frederick Douglass, ever since Marcus Garvey, ever since Martin, Malcolm, and Jesse, ever since any black man dared to challenge an order, a world view, a view that bestows gain and privilege to other men at the expense of the black man and stacks the odds against him in a cheat for power.

The natural stance of the black man in America, then, has become one of guarded opposition—the on-point position of the beleaguered under siege—for the black man is still most often viewed as a threat, and America's most frequent response to the threatening black man is to try to contain, control, or kill him—to render him powerless. Nothing more graphically revealed the magnitude of King's and Malcolm X's threat than the violent magnitude of their deaths, each man publicly gunned down at age 39 in the prime of his time and his revolution. And perhaps nothing speaks more to the success of Jesse Jackson and the final victory of revolution than his profound power to simply remain alive.

Haki Madhubuti: The Warrior as Artist

"Basically, we're at war," says the Chicago poet emphatically, speaking of the political and emotional state of black Americans in general and the black man in particular. "What we have to understand is that white men run it, without a doubt. Every area of human activity that black people are involved in in America and much of the world is controlled by white men—law, education, entertainment, media, sports, politics, health care, the military—all areas. We don't control anything."

This, of course, is not literally true, but if Haki Madhubuti is given to speaking in hyperbole, a certain rhetoric, it is precisely because he is a poet, and also black and male, a circumstance that has infused his art with revolutionary politics, placing him in the activist/artist position of both warrior and scribe.

Haki Madhubuti was born in 1942 in Little Rock, Arkansas, but grew up in tough black neighborhoods in Detroit and Chicago where being tall, skinny, and light-skinned kept him a perpetually moving target. "Learning how to fight, run, and rap at the earliest sign of danger got me through school with only a small razor cut and a mind that was not beyond repair," he writes in his bestselling book *Black Men: Obsolete, Single, Dangerous?* An early passion for language—specifically the written word—cultivated by his mother, who was killed when he was 15, became the catalyst that turned the poet Don L. Lee into Haki Madhubuti, the successful artist, educator, and businessman.

When Haki Madhubuti says "We don't control anything," he is speaking metaphorically, not spiritually or culturally. For Madhubuti, like other successful black men of his generation, has always controlled his politics and his art; he has always made responsible choices and exercised personal power. For such black men, power often begins with the simple yet profound act of declaring a name—an identity of one's own choosing, a definition of one's own making. During the period of black nationalism that characterized the later militancy of the Civil Rights Movement,

Haki Madhubuti became one of thousands of black men in America who has legally changed his name since 1970, dropping the appellations that designate a slave history in favor of one that connotes pride in an African heritage and new definitions. "Haki" in Swahili means "justice"; "Madhubuti" means "precise." In African tradition, a name stands for something, means something, conveys not only the line of ancestry, but the power and spirit of the ancestors.

In Chicago, a city where such diverse black male names as Jean Baptiste DuSable, Elijah Muhammad, Fred Hampton, Harold Washington, Louis Farrakhan, and John H. Johnson have come to stand for something, both the names Don L. Lee and Haki R. Madhubuti also stand for something. Don L. Lee is the name of the poet and writer still remembered and anthologized who launched a reputation with his first published book of essays in 1967, *Think Black*. Haki R. Madhubuti is the name of the same author of sixteen subsequent books of poetry, literary criticism, and essays. It is the name of the Chicago entrepreneur who for over twenty years has been director of the Institute of Positive Education, with its New Concept Development Center, a black private school, and the editor of Third World Press, a black publishing company, with the African-American Book and Art Center subsidiary, a chain of black bookstores in Chicago and the Midwest—businesses that grossed $2 million in revenues in 1990. It is the name of the professor of English at Chicago State University who has been a poet-in-residence at Cornell University, the University of Illinois, Howard University, and Central State University. It is the name of the black man who has successfully combined art and politics, business and culture to "redefine from our own African-American experience what is best for us on all levels of human involvement."

Haki Madhubuti considers himself primarily a poet, "in the Afrikan griot tradition," he says in *Black Men* . . . "a keeper of the culture's secrets, history, short and tall tales, a rememberer." Yet in the contemporary tradition of the African-American artist, he is also a thinker, a critic, a social commentator for whom art must seek to articulate solutions even as it documents history and struggle. This has made him a somewhat unusual and distinctly African-American success: an effective "cultural nationalist" whose life and art strike that elusive psychic balance between a mainstream pragmatism and an Afrocentric black male sensibility. Cultural nationalists such as Haki Madhubuti are in the system, but not really of it, for they understand that success among males is measured by the power of a man to perpetuate his own name, to build families, nations and institutions in his own image, to define his own reality and seek truth from his own base of power.

It is this drive for independent male power that continues to pit the black man against the white man in a virtual state of war, Madhubuti contends. "We've been at war ever since our first interaction with them. White men don't fear white women or black women, but they fear black men, and the fear is both historical and psychological. The great fear is that if we [black men] got in power we would do to them [white men] what they have done to us."

Madhubuti maintains that black men have always possessed the power to take responsibility—to operate out of what is best for the black family and for the race. He has been married to his wife Safisha since 1974 and is the father of five children—three by Safisha, one by his first wife, and one from a relationship he was in between his first and second marriages.

Fatherhood has traditionally represented a certain measure of male power in the black community, revealing perhaps the black man's ultimate weapon—his power, as Madhubuti puts it, "to genetically annihilate the white man," for it is in the area of sex and sexuality that the black man remains the greatest psychological threat to white males. But fatherhood without responsibility is not power, only dangerous, says Madhubuti, whose view of relationships has been shaped by the politics of both black male sexuality and black women's liberation.

Like most handsome, successful men, Madhubuti has always been desirable to other women and still finds "beautiful women tempting." Yet he is also a man whose commitment to his race and to black nation-building begins with a commitment to his family. "What I had to learn very early in our [marriage] relationship was how to say no [to other women] and not to take advantage of my position," he said in an *Essence* magazine interview in which he discussed his marriage. "It was much more difficult when I was younger, but it's not that difficult now, because I think that people know my work and they know what type of man I am, and they recognize that my commitment to my family is number one."

Sexuality is the one area in which the black man has been accorded power—often mythical in its proportion—and thus sex is typically both an affirmation of his manhood and too often the locus of his irresponsibility. The image of the womanizing black man as a sexual bandit who is "by nature" destined to "play around" is as enduring (and often endearing) a feature of African-American folk culture as the legends of John Henry and Staggolee. It takes a black man who is supremely committed—and confident —to move beyond primal definitions that would reduce his power to the thrust of a penis. "People do not speak to the clear dominance of patriarchy throughout the world," Madhubuti says of men's tendency in general and the black man's proclivity specifically not only to view power in sexual terms, but to view sex as the natural prerogative of males. Yet "What's good for men is good for women," he adds. "We're all sexual."

Haki Madhubuti is also successfully liberated, a man who knows that real power lies in a man's capacity to take care of serious business: his family, his work, his people. "We have to move toward new lives, and our thinking patterns have to be freed up to look at some of the other possibilities," he says, explaining that the old, traditional roles between men and women no longer work—"If they ever did." Still, he does take a certain strength, comfort, and liberating power from history: "We've gone through our major holocaust," he says of the war. "We've survived the slave trade and the Middle Passage. And the whole epidemic in terms of AIDS and drugs—we're going to survive that, too."

Successful black men seem instinctively to understand something of the nature of power—that while it may be denied, it can also be assumed, claimed, seized, and exercised, for it is neither finite nor ordained. Power is eternal, yet also elusive and fleeting, as much an act of courage as an exercise of will.

For black men, power and success are frequently also very much a matter of style. The black man who succeeds in America has usually developed a style of interacting and relating that not only suits who he is personally but allows him to be effective enough to succeed professionally. Whatever the style, however, it is always tempered by the recognition that to be black and male in America is to be perpetually at risk—to be in danger, no matter how accomplished, of being viewed at best as a stereotype, and at worst as a "nigger," a threat.

Success for the black man, then, inevitably involves the tricky psychic proposition of balancing who he knows he is against how he knows he is seen, of sometimes being forced to compromise a position, yet managing to seldom compromise power.

Ramon Hervey: Amazing Grace

Graceful as a panther, low and sleek, the black Porsche deftly winds its way through the jungle that is the freeway system of Los Angeles. Passing palm trees and exit signs leading to fantasies with names like Mulholland Drive, Laurel Canyon, Bel Air, the car finally comes to rest at a stop in Hollywood, in the empty parking lot of Ren-Mar Studios' sound stage 2. Driver Ramon Hervey is paying an evening call on his sister, Winifred Hervey Stallworth, a producer and scriptwriter for "The Golden Girls" television show. It is 1987 and the NBC show is an Emmy Award–winning hit, which has left Stallworth with less time than ever to spend with her brother, himself a busy, successful, independent Hollywood publicist.

"I'd like to make an appointment for us to take a meeting," Hervey says to his sister with a big, boyish grin, in the Hollywoodese that has come to characterize dealmaking in Tinseltown. He commandeers the desk in her large, sparsely furnished office and sits leaned forward, slowly turning back and forth in the swivel chair as if trying it on for size, then rocks back, Hollywood-mogul style. He is being campy, a bit ironic and self-mocking—a tall, gold-skinned, dashing night rider, dressed in black leather and black silk, who has the power to disarm with the magic of a reassuring smile.

For every black man who strikes a note of threat in the hearts and minds of whites, there is that unexpected black man who succeeds because he manages to be a comfort. He diffuses the threat of his black male physicality with the power of his equanimity, his even-tempered spirit, his charm and sense of humor, his soothing capacity to put others at ease, to act with a kind of natural, amazing grace.

Both Ramon Hervey and his sister, two of five siblings who grew up in a middle-class household headed by a father who was in the Air Force, came of age during a civil rights era that would lead to more roles for blacks in the high-paying, behind-the-camera industry positions in Hollywood that had previously been more off limits to African-Americans than even roles on camera. Hervey got into public relations in 1976, at age 26, writing press releases for Motown shortly after the black-owned recording giant made its crossover trek from Detroit to Los Angeles. He was laid off less than a year later, but was soon hired to work on a freelance project with Rogers & Cowan, one of the largest entertainment agencies in the business. His first assignment was to prepare press materials for a special salute to the life of Buddy Holly spearheaded by Paul McCartney. "Rogers & Cowan was impressed by my work," Hervey says, "and ended up offering me a job in the contemporary music division."

Hervey took the job and continued writing press releases and news stories. Then he started developing press column items and assisting account executives. He became an account executive himself, then the West Coast manager of the firm's music division. Then, at age 28, two and a half years after being hired, Hervey was made vice president of the company talent division. He was the first and only black ever to reach that position at the agency.

Critical to Ramon Hervey's success has been his own personal likability factor in the very personal business of public relations. "I'm comforting to clients because I have a nice temperament and a self-assuredness that says everything is under control," he explains in his nice, even voice. It is the voice of calm and reason—strong, unflappable, a voice to be trusted.

Nice guy that he is, Hervey nevertheless had to go to the mat to get his vice presidency. "They [management] didn't just come to me and say, 'Ramon, you're doing such a great job and we want to make you a vice president.' I presented them with a memo basically asking for more money and justifying why I thought I deserved it." At the time, Hervey had personally brought six clients into the firm himself, becoming in the entertainment industry's seventies crossover era the comforting main attraction for such high-powered clients as Richard Pryor, Bette Midler, Daryl Hall and John Oates, George Benson, Herb Alpert, the Bee Gees, and Peter Frampton.

Public relations is one of those "soft" professions, providing services as subtle and intangible as image, goodwill, and taste. "I think taste has a lot to do with public relations and people putting their careers and their image in your hands," Hervey explains. "In a sense, they're making a statement about their taste *in you;* that you're going to be able to reflect their taste or reflect the type of image that they want expressed to the public." What clients seem to find most tasteful about Hervey is his judgment—his ability, as he states it, "to protect a client's image and also enhance it. Those are probably the two most essential functions [that I perform] as a public relations consultant."

This is essentially what he did for the client who represented his most challenging P.R. task and became his most widely publicized relationship. The client is Vanessa Williams, the first black woman to be crowned Miss America, and the only Miss America forced to give up the crown prior to the completion of her reign due to a scandal; the woman who in one year came to represent historic success and stereotypical failure. She was not only the woman whose image Ramon Hervey would rebuild, but the woman he would fall in love with, marry, and successfully manage.

In 1981 Hervey left Rogers & Cowan to launch his own independent public relations consulting firm which later also took on personal management. Initially Vanessa Williams was simply a prospective client whose business he was soliciting when he flew out to New York in the summer of 1984 to take a meeting with her black attorney, Dennis Dowdell. "My firm was recommended to him as one he should consider [as a representative for Williams], although it was up to Vanessa to ultimately decide. She was nearing the end of her term, and her attorney was interviewing potential public relations firms to work as part of a team to manage her professional career after her reign ended. He said he liked me. He definitely wanted me to meet Vanessa, and said that he would highly recommend me to her."

Several months later Hervey heard from the attorney, who called him on the phone, sounding worried. There were rumors that compromising photographs of Williams were about to be published. "How do you feel we should handle this?" the attorney asked of the black man he had instinctively called for help.

"I suggest you not do anything right now," Hervey advised calmly. "First, let's find out if the rumor is true; second, let's wait until you see the pictures—maybe they're not that bad. You really shouldn't comment to the press until you at least know what you're commenting about."

The attorney called back. "Ramon," he said tensely. "There *are* pictures. The pageant officials have seen them and they're holding a press conference today to say they're going to ask Vanessa to resign. What should I do?"

The measure of a man, as Rudyard Kipling wrote, is his ability to keep his head while those around him are losing theirs. From his office in Los Angeles Ramon Hervey started planning the press conference Vanessa would hold the following Monday. Later that night he caught the red-eye to New York and met Vanessa Williams for the first time Saturday morning at seven o'clock.

The pictures, as it turned out, were very bad. Taken when Williams was 19 and an aspiring model, they showed the current Miss America in various nude & pornographic poses, and were scheduled to be published in the September issue of *Penthouse*. A press conference, Hervey explained to Williams and her attorneys, would maximize her response and give her the most controlled exposure. And until she responded there was nothing the pageant could do. "We didn't have to tell the pageant what we were going to do for seventy-two hours. They were waiting for us, so we had some leverage. They didn't know if Vanessa would fight to hold her title or accept their request to resign."

Hervey was one of the advisers who recommended Vanessa Williams resign. "I just had to gamble on my intuition," he says. "She was about a month away from the end of her term and didn't have much to gain by trying to retain the title for a month, and she wasn't going to lose her scholarship, and I felt she should put the whole incident behind her and get on with her life."

Hervey's instincts proved right. When Vanessa Williams, then 21, appeared at the Sheraton Centre Hotel in New York City that Monday morning on July 20, 1984, to read the resignation statement he had written before the crowd of journalists and television cameras, she was the model of coolness and grace. It had the effect of deflecting much of the media's bloodthirsty passion. It was a masterful public relations stroke, "my biggest challenge as a professional," says the black man who successfully pulled it off. "I couldn't recall many other black professionals getting an opportunity to handle something of that magnitude," Hervey adds with a faint trace of pride. "I felt an obligation to not only Vanessa because of what I thought she had accomplished as a black woman, but to blacks in general, because I knew if I didn't handle this [Williams' response] right, it would have an impact in a lot of ways in many other areas. The funny thing is, very few clients that I've worked with could have handled the situation as well as Vanessa did. As much as I gave her direction, she delivered what had to be done."

Ramon Hervey understands it is in the press that the most powerful images are communicated regarding black success or failure. "I think the media oftentimes responds more enthusiastically to failures in the black community than they do to successes. The standards are never really the same for blacks, you know. We don't have the same social access and the same privileges that go along with our success. So blacks rise and fall much faster and are more susceptible because there is always that element of people either target-shooting or trying to make blacks live super lives. There's somewhat of a double standard, but unfortunately, a lot of high-profile black professionals don't realize it until it's too late."

Nor do blacks tend to have the same psychological and social supports as whites to buttress their ambitions or cushion their setbacks, which is why the love and support of Ramon Hervey for Vanessa Williams has been key to the success in both their careers. It was Hervey's calm direction and firm belief in her talent as an entertainer that rescued Vanessa Williams from one moment of notoriety and put her singing and acting career on a clear path to success. He was the one who advised her not to accept the book offers and movie and television projects that would have brought her considerable money, but also only further exploited the notoriety that followed the *Penthouse* photos. He was the one who told her reassuringly, "You're young, you've had this one crisis, but you'll survive it. You have more ahead of you than behind you." When their professional relationship turned personal, it was not surprising that Vanessa Williams had grown to love the one man who was there when she most needed someone to be there—someone to rescue her, protect her, enhance her image; to do what men do who are successful in their relationships with women.

And so, on the evening of December 1, 1988, in the year her debut album "The Right Stuff" went gold, in the year she was nominated for two Grammy Awards, it was a jubilant and vindicated Vanessa Williams who rose and went onstage to accept the 1988 Image Award for Best New Female Vocalist given by the Hollywood branch of the NAACP. "Ramon, honey, we did it," she said tearfully to resounding cheers in the packed Wiltern Theatre. Holding her award for image high in triumph, she cried out to her husband who smiled reassuringly from the audience: "Baby, this is for you!"

Christopher Edley, Jr.: Presumptions and the "Smart-Ass White Boys"

Ramon Hervey's opportunity to help turn around the image of Vanessa Williams was due as much to the assumption by the black man who enlisted his aid—her attorney Dennis Dowdell—that he could do the job as it was to his own skill in public relations. In their interactions with white men, however, black men typically suffer from what a black Harvard law professor calls "a presumption against my competence"—the feeling by white men that black men are somehow less than competent, less than qualified, don't really know what they are doing in any situations beyond entertainment or athletics that require judicious thinking and decisive action. It was this arrogance of white male presumption that Mayor Andrew Young publicly denounced at a convention of black journalists in Atlanta in 1984, making headlines himself when he called the white men in media and politics who had underestimated the power of Jesse Jackson's candidacy for president "a bunch of smart-ass white boys."

A bunch of them are overrunning the small, cramped Dukakis-for-President campaign headquarters on narrow Chauncy Street in downtown Boston in the spring of 1988. Mainly young and ambitious, preppie and confident, they sit clustered in planning meetings in makeshift conference rooms or hurry about scheduling appointments, taking and making phone calls, setting up convention logistics, tending to the press. Jesse Jackson is running for president again, and this particular crop of white boys is betting on Michael Dukakis as the favored new hope of the Democratic Party.

There is one lone black male in the place—sitting somewhat apart from the others in his own tiny office, taking calls, giving instructions. It is one month to rollcall at the Democratic National Convention in Atlanta where Michael Dukakis, currently the governor of Massachusetts, is certain to get his party's nomination for president.

At 35, Christopher Edley, Jr., is probably ten years older than most of the campaign workers who surround him, though with his trim, slight build and open, boyish face, and wearing glasses and a beard, he looks more like the Harvard law student he used to be than the Harvard Law School tenured professor he now is. He has taken a year's leave from the university to work for Dukakis—serving as the issues director of the campaign. It is the kind of ironic behind-the-scenes power position that has brought him to the attention of the press in an election year marked by the symbolism of Jesse Jackson on one hand and by Willie Horton on the other.

Edley is the black male "paradox within a paradox," reported the *Wall Street Journal* in its April 7, 1988, profile of him. "As the issues director, Mr. Edley's main job is to translate Gov. Dukakis's thoughts into precise positions . . . and to help Mr. Dukakis beat a black man—Jesse Jackson." Edley has no illusions about either challenge, for like most successful black men, he understands the nature of paradox. He understands, for instance, that while he has contacts and credentials, "you can't focus on that as being the measure of success" if you are black and male.

The son of Christopher Edley, Sr., a Harvard-educated attorney and former president of the United Negro College Fund, Chris Edley, Jr., grew up in the black upper middle class of Philadelphia with a sister ten years younger, "where the conversation at the dinner table was usually about doing things that make a difference in people's lives." Edley attended Swarthmore College, Dukakis's alma mater, as an undergraduate. The two met in the mid-seventies at an alumni event when Dukakis was in his first term as governor and Edley was a law student at Harvard. They met again when Edley was working for the Carter Administration in the late seventies as the assistant director of the White House Domestic Policy staff. And in 1981, when Dukakis was out of office and teaching at the Kennedy School at Harvard and Edley was teaching in Harvard's law school, they crossed paths once more. In 1986 Dukakis let it be known he was thinking about running for president in 1988, and Edley let it be known he would like to be helpful if he did decide to run. "He [Dukakis] called me just before he announced in 1987 to come over and talk to him."

Why did Michael Dukakis, the unassuming, soft-spoken Greek-American, choose Chris Edley, the unassuming, soft-spoken African-American, out of all the other possibilities to be his "issues" man? First of all, "He wanted to have a couple of minorities in top jobs in the campaign," Edley admits. "Inclusion was very important to him." But Dukakis was also attracted to Edley's "particular mix of skills and experience": his sharp, analytical thinking reflecting his training in law and mathematics, his policy experience resulting from his work in the Carter White House, his Harvard law degree, and his tenured position on Harvard's law school faculty.

Yet like another black Harvard man, W. E. B. DuBois, who wrote nearly a hundred years ago of the "two-ness" blacks experience trying to reconcile the dissonance of their blackness within the conflicting context of white culture, Chris Edley speaks of the "sense of otherness" he feels in the worlds of both politics and academia. It is the dissonance that comes partly from being an academic and an intellectual, rather than a "political junkie," he says of the otherness he feels on the campaign, but it is also a general dissonance created "largely because of race."

"As a black man, whether it's teaching or working in a campaign, I know that when I go in front of a group of whites for the first time and even the second time, there's a presumption against my competence," Edley explains. "And that I therefore have to earn their [whites'] respect, or earn their deference, or their inclusion." Chris Edley knows that despite his credentials and experience, his contacts and connections, his academic and intellectual prowess, he still has to repeatedly prove his abilities to white men against what he calls a "prejudgment—a prejudice."

This knowledge has helped ground Edley's success, however, for it keeps him clear about his own positions and issues as a black man in white America. He has learned, for instance, how to distinguish substance from politics, and how to know the difference between having a sense of presence and a sense of place. "If you talk to a black faculty member at a major institution, or a black student, I think that by and large, if they have any political consciousness about them, they will tell you, 'Yeah, I'm here, but this isn't my place,' " he says of integrating the halls of academia as well as politics. "They may have a membership card, but they don't own the place. For my generation our parents knocked on the doors to get us in. And now I'm in without having to fight too hard, but I still don't have any sense of ownership or personal investment."

Yet Chris Edley does have a sense of winning, which is why he chose to throw his hand in with Michael Dukakis, the white man, and not Jesse Jackson, the black man, in the presidential campaign of 1988. "Race is not the issue," he argues. "I think the question is, Who's in the best position to help black folks? The answer is Dukakis, because he can win." Edley, the successful issues man, knows how the smart-ass white boys are likely to vote, just as he knows how they are likely to think.

Gregory T. Baranco: The Master Dealer

Knowing how white men think has always been crucial not only to black male success, but to black male survival. Indeed, it has very often been the black man's ability to outthink white men that has meant the difference between success and failure, winning and losing—between making a deal, or blowing it.

Success for Gregory T. Baranco has largely meant understanding what white men want. He discovered early on that even "the most racist folks in the world want to be good for themselves," a fact that led him "to choose only the higher ground" in his dealings with people, particularly the white men who were his customers when he started selling cars in Baton Rouge, Louisiana, in the mid-sixties. One customer back then happened to be a member of the Ku Klux Klan who made it clear he didn't want to deal with Baranco as his salesman.

"I understand," Baranco told him truthfully, as he had told countless other Southern white men coming in to the dealership with similar prejudices. "My job is not to sell you a car," he said in his slow, halting drawl. "I'm only here to help you find the right car. My training is in mechanics. The only thing I'm going to do is help you select the right car for your needs, and when you find something you want to buy, I'll get Johnny over there [who was white] to write up the order. He'll be the one who actually closes the deal."

It always worked. And the line that always landed the deal was Baranco saying very comfortably, "I'm going to do all the work, and by my doing the work, it will save you money. Now, if you want Johnny to do the work, it's going to cost you more money."

Baranco used to get a certain perverse pleasure out of knowing exactly how to play the white man. Initially, after every deal had closed, Baranco would make sure the customer knew who was actually getting the sales commission. "I would go over and tell them, 'This is my commission. You paid me. And I'd like to thank you from the bottom of my heart.' The only way I got even was to get their money."

But that was when he was younger. Now at age 41 in 1988 he explains, "As I progressed I realized I didn't have to slap them [white men] in the face to make a point. I realized if I just tried to make them feel good, genuinely gave them what they wanted, represented what was good for them, they would tell their friends about me and I would make even more money." Baranco quickly became the top car salesman at the dealership. He was made a manager at the age of 22, the first black manager, but as he likes to point out, "not the last."

Baranco went into car sales intending to own a dealership, which he wasn't given an opportunity to do in Baton Rouge. So he headed to Atlanta, and in 1978 opened his first car dealership with the General Motors Corporation in the suburb of Decatur which he runs with his wife Juanita. By 1990 Baranco ran the largest black-owned automobile dealership in the country, posting 1990 sales of $190 million. His enterprises now include a Ford and Accura dealership, as well as interests in residential and commercial real estate developments and a bank and insurance business.

Standing over six feet tall, with an easy smile and the gentleman's air of a Dixie aristocrat, Baranco has the low key, almost self-effacing style characteristic of many Southern black men who work at not being intimidating. Yet natural power cannot be denied or masked. The numerous professional and civic awards that line the wall of his sleek, computerized office at his Decatur dealership, the framed business magazine cover that reveals his photograph, the wall-to-wall picture window that showcases the gleaming cars and trucks lined up outside, the television and radio ads that flash the Baranco name throughout the Atlanta metropolitan area—all confirm that this is a man who is a major-league player in the game of American business.

Seated on the window ledge facing the huge mahogany desk in a corner of his office, Baranco occasionally glances out the picture window, watching as one of the salesmen on his integrated staff of three hundred who has steered a customer through the lot to a flaming red Firebird does the spiel. Baranco's GMC-Pontiac dealership has been designated a "master dealer" by its General Motors manufacturer, the highest citation for overall excellence given to automobile dealers in the area of sales, customer satisfaction, and responsibility. "We were the only master dealer in the Atlanta region last year," Baranco says proudly, "and we've been a master dealer four years running."

Like all entrepreneurs, the black entrepreneur seeks power and independence—perhaps a more supreme sense of power and independence than even his white counterpart. The idea of being your own boss, accountable for your own potential with earning power as great as your capacity to succeed, is as American an ethic as democracy. For to work for yourself and be successful is to realize the oldest ideal of the American dream: freedom.

The number of black-owned businesses grew 38 percent between 1982 and 1987, nearly three times the growth rate of 14 percent for all U.S. firms, according to the Survey of Minority-Owned Business Enterprises, published by the U.S. Department of Commerce in 1990. Nearly half of all African-American business enterprises are concentrated in the service sector, and much of the growth in black entrepreneurship during this five-year period represented the growing number of dissatisfied black professionals who left corporate America to start their own businesses. A black-owned business traditionally has not only been an indicator of black economic power in the African-American community, but provided a black economic base. And historically the black entrepreneur has been more successful than the black wage earner in amassing real wealth in America.

"I had every reason to succeed," Baranco says of his middle-class upbringing in Baton Rouge as the son of a father who was a dentist and mother who was a teacher. He was the oldest of eight children, and the only son. "So it was always a negotiation," he says of growing up in a family that never had much money despite its professional status because of so many children. "I grew up in a family with kids where we always hustled. We were trained for business just growing up. You had to work in order to get something. My training and exposure from my parents told me that basically I could achieve anything I set out to accomplish."

Early on, Baranco made "a conscientious decision that I was going to work within the system." As a black Southerner who came of age in time to "have the privilege of integrating schools," he says what is important is "that we have access to everything." Baranco also believes in the system—has faith in its people, both black and white—for he has made the system work for him. "It's been uphill," he says of his climb in business. "But that's good; that's what builds success. I'm an uphill guy."

Les Payne: Shooting the Wounded

If black men such as Greg Baranco succeed by making whites feel good, by giving them what they want, or as author Shelby Steele puts it in *The Content of Our Character,* by "granting whites their innocence," there are occasionally black men with gunslinger styles, such as newspaper columnist and editor Les Payne, who manage to be a success and still take no prisoners. As Payne once cracked with characteristic hard-line wit upon accepting yet another award for excellence in journalism in the category of commentary: "The job of the critic is to ride down from the hills after the battle is over, after the smoke has cleared, and having surveyed the damage—shoot the wounded."

Les Payne has always had a way with words, and if he is a black man who happens to be a journalist, he is more notably a black male success who happens to be a straight shooter.

As the assistant managing editor at *Newsday,* the Long Island, New York daily newspaper that reaches a largely white, suburban readership of 700,000, Payne is responsible for assigning coverage on the national, foreign, state, and science desks. He also writes a weekly column that appears in the paper's Sunday edition. He has been with *Newsday* for over twenty years, the only place he's ever worked since leaving the army as a captain and Vietnam veteran in 1969 at age 26.

Payne always knew he wanted to write, though "Journalism was not open to black people of my generation," he says of growing up in Hartford, Connecticut, during the fifties, where neither of the city's two papers had ever hired a black reporter. By 1969, however, there were urban riots and the Kerner Commission Report grimly announcing that America was in danger of moving toward two societies—one white, the other black. Both developments led to white media hiring more blacks to cover the riots in ghettos where white reporters feared to tread, and to bring a larger, more black perspective to news coverage in general.

It is the black perspective on which Payne has built his reputation and success. "Someone has to advocate on behalf of black people. I wanted to write to express certain things that I felt about conditions that affected me and other blacks." In the tradition of Frederick Douglass, the black journalist and abolitionist whose spirit his own seems to most closely match, Payne is one of those black men who agitate, agitate, agitate.

The weapon that has made Payne a successful agitator is the very craft of journalism. "When my white counterpart came to work for *Newsday* in 1969, all he had to do was learn journalism. That's all he had to do. Now, I had to do that, plus work to organize on behalf of blacks, work to get more blacks hired so there would be better coverage of blacks in the community." The secret, Payne says, is that he always kept the struggle separate from the craft, yet he has perfected the craft in order to carry forth the struggle.

"The trick was learning the craft in a system that was hostile to me and other blacks. The way it normally works is that an editor will take a young reporter under his or her wing and pass the craft along, give him good stories, show him what mistakes he made. But the craft was not taught to black people—so I stole it. I was in a newsroom where journalism was practiced—in some cases very well. Maurice Swift was a rewrite man very good in foreign interviews. I sat three chairs away from him. So I used to listen to him.

John Pascal was a beautiful writer—I never saw him write a bad sentence—and I would clip his stories and study them."

Payne watched, listened, and read, read, read. The floor-to-ceiling bookcases that run the length of a dining room wall in his Huntington, Long Island, home contain the writings of Abraham Lincoln; there are the works of H. L. Mencken, A. J. Lieberman, DuBois, Douglass, both Walkers—Margaret and Alice, the black writers, the white ones, the men and the women, the journalists, the novelists, the poets. "I wanted to be the best at *Newsday*," Payne says simply of what drove him to perfect his craft. "I wanted to write better than anyone who is a better reporter, and I wanted to report better than anyone who's a better writer."

In 1973, Les Payne—by then a tough reporter who could write and a stylish writer who could report—was selected to be part of a four-person news team doing an investigative series on the heroin trade from its origins in Turkey to its distribution through the French Connection. The series, titled "The Heroin Trail," won Payne and his colleagues a Pulitzer Prize in 1974, one of over two dozen writing awards that have distinguished his career.

Payne's mastery of his craft has made him formidable as an advocate. As a reporter he covered stories ranging from the Soweto uprisings in South Africa to the plight of migrant workers on Long Island, the drought in Africa (for which he won the prestigious and most lucrative journalism honor in 1983, the United Nations Hunger Award, with its $10,000 cash prize) to interviews with Huey Newton and Bobby Seale of the Black Panther Party.

As a columnist Payne has taken aim at Reagan and Bush in Washington, Koch and Dinkins in New York, and dictatorships in Uganda and Haiti, firing with equal opportunity at both black and white offenders. In a column written shortly after the videotaped police beating of a black man in Los Angeles in 1991, he led off with this swipe at the city's black mayor: "After millions of Americans had endured a month of reruns of the savage police beating of Rodney King, Los Angeles Mayor Tom Bradley finally found his voice and what passes for his courage to call for the police chief to step down."

"They used to call me a supernigger," Payne says of both his black and white colleagues at *Newsday.* "Never to my face, but behind my back." The reference speaks in part to the grudging respect given to a black man with the temerity to be outspoken—and get away with it. It also speaks to the tendency of whites, says Payne, to give a top slot to only one black. "And the worst part about it is that blacks accept it. When they [other blacks] call me 'supernigger,' that's what they meant—that they had let white folks anoint me to be the top."

Payne, who is in fact the highest-ranking black at the newspaper, knows, as a top black man, that the power of a position does not lead to the power of success unless it is used for change. In his current position as an editor, then, he has used his power to name Marilyn Milloy, a black woman, to head the paper's Atlanta bureau, and Derrick Jackson, a black man, to head the Boston bureau. He assigned Morris Thompson to run the Mexico City bureau, sent Dennis Bell to cover the drought in Ethiopia (for which Bell won a Pulitzer), assigned Ron Howell to cover the Caribbean and then the war in the Persian Gulf—all black people, black journalists, who now get good assignments, top slots. "There is no one supernigger in the areas I control," Payne says.

Of course, in many ways Payne himself remains the super black man at *Newsday.* A black man whose natural style is confrontational, his manner intimidating. Tall, dark, and imposing, with heavy-lidded, piercing crescent-shaped eyes that seem always to be assessing, sizing up, Payne has the imperial, impervious bearing of an African chieftain. A bearing not unlike that of Idi Amin's, the former Ugandan dictator about whom he has written some of his most scathing articles. Les Payne is, quite simply, the kind of black man who scares white men.

"I'm told all the time that white people are afraid of me," Payne says, speaking in his deep voice, rumbling with the velocity of an uzi. "They see me as being intimidating, but I think the intimidation is that I know their number. I studies white people. And what's intimidating to white people is a black person who is sure of himself and feels equal to them." Yet Payne also concedes that *Newsday*'s corporate culture has probably accommodated his own style better than, say, a paper like the *New York Times* or the

Washington Post. "It's a young paper," Payne says of *Newsday,* which is owned by the Times-Mirror Company of Los Angeles. "It was only founded in 1940 and has been successful because it's taken chances. It was not straitjacketed or locked into one style. What I'm saying is that the style of the paper is compatible with my own."

It is rare that Les Payne ever concedes white institutions anything approaching compatibility. Like other black men who have managed to be successful and also continued to agitate, Payne has chosen to work within a system in order to change it. He has also become very good at playing by its rules—not just learning the craft, but excelling at the craft, which makes him one of those successful black men who is both feared and respected because he is good. "The reason I'm so constitutionally suited for journalism is that I'm basically a critic. I think temperamentally I'm kind of an iconoclast. I see warts, contradictions, and imperfections very clearly." And Payne knows his job as a black man, if he is to be successful as an agitator, is to shoot them down.

Jamil Sulieman: The Revolution Will Not Be Televised

For many black men coming of age in a civil rights era characterized by a thrust for integration in the South and the revolutionary furor of black nationalism in the North, success sometimes appears to be the sum of its own contradictions—the full circle that comes around to end at the beginning, complete, yet altered.

Like other revolutionaries of his generation, Jamil Sulieman, M.D., has changed, reassessed. The activist who was student body president of Montclair High School in predominantly white suburban Montclair, New Jersey, the same year he was chairman of the school's black student union and captain of the football team is now a doctor. However, he did not go to practice medicine in Africa or the Caribbean, as he once envisioned, planning to join the idealists in the black diaspora "who were building a new tomorrow." Instead, he went west to Oakland, married Kathleen Carney, a dentist, became a specialist in pulmonary diseases, and went into private group practice with three other doctors, all white men. Such reversal of perspective reflects the kind of irony that leads Sulieman to conclude with a low, dry chuckle: "When I was 18, I had all the answers. Now, at 35, I don't know the question."

In the seventeen years between the time he graduated from high school in 1970, went to Dartmouth on a full scholarship and medical school at the University of Cincinnati on another scholarship, and opened what is now, in 1987, a lucrative practice on Oakland's Pill Hill, there have in fact developed more questions than answers for black men such as Jamil Sulieman. What, for instance, has been the final cost of revolution, the price of victory and success—and who has paid?

As he sits leaning forward on the couch in the waiting room of his wife's office, thoughtfully stroking his beard, Sulieman, who has the large, compact build of a linebacker and the reflective introspection of a thinker, knows that his success has been shaped by the accident of history that put him at the right time and place of revolution. "My wife and I have often said that we owe our ability to be here to Martin Luther King and to the greaseheads who threw bricks in Detroit, Newark, and places like that," he says. "The ragheads, the blockheads—whatever you want to call them—who brought about this action that was the experiment."

Sulieman is referring to the masses in the black underclass whose urban rioting in the late sixties and early seventies led to a move toward social change and what he calls "the experiment"—that moment of equal opportunity in American history marked by policies such as "minority scholarships," affirmative action, and open admissions that cracked a door through which more blacks were able to enter American institutions. By the mid-seventies, however, the door was starting to close, Sulieman contends. Nontraditional "underprivileged" students, both black and white, who often challenged the status quo, were increasingly being replaced by black and white students who had a "vested interest in the institution, would respect the institution and maintain the institution," he says.

"Between the time I was a senior in undergraduate school in 1974 and finished medical school in 1978, things had already started to change. I didn't have the same sense that we [blacks] were committed as a group of people regardless of class, or thought of succeeding in a collective sense. The attitude of those who came behind me—and this is a generalization—appeared to be more concerned with getting themselves through and taking care of themselves as individuals, so there was not this mass sense of 'we.' "

Jamil Sulieman would be the first to admit that he, too, has changed. "I no longer have the self-assurance of youth and the feeling that what I believed before was right." He remembers the days Malcolm X and Martin Luther King were killed, and though he considers both men his influences, he is a Northern black who was shaped by the cultural nationalism Malcolm X evoked. He joined poet and activist Amiri Baraka's New Ark political organization in Newark when he was 15, became a Black Muslim while in college, and changed his name from Edgar Satterwhite to Jamil Sulieman after a trip to West Africa in 1971. "Jamil" is an Islamic derivation that means "purity," "strength," and Sulieman is the Islamic translation of his father's first name, Solomon. He kept his middle name, Sterling, after learning that his mother, who died when he was 12, gave him the name because it meant "quality."

Yet the politics of revolution that became a rite of passage in Sulieman's youth has led to a certain disillusion in his coming of middle age. The black men he once followed, believing they did indeed have the answers—Amiri Baraka, Ron Karenga—turned out to be only men after all, human, given to mistakes and their own contradictions. It has been one of the hard lessons learned in the struggle.

Sulieman still believes in a black value system as articulated by Ron Karenga, leader of the sixties California-based US nationalist organization and creator of Kwanza, the African-American holiday observed during the Christmas season that affirms seven principles of African unity. "I still think black people need to have a value system that gives us as a people predictability to our words and actions—a predictability based on the values that we are all one people, of coming together. But if you ask me if I feel a need to develop alternative [black] institutions for every aspect of life as I once felt, I'd say no. The hope and desire that time and circumstances would bring black people to a point of commonality has not occurred. Black people are as diverse as ever, and if I have changed, it's because I now know we are never going to extract black people in any large way from the larger society to create alternative institutions."

With age and revolution has come not only maturity, but an appreciation of complexity and an understanding of "just how long that road is" to black unity, to freedom. "There has been a clarification of my attitude over the years based on my experience that people truly have to be judged as people. There are white people who have gone through their own experience and appear to have gotten to the same point of saying people have to be judged as people."

Jamil Sulieman is a black man who would probably have been a success with or without a Civil Rights Movement in the South or an urban revolution in the North. The third of four siblings from a working-class family with middle-class aspirations "who had an unspoken, unwritten commitment to civil rights," he grew up with a sense of history and a sense of mission—and that, as much as anything, has defined his success. "I learned that my success was part of other people's activity," he explains of those who have gone before—from the "greaseheads" in the ghetto to the preachers in the church—agitating for change. "And the pride I take in other people's success is part of the same continuum."

Jamil Sulieman knows that as a successful black man in America he is a minority within a minority—an exception to the statistics that project failure as the most common rule in the lives of black men. The real question, he says, is not whether the Civil Rights Movement made it better for some people within a generation, as it clearly did for him and for other black men who had the advantage of certain opportunities. "The real question is, will {our success} in turn make it better for more black people? We don't know yet."

GETTING
DOWN

The word has no real meaning . . . whatever integration is supposed to mean, can it be precisely defined?

Malcolm X

A DREAM
DEFERRED?

*I*f nothing succeeds like success, nothing quite disappoints or defeats like a dream deferred. During the second half of the twentieth century perhaps the most salient dream of the African-American has been the vision of integration. And with the vision have come certain expectations and assumptions, certain wistful thinking, fueled by an element of fantasy inherent in the nature of all dreams. Among the integration fantasies that have become self-evident during the last thirty years, the most enduring have been these: that race will not matter; that education will make all the difference; that class will count more than color; that blacks will be free at last.

PAYING THE PRICE OF THE DREAM
Janet Cooke, Leanita McClain, and Edmund Perry

By the end of the eighties it was clear that such fantasies had exacted a certain price and taken a psychic toll on a new generation of African-Americans pursuing the integration dream. And perhaps nothing more dramatically revealed the dark side of the dream than the personal tragedies of three young black Americans whose success stories in the eighties became disturbing morality tales for an integrated age, a metaphor for the excesses of expectations and assumptions.

In 1981 a 26-year-old black reporter for the *Washington Post* named Janet Cooke was awarded the Pulitzer Prize for her story "Jimmy's World," a shocking, investigative portrait of an 8-year-old heroin addict. It was soon discovered that her story was a hoax. Cooke herself was then discovered to be a hoax. She had not graduated from Vassar College, as her résumé stated, nor had she attended the Sorbonne or speak several languages, as she had claimed. The Pulitzer was yanked back, Cooke resigned from the *Post* in disgrace, and the black community felt alternately angered, betrayed, and shamed by both Cooke and the whites who seemed so quick and eager to believe her farfetched story of an 8-year-old drug addict.

In 1984 another black female journalist made the news: Leanita McClain, not a hoax, but a bona fide success story. She had escaped the projects of Chicago's South Side, earned a master's degree from Northwestern University's prestigious Medill School of Journalism, and arrived at the *Chicago Tribune,* where she worked her way up from a classified ad taker during college to become the first black member of the *Tribune*'s editorial board. Yet education and the climb up from poverty into the middle class could not pry loose McClain's unshakable belief that she would always be viewed by whites—and by blacks—as an "uppity nigger." In a "My Turn" column she wrote for *Newsweek* in 1980, she made this anguished observation: "I am a member of the black middle class who has had it with being patted on the head by white hands and slapped in the face by black hands for my success . . . I have a foot in each world, but I cannot fool myself about either. I know how tenuous my grip on one way of life is, and how strangling the grip of the other way of life can be."

On May 29, 1984, Leanita McClain, unable to reconcile the dichotomies or find psychic comfort, killed herself. She was 32.

A little more than a year later, on the evening of June 12, 1985, Edmund Perry, a 17-year-old black youth, was shot to death on a street near New York City's Columbia University by an undercover police officer who said Perry had tried to mug him. It didn't figure. Perry, a recent graduate of the elite Phillips Exeter Academy in Exeter, New Hampshire, had been a shining example of all that was right with integration. Growing up in Harlem, Perry was a bright and ambitious boy who dreamed of becoming a doctor in the new age of equal opportunity. He was awarded a full scholarship to Exeter through A Better Chance (ABC), a Boston-based program that places gifted minority students in prep schools. Although he was one of only forty black and Hispanic students out of Exeter's total enrollment of 980, he excelled academically, and by the time he graduated in the spring of 1985, he had been offered full scholarships to Stanford, Yale, Berkeley, and the University of Pennsylvania. But ten days after graduating he was dead, shot by a plainclothes police officer who charged that Perry and his older brother, Jonah, also a prep school graduate and a sophomore at Cornell University, had attacked him, demanding money.

All three tragedies—Janet Cooke, Leanita McClain, and Edmund Perry—raised the same alarming question: Why? Why did such promising blacks, who represented the best and the brightest of the black future—all under 35, all on fast tracks to success—become in a shattering instant of deceit and despair instruments of their own destruction? The answers were both obvious and oblique, simple and complex.

What was most obvious in the case of Janet Cooke was that a black woman thought she had to make herself over to be exceptional in order to be acceptable, successful. She was shrewd enough to know what constituted an exception: an Ivy League degree, a European education, and fluency in more than one language were the kind of credentials she knew impressed white America, just as she knew which black stereotypes would not be questioned in a fabricated story.

The not-so-obvious irony here is that Janet Cooke was exactly right. With her phony credentials she was indeed perceived as an "exceptional" black woman—attractive, talented, an integration success story. Her story of an 8-year-old drug addict, implausible at the outset, was not only believed but bestowed journalism's highest award. Cooke's success, however, was the very phenomenon that led to her undoing, which came from a least expected quarter: Vassar College. When word came that a Vassar alumna had won the Pulitzer—and was a black woman, too—the school's public relations machine swung into gear, eager to claim this exceptional twofer. It didn't take long for the school to check its records, and finding none for Cooke, blow the whistle.

The tragedies of Leanita McClain and Edmund Perry raised more disturbing, troublesome questions. Here were two outstanding blacks whose credentials were real and whose accomplishments unassailable, yet they apparently could not cope with integrated success. McClain's success seemed only to deepen her despair. Her writing toward the end of her life took on a haunted, brooding cynicism, exposing a tormented soul, as W. E. B. DuBois put it, "warring with itself," and in the end destroying itself.

The Edmund Perry case was a deeper mystery, for there were fewer clues to why a young man so full of promise at the beginning of life, already heading to the top, would take a sudden detour down the dead-end alley of street crime. Of the three, Perry seemed the one most truly caught between two worlds. Investigative reporter Robert Sam Anson, a white journalist whose son attended Exeter with Perry, spent a year interviewing nearly a hundred people, from the police officer who shot Perry to the victim's mother, attempting to piece together what had happened to a dream. His search resulted in the book *Best Intentions: The Education and Killing of Edmund Perry,* an exhaustive compilation of facts, details, theories, and speculations in which everyone, it seemed, had an opinion on what had gone wrong with the integration of Edmund Perry.

"He didn't want to be different," Bill Perkins, leader of a local democratic club, told Anson when he was interviewed, giving his opinion on why a successful black prep school student would come back to the old neighborhood and attempt a mugging. "It's a prove-yourself age [Perry's teen years], and like everybody else, Eddie wanted to fit in. . . . [But] after you've been to one of these schools [Exeter], you never completely fit in anywhere."

"It was the streets," explained Detective Billy Carreras, a hard-nosed veteran cop who was the first to arrive at the hospital after Perry had been shot. "The fucking streets ate him alive."

"The trouble is, you really aren't a part of your neighborhood anymore . . ." explained a black woman who had herself been through the ABC program and gone to prep school. "After you see the kind of wealth that Eddie saw at Exeter . . . you know that there is more to life than hanging out on street corners, having babies, and getting welfare checks. Still, you've gotta fit in with your friends . . . You've got a week to prove you are black, before you're on that bus Monday morning, heading back for class. A place like Exeter can't help you make that transition."

"Eddie had problems that went beyond Exeter, especially about race," said an older black male friend. "You know how a schizophrenic talks? . . . That's the way Eddie talked about race."

In the end, Anson himself could conclude only that race, in fact, was at the heart of the tragedy. "The only villain I found was something amorphous," he wrote, "not a person or a thing, just a difference called race. It was race—not the fact of it, but the consequences flowing from it . . . It was ironic as well that race had given Eddie his chance for betterment, just as it was race that had prevented him from making full use of it. Every moment of his prep school career was reminding him he was different; every moment, race was allowing and encouraging others, black and white, to treat him as different."

Race underscored the tragedies of Janet Cooke and Leanita McClain as well, and for all three, race was the circumstance that led to the failure to integrate. Cooke thought she had to become someone else—if not white, then certainly white-identified—to succeed; McClain and Perry failed to be comfortable as blacks in either the black world or the white world. The conflicts were extreme, pathological—dooming even the most potentially successful to destructive failure.

Such conflicts, though perhaps not as debilitating as those ending the careers and lives of Cooke, McClain, and Perry, have taken a toll throughout black America. The integration generation has learned, often at great pain and psychic cost, that race always matters if one is black; that education and credentials help but don't necessarily guarantee success or really ever change racist attitudes; that class makes a difference, but the changing of class often carries an emotional price; and that blacks can perhaps be free at last only when they learn to let go of integration fantasies.

Charles Morrison: Integration and the Real Thing

The booming voice reverberates through the hushed mauve reception area on the eleventh floor of 1 Coca-Cola Plaza, begging the question before it can even be asked: *"What does it take to be successful in America? I'll tell you what it takes—being white, that's what!"* thunders Charles (Chuck) Morrison, who looms as large and expansive as his voice. His portly frame is seated on the couch in his corner office, his feet propped up on the coffee table. He has the sly grin of a cat who has just swallowed a mouse, a shock of stand-up graying hair that resembles fight promoter Don King's, and the blunt humor of one who uses facetious wit to deflect impatience and frustration.

Morrison, 42 in the spring of 1988, is vice president in charge of black and Hispanic consumer marketing at Coca-Cola U.S.A. in Atlanta's corporate headquarters, a sprawling complex of office towers, warehouses, and parking areas that make up a company which proudly proclaims "Coke is the real thing." Morrison is one of the highest-ranked blacks in the company—a corporate officer with bottom-line responsibilities that account for over one-fifth of Coca-Cola's business. When he joined Coca-Cola six years ago, he made it clear he didn't intend to be "one of those spooks who sits by the door," a black hired in the face of a boycott threat who is given an impressive title but no power. Coke was in fact under a boycott threat from Jesse Jackson's Operation PUSH organization at the time it hired Morrison. PUSH charged the company had a poor record of hiring and promoting minorities, given that a core base of Coke's market is the black and Hispanic consumer.

To show he meant business, Morrison initially turned down Coke's offer. "I'll be candid with you," says the man who's had a successful career seldom being anything else. "I came down for an interview, looked around. I give companies what I call the Chuck Morrison Business Test, if you will. I walked around the four corners of the floors looking to see how many minorities were sitting in what I call the power positions. Corner offices. There were no men. No black males. No black females. And I said to myself, This isn't good. I was realistic, because having been out here for a while you understand a corporation's attitude by what they do . . . not by what they say."

Jesse Jackson eventually talked Morrison into taking the position with Coke. Morrison, who is from Dallas and a graduate of all-black Bishop College, started his career with Procter & Gamble working in marketing in the company's Dallas office, then was recruited by the Schlitz Brewing Company, where he worked in the areas of sales, brands, and promotions, becoming a district manager in Cleveland and Chicago, and finally running the Illinois division. He was recruited in 1977 by Thomas Burrell to work for the black-owned Burrell Advertising in Chicago, where he learned advertising and was introduced to the black consumer marketing concept. Then, in 1979, Schlitz lured him back to head up its black consumer marketing department.

Morrison admits he has benefitted from being a black man with a marketing background and a proficiency in Spanish at a certain point in history, namely the point at which consumer product companies recognized a giant ethnic market to be tapped. But if Morrison now occupies a power position on Coca-Cola's executive eleventh floor, he does not inhabit his corner office easily. The black and Hispanic markets represent more than 20 percent of Coke's business, yet most corporations "still do not understand that blacks and Hispanics are important," Morrison charges, "and even if they do understand, they don't want to give you that respect." The numbers alone, however, would seem to dictate respect. Though Morrison won't give specific figures for either Coke's market share in the black and Hispanic markets or black and Hispanic overall consumption of the soft drink, he does say that about 25 percent of total cola consumption in the United States is by blacks and Hispanics, and that their total percentage consumption of Coca-Cola is "significant."

In other soft drink categories, as he points out, the figures for black consumption are even more than significant. Blacks account for roughly 12 percent of the total American population, yet they represent 42 percent of the total red soda consumption in the country, and they consume 44 percent of the orange sodas and 56 percent of the grape soda drinks. Still, despite the bottom line numbers, Morrison finds himself in an uphill fight to target a market that is taken seriously. The dilemma speaks to both the enduring racism of larger society and the particular bind the integrated corporate black executive often finds himself in.

While Morrison knows he is not exactly an affirmative action hire, he is nevertheless one of those high-ranking corporate blacks consigned to "an ethnic area" corporate whites, and even some corporate blacks, tend to disdain. His particular area happens to represent a sizable portion of Coke's revenues, however, a fact Morrison says top management understands, but middle management often refuses to. "When I came here Coca-Cola's image was down, the sales volume was down, market share was down. And we changed all of that," he says, noting that Coca-Cola has come from second place to surpass Pepsi Cola in market share in the black and Hispanic community since he has been with the company.

Morrison's own professional success stems from not only recognizing the value of the black and Hispanic market, but making sure that value is known to Coke—and making sure Coke does not develop a "problem" with its black and Hispanic markets. "I've always taken an aggressive approach," he explains. "I feel that my job is to tell a corporation what it needs to know—not what it wants to know."

What all corporations need to know, Morrison points out, is that by the year 2000 it is estimated that blacks and Hispanics are going to be 30 percent of the population and in some product categories will represent more than 50 percent of total sales. "That's what we have to deal with. We have to come in here and change attitudes. The average white brand manager sits down and does not consider blacks and Hispanics."

Morrison has found that changing white attitudes toward blacks remains as formidable a proposition as it did thirty years ago, when ideas such as affirmative action, equal employment opportunity, and integration may have been in vogue but never quite became internalized. Today, while corporate blacks are more likely to achieve success, they are just as likely to experience the frustration that comes with rising expectations in the face of inevitable limitations. Emotionally healthy blacks, however, understand the difference between what are certainly the limitations of race and integration and what are also the real limitations of life in corporate America.

Like many executives, both black and white, Chuck Morrison knows he has hit the proverbial glass ceiling in corporate America, that level beyond which there are probably few more raises or promotions. "If I stay at Coca-Cola, they'll make me a senior vice president of black and Hispanic marketing and I'll report then to the president of the company. Whoopee," he notes wryly. But if Morrison is somewhat facetious about his future prospects, he is also sanguine about the present, for he recognizes that in the total scheme of things he has done quite well, been quite successful. "I think I compare favorably with other men of my age [black or white]," he admits, "particularly when you consider the company I'm working for. This is a formidable company with a great reputation. Being an officer of Coca-Cola is a great and significant achievement. One of the things I said I wanted to do was be a vice president at a Fortune 500 company, so I'm satisfied."

Yet there is also the unavoidable element of dissatisfaction, the note of resignation and frustration that is a common refrain among black corporate executives. On the one hand there is the intellectual recognition that only a few can make it to the top—"Let's be realistic, I'm not going to be a CEO of this company. At 42, my time has passed," as Morrison says—but there is also the realization that being black is still its own limitation on corporate advancement. It is the kind of realization that leads Morrison to say, without rancor or bitterness, just a certain matter-of-factness: "I really think if I had been white I would have been ten times more successful. In every job that I've had I've been very successful, but I never feel I get the credit that's due me. I know a lot of blacks like me who feel that same way. I built a department, but I still do not feel that I've been accepted as a full member of what I call the club. No matter how much of a contribution we make to the corporation, no matter how hard we work, no matter how skilled we are, we're always thought of as black first rather than being fully integrated into the system."

The problem goes beyond ordinary racism. It is a problem of ignorance, coupled with the problem of invisibility—white America so seldom actually *sees* ethnic America. "You have to understand that the most corporate America is ever exposed to black and Hispanics is in the office," Morrison explains. "Then they [whites] go home to the suburbs. The major difference between white executives and us [black executives] is that if you're black you cannot be successful in corporate America without knowing a lot about whites. You've got to learn the majority culture. White people have made fortunes and had this great career knowing nothing about blacks and Hispanics—and that's the problem."

It is perhaps the central problem underlying the concept of integration—the essential dilemma that perhaps best explains exactly what has gone wrong with the dream. By definition, to integrate means "to put or bring (parts) together into a whole, to unify," according to Webster's New World Dictionary of the American Language. Yet integration as practiced in American society has most often meant black assimilation, "to be absorbed and incorporated." This is a distinction with a great difference, and for the African-American the distinction has often led to great dissonance.

It has led successful corporate blacks such as Chuck Morrison, who earns a six-figure salary and has stock options and visibility and responsibility in one of America's Fortune 500 companies, to make this bittersweet observation about success: "I know in what I do I'm good. I know it. Now, if I'm white, I'm not arrogant. I'm a self-starter, a go-getter. I want to make that clear distinction. But because I'm black, I'm considered arrogant. Clearly, I don't think I'm arrogant. I'm aggressive. I'm competitive. I want to whip Pepsi-Cola's butt. I want to win."

WINNING AT RACE

The degree to which blacks win in the corporate workplace—succeed professionally—is often a function of how well they handle the dissonance caused by race and racism. Blacks spend so much emotional energy dealing with race that it has become almost a visceral reflex, rarely examined, though it contributes enormously to the high incidence of black stress in the corporate arena. The fact that most people, both black and white, are less comfortable talking about race today than they were twenty years ago only adds to the "black tax" African-Americans experience, a feeling that society, for the most part, treats race as an issue that is passé, no longer requiring the uncomfortable exploration of racial attitudes. As a result, blacks usually adopt one of three modes of "dealing" when confronted with the possibility of racism in the workplace.

1. **The knee-jerk reaction.** This is the most debilitating response, for it assumes that racism is behind every criticism or negative reaction a white person makes toward a black. It is an angry position that keeps blacks who react in this mode always on the defensive, and thus frequently unable to listen, gain information, or learn. The assumption here is that whites are always guilty until proved innocent, an especially damaging and stressful, to say nothing of incorrect, attitude for the corporate black who may be one of few blacks or even the only black in a white work setting. They are the least likely to be successful in such circumstances.

2. **The measured response.** This is a healthier mode, one in which blacks consider each instance of interaction on a case-by-case basis. Those interactions that seem clearly racist are similarly evaluated on a case-by-case basis, for most blacks understand they cannot "go to battle" over every racial slight. The stress often comes, however, in determining what can be forgiven and what should be challenged, and then figuring out how best to fight back.

3. **The operational trusting mode.** This mode gives both

whites and their institutions the benefit of the doubt. The expectation here on the part of blacks is that whites, regardless of how they may feel personally, will at least "do the right thing" by blacks and other minorities in the workplace, i.e., be fair and civil. Blacks with this attitude know that racism on the job exists (just as it does everywhere else), but don't really care as long as it doesn't get in the way of their reaching their personal goals. This is the mode that allows blacks to take "the larger view" in matters involving race, to ignore racial slights and innuendo when they have no bearing on attaining desired results. This is the healthiest attitude, for it takes the "burden of race" off the backs of blacks and puts the responsibility of racism where it belongs. Blacks who act with "operational trust" tend to be the most successful, for their attitude regarding white racism is usually, "That's their problem, not mine."

Race, however, is still largely a problem for both blacks and whites. And integration has not only failed to solve the problem, but in some ways it has actually exacerbated it. Policies, for instance, such as affirmative action, created to remedy the past history of race discrimination are now being used to indict a race as inferior, to level charges of "reverse discrimination" and "quotas," as if twenty years of "preferential treatment" could eradicate the effects of 240 years of slavery or a hundred years of race discrimination.

More insidious, however, is that the concepts of equal opportunity and affirmative action have now become synonymous with a "lowering of standards." The inference here is that American democracy is only for those who measure up, who prove "worthy" of equality and opportunity. The larger inference, of course, is that blacks seldom measure up. It is the old story, tarnishing a new dream. Yet for this integration generation, which has had equal opportunity and affirmative action, there is very often a new story —a story of dreams lost and found, of actions taken and affirmed, of fantasies shattered and success reexamined with a view toward that which is real.

Craig and Gloria Smith: Taking Affirmative Action

Craig Smith and Gloria Mitchell-Smith have the prosperous look of winners. He is 40, she is 42; both are St. Louis, Missouri, natives, small and slim, tan brown, attractive, the kind of blended couple who have been together so long they start to look alike. In the sixties and seventies they epitomized the integration dream: he graduated from the exclusive preparatory Kent School, then attended Howard University and Harvard University, where he got an MBA; she attended black parochial elementary schools in St. Louis before the Supreme Court decision of 1954, then went to an integrated school across town, graduated from St. Alphonsus High School, a former Catholic boarding school for wealthy white girls, and got an MBA from St. Louis University. Both have spent most of their work lives in high-paying, high-profile corporate careers, often as the first blacks to integrate a particular department or a particular company.

In the eighties, the Smiths and other black professionals of their generation were tagged Buppies—a label that became at once a badge of black success and a pejorative variation on the theme of white success. Black upwardly mobile professionals, like the Yuppies their designation was modeled after, defined the era of the "good life" in an eighties gilded age marked by corporate fast-tracking and rampant consumerism.

The Smiths are one of those DINKs—dual income, no kids—family units whose good life is tastefully reflected in the elegant brownstone they own in an integrated, gentrified section of Brooklyn, New York. Epitomizing the "urban homesteaders" of their age, they purchased a burned-out shell for next to nothing in 1978 and used a combination of corporate savvy and bank connections to finance a renovation that's resulted in a five-story real estate gem: an owner's triplex and two rental income units. The black art collection that lines the wall, the eclectic display of books and records that occupy the top floor open loft-space study, the gadgeted gourmet kitchen with its two sinks to accommodate workspace for both, the photographer's darkroom to indulge a hobby—all reveal the conspicuous touchstones of a black generation that has arrived.

And yet on this fall day in 1989, the Smiths are taking leave. The triplex has been rented. The books and records are in boxes, marked and catalogued; the art sits neatly bundled against a wall. The movers have already taken the bigger furnishings—the sleigh bed bought at Bloomingdale's, the billiards table, the dining banquette the Smiths made themselves. Craig and Gloria Smith have packed it all in—the big city, the big careers, the dream—and are switching tracks.

Craig has been offered a fellowship to the University of North Carolina at Chapel Hill to pursue a doctorate in psychology. Gloria, who has put a five-year-old business on hold to facilitate the move, plans to look for a consulting job and a house large enough to accommodate three floors and fifteen years of New York City living. It is the kind of drastic career change in midlife typically associated with a "crisis." For the Smiths, however, the change represents an opportunity to redefine a dream and retreat from the battlefield, to take stock, reassess, wind down. They are at an age when there is little left to prove, for having proved they could successfully integrate, be successfully black and middle class, they can now afford to redefine success on their own terms.

For Gloria, success has meant striking out on her own—going back to roots she once thought she would leave forever. The daughter of a part-time seamstress and a construction worker, she came from the working-class side of the tracks in St. Louis and grew up wanting the lifestyle she associated with the college-trained professionals who worked in corporate industry. Yet when she got her accounting degree from St. Louis University in 1971, she did not get a job offer from any of the Big Eight accounting firms, "which was the whole goal of an accounting major," she notes. "One recruiter told me the real deal—off the record, of course. He explained the big accounting companies could not risk me. One, to have a woman is bad enough, two, to have a black woman, and three, to have a young, attractive and single black woman—the firms just couldn't take the risk. Three strikes and you're out."

Gloria was hired by Monsanto, the St. Louis–based chemical

manufacturer, as a treasury analyst in 1972 with the help of a white
man at the Ralston Purina Company who was committed to integrating business and interceded with colleagues at Monsanto on her
behalf. Her first day on the job, however, her boss ignored her,
subsequently withheld information from her, and in general tried
to sabotage her work. "He later said, in effect, that he had been
forced to hire me, but that he didn't accept me. I didn't fit the
mold." Gloria nevertheless learned the job—in fact, made herself
indispensable. "I created a niche for myself," she explains, becoming the only one in the department who knew how every activity,
every piece of paper, every check fit into the scheme of things. "I
learned in depth what was going on, and during one of my performance evaluations my boss admitted we did not have a great beginning and suggested we start over again. He came around and we
developed a great working relationship. By the time I transferred to
another area in the company, he considered me an important part of
the team."

Proving herself, however, had started to take its toll. In order to
succeed, Gloria had to be more than competent; she had to have the
ability to uncover information that was actively withheld. She had
to spend time and energy figuring out how to succeed in an environment in which she was constantly being set up to fail.

During the next ten years, from 1973 to 1983, Gloria worked in
a variety of high-powered financial positions that included internal
financial consulting with the Honeywell Corporation, managing
cash and banking for the Singer Corporation, overseeing $2.5 bil-
lion in corporate assets, and managing and overseeing investments
in South America and the Far East at Avon Corporation.

It was at Avon that Gloria ran up against the politics of race and
cronyism, encountering a boss who refused to promote her, who in
fact put her on probation after she had been in the job several years,
claiming he was not happy with her work. "What it came down to
was that I had been getting bids for jobs that he wanted for another
woman he had been pushing. So rather than promote me out of the
group where I might have some options, he decided to kill me off.
It was wild."

The experience was the final blow that propelled Gloria out of corporate America and into her own business, Sparkle Productions, a resurrection of something she had done with her mother back in high school: make "fat man's shirts" for her father and other big-sized men. She now designs a line of intimate apparel geared for the large-sized woman which are sewn by hired seamstresses and sold in specialty boutiques. Gloria's corporate experience in finance and marketing have been successfully transferred to her own business where the pay may be less but the satisfactions are greater. Like other black professionals who have made similar entrepreneurial moves, Gloria has found that the trade-offs in leaving the security of a corporate position for a business of one's own include a greater sense of freedom, personal control, and peace of mind. As she says ruefully of the corporate career she left behind: "You may have a successful corporate career by outside standards, but you're battling all the way."

Craig Smith's battles with integration began before he set foot in corporate America. It was in the halls of privilege at the elite Kent boarding school that he discovered the limitations of race despite his status of class. The son of a prominent St. Louis physician, Craig grew up among the city's black middle class, and he and his two brothers were regulars on the social scene: active members of the Jack & Jill Social Club, which consisted of children of the black advantaged, and perennial escorts at the black cotillions and debutante balls.

At 14, Craig left home to attend the all-male Kent School, a boarding school in Kent, Connecticut, populated by the scions of the rich and powerful from this and other countries. Craig had always been an excellent student, so he had no trouble holding his own academically, and made the honor roll his first three years. He was also an athlete of some note, making the junior varsity teams in both wrestling and crew. None of this, however, translated into social success, for at Kent Craig never really became part of the crowd. The white friends and acquaintances he studied with during the week, and competed against in sports virtually disappeared on the weekends, caught up in a swirl of parties and dances to which he was seldom invited. The expectation was that he would date the one black girl who attended Kent's sister school; to date interracially was an unspoken taboo. The pressure resulted in Craig most often spending weekends in the dorm alone, reading. Moreover, Craig found the school's cultures and customs—the music, the food—different from his own, strange. But like all adolescents, Craig wanted to fit in, he wanted to belong, which is why when it was time for college, he chose predominantly black Howard University over predominantly white Harvard. He was tired of feeling isolated, of being the only black or one of few blacks in most situations. He wanted to be in an environment where his needs were reflected as a matter of course and not as a matter of exception.

While Howard provided Craig with a social atmosphere that was more comfortable, more like the one he'd grown up with in black middle-class St. Louis, he found the school's academic program less rigorous than what he was used to. "Howard wasn't as academically focused as I needed it to be," he says. "If I spent four years at Howard's pace, knowing what my white peers were experiencing at other schools at Kent's pace, I felt I'd never catch up." Craig's compromise was to transfer to Washington University in his hometown, where he completed his bachelor's degree, and then to attend Harvard for an MBA.

Integration has itself often become a compromise for blacks who must frequently choose between the psychic comfort of an all-black environment and what is often the real competitive advantage of a white one. It was Craig's integrated experience that prepared him both academically and emotionally for a corporate career starting in 1976 at Citibank in New York, where he worked in the area of corporate lease funding. "Citibank was an excellent training ground," he says, "whether in investment banking or on the commercial side, and they had excellent creative people."

In 1979 Craig moved to the International Paper Company, where he was manager of western land sales. International Paper was the country's largest private landowner, and Craig's job was in the areas of marketing, leasing, and selling land, a position then central to the firm's corporate strategy. By 1983 corporate strategy had changed, and Craig, finding himself no longer at the nerve center and with a new boss he never jelled with, left International Paper and went back to Citibank. "I had done my job, had some fun, and it was time to move on," he explains of his "mission" at IPC—a place where he felt he had really made a difference.

Back at Citibank, Craig became product manager, developing the securities that were traded in the financial markets. Similar to his position at IPC, he was at the hub of the information flow and prospered both financially and intellectually. But once again a new boss led to a reversal of fortune.

In all of Craig's professional situations the quality of his work environment turned out to be one boss deep. Such are the vagaries of life in any corporate setting, but for the black professional the burden only adds to the "black tax"—the toll race exerts in the workplace. For Craig, like his wife Gloria, switching professions at middle age reflects an attempt to reduce that tax by regaining control, by looking beyond the materialism of money to the power of self-affirmation in deciding what is really important, what work one is really suited temperamentally to do. It is a luxury no other generation of blacks has had before, this "dropping out" to find yourself, to explore other options and make other moves—to take affirmative action. It is perhaps the true hallmark of freedom and success for the integration generation.

Earl G. Graves, Jr.: The Dream Continues

The firstborn son is seated at the Queen Anne desk in his mother's pink and lavender office in the executive wing on the corporate floor, eating lunch ordered in from a deli. He has the same large hands and long, elegant fingers of his father, made to dunk a basketball; the same tall, athletic build, toned skin, and discernible air of power and privilege. Though the father was not born to power or privilege, it is a birthright he has secured for his three sons. Embodied in them is the dream—realized, actualized.

"Graduating from Morgan State University in the fifties, my father could have joined the social security administration, the post office, or the military. Those were his options," says the oldest son.

"It wasn't as if he could say 'I think I would like to work in a consulting firm,' or decide, 'I'm going to take a trip to Europe and then I'm going to law school.' Those were not options. But these are options for us [blacks] today. They are taken for granted if you don't really investigate what happened in the past."

Earl G. (Butch) Graves, Jr., eldest son of Earl G. Graves, Sr., has learned to take nothing for granted. Not his Ivy League degrees from Yale and Harvard. Not the thirty-room mansion he grew up in in New York's affluent Scarsdale. Not the year he spent playing professional basketball for three teams. Not the corporate vice presidency he secured at age 26 in his father's company. He knows that dreams cost.

Born in 1962 at the closing of the baby boom era, Butch Graves is in that tail-end of the generation caught between the militancy and excesses of older baby boomers and the floundering "lost generation" of twentysomethings coming up behind. He has the psychological advantage that a sense of history always gives and the grounding that a strong, successful family typically instills. His father is chief executive officer of Earl Graves Ltd., the holding company for *Black Enterprise* magazine, started in 1970, a Pepsi Cola franchise acquired in 1990, a video division, and a professional networking/seminar subsidiary. In 1990 the company ranked 58 on its own list of top 100 black-owned companies published every June, with sales totaling $16 million.

Unlike most blacks of an integrated or any other age, Butch Graves and his two brothers grew up against a backdrop of entrepreneurship, discussing stocks and bonds along with sports and racism at the breakfast table. "When I was ten or eleven my father gave my two brothers and me three hundred to four hundred dollars' worth of stock in different companies to invest. He wanted us to learn how investing works. I took an interest in it more than my brothers, learning how the value of things change over time, how you could save, invest, make money. I really got into it."

At the time he graduated from Harvard with an MBA in 1988 and a specialty in investment banking, investment banking was the "glamor" field and Harvard the magic name to have attached to one's MBA. In a word, this gave well-heeled and well-connected integrated blacks like Butch Graves options. The fact that he opted to go into his father's business—he is currently vice president of advertising and marketing for *Black Enterprise*—speaks to a new perspective the integration generation is now often taking.

"I didn't like the investment banking industry all that much," Graves says of his decision not to pursue it. "And what I didn't like, frankly, is that I had not seen a lot of blacks in the industry, and certainly not a lot in terms of any positions of power. That was the light that went off that said to me something was not right. And it's obvious what it is: racism. It's what I call institutional racism—not the overt 'Get-out-of-my-face' type of racism. But the kind where you have a recruiter saying 'We want you. You've gone to good schools. We're equal opportunity employers.' But then what happens inevitably as you move up through the ranks, that invisible glass ceiling seems to come before you make partner, managing director, or whatever the euphemism is for someone who has a stake in the business. Suddenly, all the work you've done positively up to that point becomes not-so-good."

Reaching goals he has set for himself is how Butch Graves measures personal success. One goal—and huge dream—he had as far back as high school, where he was an outstanding basketball player, was to play for a professional basketball team. "As time went on I became more realistic about it," though he was good enough to make the dream come true for a year, getting drafted by the Philadelphia 76ers in 1984 after finishing Yale as an undergraduate. Despite the rigorous sports competition he experienced throughout school and throughout his years growing up with a father who was both hard-driving and "adored sports," Butch found pro ball "to be much tougher than I thought." He was bounced around to three different teams that year—the Philadelphia 76ers, the Milwaukee Bucks, and the Cleveland Cavaliers—and spent most of the time on all of them warming the bench. The experience was daunting for an athlete used to winning, but also eye-opening for a young black man who had a somewhat naive view of the pro game.

"From the outside looking in, all of pro athletics is so glamorous. It is in a monetary sense, which is why so many black youths think they don't have to worry about things like finishing school or

going to college—they all think they can just play pro ball."
Butch, however, who had the benefit of other options, found that if
he couldn't play, he didn't want to stay, despite the great pay—
$65,000 a year minimum to start when he joined the 76ers in
1984. "I'm the kind of person who's realistic," he says of letting go
the dream to play pro ball, "and I'm objective about myself. I can
recognize my strengths, and I can also recognize my weaknesses.
Everyone would like to think they can do everything well, but the
reality is, no one does everything well."

Graves always knew, regardless what he did beforehand, he
would eventually go to work in his father's business, where, since
the age of 8, he had watched the elder Graves "build a company
from scratch into something that was now very well respected in
not only the black community but within the society at large." It
was natural, if not expected, that the sons would carry on a business
in which they had a ready-made stake. "My father did not groom
us to work in the business, though I think he would be disap-
pointed if none of us did. [In addition to Butch, youngest son
Michael works for the company in the Pepsi-Cola franchise, and
middle son Johnny, an attorney, is expected to join the firm one
day as legal counsel.] The only thing he wanted to ensure was that
we got the best education possible so that we could have
choices."

Pursuing "the best education possible" took the Graves family
from the black community of Bedford-Stuyvesant in Brooklyn to
the all-white suburban community of Armonk, New York, corporate home of IBM, when Butch was entering second grade and his
brother Johnny was going into first grade. "My brother and I are
close in age and also close emotionally, and I can remember us
walking out of school that first day. He sort of whispered to me,
'Did you see anybody who was black?' I told him No, I hadn't seen
anybody in my class who was black. He didn't see anybody black in
his class either. That was it. We were it. We were the only blacks
in the whole school. Kids looked at us strangely. They tried to play
with our hair."

In 1975 the family made a final move to Scarsdale in New York's
Westchester County. Again the purpose was to secure a quality

education for Butch and his brothers and to also provide a lifestyle in keeping with the growing success of their father's business. "Scarsdale was not necessarily any better in terms of the number of black students the school had," Butch says. "But we now lived in an area that had many blacks around us. In the Westchester area we had the cities of White Plains, Mt. Vernon [both with sizable black populations], and we weren't that far from New York City and our family in Brooklyn. We were given back that black identity we had sorely missed."

Graves points out that neither his father nor his mother would ever "tolerate" their sons losing their sense of identity. "They were uncompromising in us getting the best education we could and they were uncompromising in us maintaining and being proud of our black identity. And I know in my mother's scheme of things, as we went into our teenage years, she was not going to stand for us bringing home white girls—not that there's anything wrong with someone who happens to be white—but as far as she was concerned, they were not to be who we dated."

Such messages, along with activities in black social clubs such as Hansel & Gretel and Jack & Jill, where the Graves boys could meet suitable black girls, practically guaranteed that they would grow up to marry black women much like their mother, Barbara Graves, who is the business manager in her husband's company. Butch Graves terms his own wife, Roberta, who graduated *summa cum laude* from Yale, received an MBA from the Wharton Business School, and is a product manager for Clairol and the mother of their twin daughters, "pretty, sweet, humble—and very, very smart."

If the family's focus on race and identity seemed at odds with an integrated lifestyle, it reflected the reality of racism as a recurring fact of life, even in an integrated America. Unlike many black middle-class parents who try to shield their children from the pain and wounds of racism, "My parents never tried to shirk from the fact that racism existed. It was a constant topic of discussion from two ends—the social and school end, and also from the viewpoint of my father, who talked about the racism he endured in the business world." There was white racism, which the Graves experienced as blacks living in a predominantly white, well-to-do community —from instances of Butch being pulled over by the Scarsdale police, to going to a supermarket dressed in a suit and tie and still being mistaken for a stock boy and asked to fetch a bottle of milk. There was black racism, leveled at the Graves from other blacks who resented the family's *ability* to live in a predominantly white, well-to-do community. "Any insult that could possibly go on, went on," Butch says. "It really gave us an acute sense of people, both black and white, and of the level of racism, the resentment."

And yet it is success, both family and personal, that has given Butch Graves his psychic strength, his liberating awareness and power. "I recognize the fact that we were given opportunities and privileges that a lot of people were not. Do I apologize for that? No. Do I realize it? Yes. But I think the best thing my parents ever gave us was the opportunity to be the best we can be. I am really fearless now. I don't fear a great deal in terms of going into the business world—I fear nothing, which is why I am so fascinated by blacks of my father's generation and before. The things they had to go through—to start a business, to do anything. People of my generation can't really fathom that, but we have got to respect and honor what our predecessors were able to do. We have so many more opportunities today because of that."

This is perhaps the final legacy of black success: to pass on to succeeding generations not only the opportunities that come with integration, but the race memory that comes with struggle and the respect that comes from understanding history. Earl Graves, Jr., is of the generation that has inherited the dream—of opportunity, of advantages and choices, of integration. He has chosen to live out the dream in the arena of black business, family business, the kind of enterprise on which power is built, wealth is made, dynasties are established and perpetuated. This makes him not only heir to the fortunes of a family, but a major asset to the fortunes of a race. In the final scheme of things, a dream come true.*

---

* In June 1991 Earl Graves, Jr., at age 29, was named a senior vice president at Earl G. Graves Ltd.

HOW WE HAVE OVERCOME: THE PSYCHOLOGY OF BLACK SUCCESS

*T*ruth be told, black success is as much the norm as the exception, though it tends still to be regarded as one of those recurring contradictions that flies in the face of popular perceptions. The most persistent perception is that blacks in America remain an oppressed and downtrodden class, their proportion of pathology out of sync with their numbers in the population. Unemployment rates, single-headed households, crime, teenage pregnancy, drug addiction . . . whatever the index used to measure personal and/ or moral failure, blacks, it is sure to be pointed out, are always represented in disproportionate numbers.

The trouble with portraits that focus mostly on the negative is that they never give a complete or even accurate view. The larger view and essential truth is that despite America's history of slavery and its continuing malignancy of race discrimination, there have always been blacks who overcome, who succeed. In the jungle of oppression, there have always been blacks who prevail, surviving as the fittest. They not only go against the odds to survive, but succeed against the odds to triumph.

What is it about successful blacks that leads to achievement? Are there personality traits or particular points of view, attitudes or rules that "select" out some blacks for success over others? Clearly, yes.

Those blacks who move forward to success possess traits that are at once solidly rooted in American culture and values and also racially colored by the experience of being black in America. The extent to which blacks successfully accommodate the dynamics that race inevitably exerts in their life and work, the more successful they are likely to be both professionally and personally.

We have identified ten characteristics that are, to differing extent, present in all successful blacks. The primacy, salience, and magnitude of the traits vary from person to person and situation to situation. They are almost never articulated as being important to individual success, yet upon close examination each emerges as a recurring riff in a melody played consistently throughout the life of a successful black. These riffs constitute the background notes through which achieving blacks come to understand and organize their interactions in the world. As with any melody, the notes are sometimes intrusive, sometime not, but always present.

Note 1: Personal Responsibility/Integrity

Successful blacks treat their lives as a matter of personal responsibility. That is, they take responsibility for everything that happens or does not happen in their lives. It is an attitude that says, "If it exists in my life, then I allow it to exist. If there are changes that need to be made, then it is my responsibility to identify the changes and to do whatever is necessary to effect those changes."

Here, the perspective, the attitude, is more important than the absolute ability to control. It is this perspective that positions someone to have maximum impact on the way in which he or she interacts with the environment. It is this posture that gives access to the wider range of personal potential which is commonly referred to as personal strength and ability. It leads to the ability to make a way out of no way, to build where nothing was erected, to achieve where no success seemed possible. Personal responsibility and integrity harnesses the control, the potential of life, into the hands of the striving achiever. It wrests fate from that which is defined by societal circumstance. For such people, the impoverished circumstances into which they may have been born does not mean that they themselves also must be impoverished.

Exactly why personal responsibility and integrity are pivotal to black success is very clear. On the whole, blacks do not get the benefit of the doubt in American society; they must demonstrate their worth and ability rather than have it presumed. If ability is not consistently demonstrated, then it is assumed to be nonexistent rather than dormant or underdeveloped, as is the case when one is given the benefit of the doubt. Indeed, the margin for error among blacks is much smaller than for others in American society.

Blacks who take personal responsibility are easily recognizable by their very conversation. The attitude they express says: "If I want it, I have to go for it, work for it." This is the person who has learned to postpone gratification and rarely talks in terms of "luck" —winning the lottery or hitting the number—as fundamental to succeeding. They talk instead in terms of "self-improvement," "discipline and planning," those life assets that are within their power to achieve and control.

Among successful blacks taking personal responsibility is so reflexive, so much a part of their lives, that it rarely occurs to them to articulate it an essential ingredient that has been key to their achievements. It just is.

General Fred A. Gordon: Taking Command

The forty-first black man to graduate from the United States Military Academy at West Point received his sheepskin in 1962, exactly twenty-six years after the first black man to become a military general, Benjamin O. Davis, had graduated—enduring four years at the Academy being "silenced" (not talked to) by the white cadets who refused to acknowledge his presence.

If General Benjamin O. Davis was the pioneer, Brigadier General Fred A. Gordon represents the legacy, for in 1987 this forty-first black graduate of West Point became the Academy's sixty-first commandant of cadets, the first black man to command the troops of the Long Gray Line.

On this hot August day in 1988, the commandant has emerged, barely sweating, looking every bit as fit as the freshmen plebes he has just led on a twenty-mile march. At age 48, his six-foot-three frame has the lean, toned bearing of the paratrooper he still is. His summer uniform, which fits him like a sleek glove, is decorated with the rows of ribbons that designate honors in a soldier's life: the Legion of Merit and the Bronze Star, awarded for bravery under enemy fire.

In his wood-paneled office that overlooks the Plain, the Academy's main parade ground, where he has just finished marching with the new troops, the general explains that it is part of the West Point tradition for the commandant of cadets to march with the entering class. Like most career military men, Fred Gordon has respect for tradition, reflected even in marriage to his wife of twenty-six years, Marsha Ann Stewart, a descendent of a Buffalo Soldier—one of the men in the elite black calvary unit that helped settle the West after the Civil War.

As West Point's commandant of cadets, Gordon is essentially the dean of students for the Academy, and as such, he has overall responsibility for the military, character, and leadership training of his young soldiers. "The purpose of West Point is to provide the United States with leaders of character," he says. "At other institutions their primary mission is to yield educated graduates. West Point's purpose is to graduate a leader who is well educated, and there is a difference."

Fred Gordon, a native of Anniston, Alabama, and himself a soldier's son, lived in Atlanta, Georgia, until he was 10 and then moved to Battle Creek, Michigan, where he lived with an aunt, although he was one of four children in a nuclear family. "She was the oldest of my grandmother's children and had no children of her own. Since my family had four children, I went to live with her." The move from the South to the North was a move from a segregated society to an integrated one. Gordon lived in a segregated community and went to segregated schools in Atlanta, but never does he think those institutions lacked a tradition of excellence.

His own family emphasized both personal responsibility and academic excellence. Academic excellence was, in fact, a must if Gordon was to attend college. His family had little money, which meant he would have to earn a scholarship.

Securing a scholarship to college is one thing, but earning an academic pass to the United States Military Academy was never even in Fred Gordon's wildest dreams. "I didn't expect to be at West Point at all," he now says. A gifted student with a facility for languages who once wanted to be a linguist, Gordon had planned to attend a local junior college for a year and then transfer to a large state university, most likely Michigan State. "It's very simple," he says, explaining how he came to be at West Point. "An opportunity knocked and I pursued it."

The opportunity actually rang. A local black lawyer called Gordon during his first year at Kellog Community College to tell him there was a competitive appointment available for a black to West Point. "The attorney had checked with the local high school and junior college faculty and they recommended me," he recalls. Yet Gordon's only frame of reference for West Point at the time was a dim recollection of a series on television called "The West Point Story."

Fred Gordon nevertheless pursued the appointment. He visited the campus, took the required exams, and a week after returning home, received a telegram from his local congressman informing him that he had received the appointment. He still didn't appreciate the full significance of it all. As far as he was concerned, it simply meant he had a scholarship to college: a free higher education.

Gordon's free higher education has resulted in a distinguished military career with assignments that have taken him to the Panama Canal Zone, to Vietnam, to Korea with the Eighth Army, and to the 25th division in Hawaii as Assistant Division Commander. Along the way he received a master's degree in Spanish literature from Middlebury College in Vermont, served in the Pentagon as a Deputy Assistant Secretary of Defense for the American Region of Latin America, and attended the Armed Forces Staff College and the National War College.

"Preparation is the key," says the general of what has underscored his success. "When doors were open for me, I was ready; and if that's what success is, I guess I've been very successful. However, I've been more focused on being prepared than on success." Fred Gordon focused on taking responsibility for doing the work it takes to be prepared, which enabled him to be ready for opportunity. "My real skill as a soldier," he concludes, "has been in advancing in the field. I have a feeling that's going to continue to play a role for me."*

Note 2: GOPAs (Goals, Organization, Planning, and Action Sequences)

The second theme that emerges in the lives of successful people is their facility to take considered action. This action is most often the result of procedural or GOPA sequences that blacks have developed to achieve: goal setting, organizing resources to obtain the goal, planning for implementing the resources, and then taking the action that will lead to the goal.

Closer examination reveals that the lives of successful blacks are also organized around a series of miniature planned action sequences that are followed by an evaluation of what has been accomplished, an adjustment of the action, if necessary, based on what the experience has taught them, and then another action. This activity has become such an implicit part of their lives that successful people do not realize they are operating with GOPAs in nearly every situation they encounter. Indeed, this sequencing of goals, organization, planning, and action underlies their fundamental approach to personal living as well as professional work.

The importance of GOPAs is usually instilled early in achieving blacks, most often first by the family who may stress such qualities as discipline, perseverance and hard work as prerequisites for success. GOPAs are also developed in the competitive arena of school

* Fred Gordon ended his tour of duty at West Point in July 1989, and was awarded his second star. Major General Fred A. Gordon is currently the Commander of the 25th Infantry Division (Light) based at Scofield Barracks in Hawaii.

in both the classroom and through extracurricular activities such as sports and student government. And they are often most finely honed through trial and error, adversity and setbacks.

Bert Mitchell: Giving an Accounting

The sprawling corner office on the twenty-seventh floor of an office tower in Battery Park Plaza glistens with wall-to-wall windows that command a stunning, panoramic view of the New York harbor. Framed in the horizon, postcard perfect, is the Statue of Liberty, beckoning still: "Bring me your tired, your poor, your huddled masses yearning to breathe free."

It was across the very ocean that lies beyond, leading to the very harbor stretched out below, that Bert Mitchell came to America, a 20-year-old country boy from Jamaica arriving in 1958 with his mother and father and a half dozen brothers and sisters. "It was," he remembers now, some thirty years later, "like coming to the Promised Land." America still has promises to keep, but from where Bert Mitchell sits in his sprawling corner office, the land of opportunity has been good, true to its word.

Bert N. Mitchell, 50, is managing partner and chief executive of the largest black-owned accounting firm in the United States, Mitchell/Titus and Company, which also ranks among the top forty accounting firms in the industry. For Mitchell, success has been the result of both a capacity for risk-taking and an affirming attitude that refuses to contemplate the possibility of failure.

"I've never been afraid of things not working," he says with confidence. "If it doesn't work, you learn from the mistakes, reorganize, and try again. I just find it difficult to accept the concept of failure; if we encounter difficulties from time to time, we have to be able to see how to turn them into benefits and build on them, so the next time around we know the pitfalls and can be better prepared."

Mitchell, like many top executives, learned an early lesson through the experience of being fired—on his very first accounting job. It was while he was a senior in college and working for a small firm. "The guy told me, 'I've got to let you go; you're too slow.' I knew that I was good, so it wasn't that negative a thing. The fact of the matter was, I *was* slower. I didn't have that much exposure to business, so when I was given an assignment, it was more than the accounting that I have to figure out. I had to figure out what was going on with the business. The other people on staff were much more experienced. I simply went out and got another job, this time with a larger firm that had different types of assignments. They didn't think that I was slow at all. I had learned a lot from the previous experience."

Through the same honest assessment, organization, and a willingness to step out and take risks, Bert founded Mitchell/Titus and Company in 1973 after management differences caused a break with his partners at the then-largest black CPA firm, Lucas, Tucker and Company. In the nearly twenty years since he teamed with the other named partner, Robert Titus, Mitchell has steered the firm on a course of steady growth and prosperity. He and Titus have grown from a two-partner, five-staff company to a 16-partner, 200-staff organization with annual billings of more than $15 million.

Tapping the largely ignored not-for-profit area of accounting, Mitchell/Titus has developed substantial accounts in auditing, management and systems consulting and small business development. To compete in a business dominated by "the big six" accounting firms, Mitchell/Titus also does a number of joint ventures with larger firms such as Peat/Marwick. In 1990 the company acquired the Philadelphia, Pennsylvania, accounting firm of Leevy, Redcross, and Company. The combined organization now has offices in New York, Philadelphia, and Washington, D.C.

Mitchell seems the least surprised by his success. "It's all been planned and projected," says the West Indian native whose route to achievement has followed that of many immigrants. When he arrived from Jamaica in the late fifties, he worked full-time as a bookkeeper during the day and took a full course load at night at the downtown campus of the City University of New York's Baruch College. Working at this pace, he completed his undergraduate degree in four and a half years, and took on the kind of extra curricular activities the popular black television show "In Living

Color" parodies in its depiction of the "many jobs" hard-working West Indian immigrants typically undertake: he founded Baruch's Accounting Society for the evening session, was a member of student government, was a class president, was a member of the Student-Faculty Committee, was on the school debating team, and wrote for the *Reporter,* the school newspaper. By 1967 he had earned an MBA from Baruch and had been elected to a school board in Long Island. Three years later, he made an unsuccessful bid for the New York State Senate.

As a working professional, Mitchell has written more than fifty articles on accounting and business and has served as president of the New York State Society of Certified Public Accountants. He is the father of three adult children, all of whom he has educated in the Ivy League, though he gives most credit for their accomplishments to his wife, Carol.

Even Bert Mitchell could not have predicted the magnitude of his success. "I expected to go further and do better than my parents, neither of whom had more than a fourth-grade education," he says, but he never expected the distance to make or to leap history. He recognizes that his opportunities as an immigrant son represent the hard-won victories of a distinctly African-American struggle. "My success has as much to do with the good fortune of coming along at the strategic time that I did, as it does with my own focus and energy," acknowledges Mitchell, who has also had the black immigrant's advantage of opportunity without the black American's debilitating psychology of oppression.

Like many black immigrants whose resolve and drive have not been stunted by a history of continuing racism, Mitchell attributes his good fortune, as he puts it, to the fact that the system of racial separation in this country never existed in his own country and thus was never a factor to warp his view of himself or what was possible.

"I think that I've benefited from my naiveté because the reality of what the system had done to black people never really affected me—although I certainly would have been affected if no changes had taken place. I came along wanting to do certain things and then had the opportunity to do them. But it was the people who fought the early desegregation battles that made the opportunity possible," Mitchell adds with his typical honesty as he glances at the charcoal drawing of Malcolm X that occupies a prominent place on a wall in his corner office.

Note 3: Managing Others' Racial Perceptions and Reactions

Critical for all successful blacks is the ability to manage the racial perceptions that others have of them. While achieving blacks don't necessarily dwell on race, they fully understand that race colors nearly all of their interactions with others—particularly with whites. White fear of blacks, white distrust of blacks, white discomfort with blacks, white disdain for blacks . . . these are just a few of the negative impulses all blacks will be hit with at some point in their interactions with whites.

Successful blacks manage not only to diffuse such impulses, but to turn whatever negative perceptions whites may have of blacks into, if not a more positive view of the black race, then at least a positive perception of a black individual. Successful blacks are the ones inevitably viewed as "exceptional" by whites—not like "those others" of their race. And indeed they very often are, for achieving blacks have invariably figured out how to raise the "comfort level" of whites, how to put them at ease and establish common human bonds that transcend the stereotypes of black and white.

Blacks who achieve tend to be as socially skilled as they are intellectually competent, for it is in these two areas that whites have some of the greatest misconceptions regarding black ability. Social skills may be learned, but achieving blacks are more likely to have a natural facility for the kind of "graces" that ingratiate—a "gift of gab," a "pleasing personality," "good manners," or a "comfortable style"—which they skillfully use to manage perceptions.

Successful blacks are most often also smart blacks—not just competent or even intellectually and academically gifted, but practical, shrewd, and flexible. They operate out of a heightened sense of consciousness which gives them a finely tuned sense of control— an ability to assess a situation, make critical judgments, and take appropriate action. Competence is the very quality that often clears up any misperceptions whites have with respect to black ability, but competence alone does not always guarantee success. Competence frequently must be accompanied by comfort if blacks are to achieve, for it is this combination—the ability to demonstrate proficiency coupled with the ability to put others at ease—that usually gives successful blacks their winning edge in managing racial perceptions.

Alfred E. Woods: Managing at the Top

R&S Strauss and Company corporate headquarters lies on the western side of the Hudson River, its office and warehouse distribution center sprawled just off Route 9 in the suburbs of Union, New Jersey, forty-five minutes from Manhattan. Company parking spaces ring the complex, with those closest to the office assigned by name and ranking to the key corporate officers responsible for running R&S Strauss stores. As with most company parking, the space nearest to the R&S Strauss headquarters entrance is reserved for the man at the top: in this case, Alfred L. Woods, president and chief operating officer.

Woods, a 44-year-old native of the Bronx, New York, is one of those people-oriented, hard-driving executives who doesn't consider his rise to head a white-founded chain of automotive stores any more remarkable than getting elected freshman class president at Idaho State University twenty-six years ago, where he was a chemistry major and one of eighteen blacks on campus. Neither achievement is surprising to the man who says quite affably, "I'm a people person—adapting and learning to accommodate the interests of lots of people and cultures without compromising who I am is what I do."

When Al Woods left the South Bronx to attend school in Pokotello, Idaho, in 1962, he left a neighborhood where Motown was the sound and found himself in the heart of Mormon country, where it was hard to get a haircut, and the sound was Bob Dylan, Buffy Ste. Marie, and Joan Baez. The fact that he continues to love the former sound and grew to appreciate the latter underscores the beat of his own success.

"Business is white, and whites are comprised of people with varied backgrounds and cultures," says Woods, a large man with the body of a football player who speaks with the slight twang of the Midwest, explaining how he has positioned himself in relation to whites during his nineteen years at R&S Strauss. "Being able to make people feel comfortable while still gaining their respect for who you are and what you represent is the key.

"I've had some interesting meetings during my career—I recall one that was in Georgia with members of a buying cooperative that we [R&S Strauss] belong to. Most of the people in the association are Southerners. The first night everyone was just being cordial. I made a point of introducing myself all around to get to know folks and let them know me. The second night folks were saying, 'Hi Al, good to see you.' By the third day it was 'Hey, when are we gonna get together and play some golf?' We were all people with similar intelligence, similar interests, similar accomplishments, and therefore there was no need for discomfort." It was Al Woods, however, who had eliminated any element of discomfort by making it a point to be sociable, to be nice and bright, proving he was like everybody else in the room. It was Al Woods who worked not just the room, but the white perceptions in the room.

Woods doesn't think of himself as being any more successful than a lot of other blacks, just perhaps more visible. "I truly believe success hinges on my being the best that I can be, realizing my true potential, exercising whatever capabilities I have. There are lots of folks doing that. If I'm getting 80 percent out of me and someone else is getting 80 percent out of himself, then we're equally success-ful."

Note 4: Pioneering

Pioneering refers to the ability to function in an environment where no iblacks have gone before—to be the first one or the only one in a position or company previously populated by non-blacks. This ability has been an essential ingredient in the success of most blacks, particularly during the past thirty years of integration, which marked the entrance of blacks into brand new, often alien fields. Pioneering blacks understand the political and historical importance of "trailblazing," of knocking down racial barriers, and thus frequently draw the strength it takes to pioneer from the rightness of what they perceive to be their "mission."

Pioneering has, at its root, the ability to adapt, to be flexible, and perhaps most importantly, to tap emotional and spiritual sources of satisfaction, reward, and power. This includes developing and nurturing a support system that helps sustain the pioneer in a new milieu. Traditionally, the black church has been instrumental in this endeavor, though more recently, blacks "networking" with other blacks in similar pioneering positions has also provided emotional sustenance.

Shellie Ferguson: Breaking New Ground

On this cold, gray day in January of 1988, Shellie Ferguson, 44, moves through his warm, inviting Hartford, Connecticut, office with surprising grace and ease for a man who is six-feet-six. The former high school teacher and basketball coach turned college professor and entrepreneur has been in the real estate development business for the past sixteen years—twelve of them at a white real estate firm where he started as the first and only black, and the past three years as president of Monitor Management Incorporated, the multimillion-dollar development company he cofounded in 1985 headquartered in Hartford's City Place office tower.

An accountant by training, Ferguson grew up in the housing projects of Waterbury, Connecticut, and graduated from the University of Connecticut with an MBA. He spent the first ten years of his career teaching, however, first at Watertown High School, where he also coached the basketball team, then as a professor at Mattatuck Community College, where he was also a consultant to an anti-poverty agency in Waterbury. In 1973 the agency was looking for property to develop into a social service center, and Ferguson's assignment was to find a suitable building and put together a package that would make acquiring the property financially feasible. The assignment would change his life.

"I found a building which happened to be owned by Stanley

Fisher, a wealthy developer. He was based in West Hartford and headed a company called the F.I.P. Corporation. I met with him, explained our anti-poverty program, what we were trying to accomplish, and explained that we had no money—we really needed to have the building given to us. I talked about how the agency could turn the building into a significant economic venture in the Hartford community." The two men eventually did the deal, and Ferguson's performance with the project exceeded all expectations. Stanley Fisher offered him a job in his own company as assistant comptroller.

As comfortable as he was teaching, Ferguson knew he wanted to do something different—to break out of the mold. He had briefly left teaching to become personnel director for a medium-sized company, but soon left when he found he was hired largely to be a token black and not because of his skills. Stanley Fisher, however, clearly recognized and valued those skills. The only problem was, Fisher was offering him twelve thousand dollars less than what he was making as a college professor—a 40-percent cut in pay.

"The interviews I had with the other company managers didn't help either," Ferguson recalls. "They knew that Mr. Fisher saw some ability in me, but they didn't think I brought anything unique to the firm and that which I did bring they didn't need. I went home and talked it over with my wife. She was leery, to say the least. But I realized that with Mr. Fisher I could learn real estate. He was one of the people who had started the industrial park concept. Here was a guy who was extremely charismatic, had tremendous presence and knowledge. Be it a day, a week, a month, or a decade, I knew I could learn from him. I accepted the job."

Already something of a success in life, Ferguson wanted more. "I felt that I could do more, and I wanted to try. There I was, thirty years old with a wife to support who, at that time, was willing to take the risk with me. I didn't realize that success was the only alternative, because at the time it was the least likely alternative. I had to stop and tell myself that now is the time, because if I'm not successful, I have time to recover. Perhaps life is being ready for something, and I think I was just ready at that moment."

Successful pioneering blacks have very often been assisted on their journey through new terrain by fair and sympathetic whites. In Ferguson's case he had the advantage of not only Stanley Fisher's expertise guiding him through the new field of real estate, but the benevolence of a fair-minded man in authority who was giving him an opportunity. Frequently, it is whites at the top who are the fairest in extending opportunity, for they tend to be secure in their own positions and therefore are not threatened by the idea of help-ing newcomers to the territory. "I started with the F.I.P. Corpora-tion as an assistant comptroller, which was nice because there was no comptroller," Ferguson says with a smile.

As it turned out, Shellie Ferguson stayed with the company twelve years before striking out on his own. "I learned from Fisher. I learned how to develop real estate, and just as importantly, I learned how to deal with people from the empowered side of the table. I didn't have that at the time I went there. I was talented, and bright enough, but I had come from a differently sophisticated world. Fisher worked on my head. We had meetings after meet-ings, one-on-one conversations where he would ask me what I thought of this person or that person—what were some of the things the person did? How did I read his body language? How did the guy respond when he was pressured? He took time to really educate me, to work with me, to be a mentor in the truest sense of the term. I couldn't have paid him enough for the experience."

It was Fisher who helped Ferguson understand the impact of height, and not just race, on business interactions. "I'm taller than most of the people that I have to deal with," Ferguson explains. "And being driven, black, and very tall can sometimes overpower people and make them uncomfortable. If I'm sitting at a conference table and lean forward to make a forceful point and stretch out my arm, my body is completely across the table and I have invaded another person's personal space. If I stand over people to talk, I don't get the best from them. I get what they think I expect, not what they really think or feel, which is what I'm really after. The challenge for me is toning down." Indeed, this is the challenge for many black men whose color and physical size are frequently a source of intimidation to others before anything else about them is known.

Ferguson successfully met the challenge in managing the perceptions of both size and color. The managers at the F.I.P. Corporation who were initially skeptical when he joined the company became his biggest supporters. By the time he left in 1985 (after honoring a commitment to remain with the firm for five years following the death of Stanley Fisher) Shellie Ferguson had risen to become executive vice president of the company and had a 20 percent ownership stake.

Note 5: High Degree of Self-reliance

A high degree of self-reliance is particularly important to blacks who achieve. High self-reliance means an ability to move in an independent, constructive direction based on an individual's unique goals, ideas, or principles. This is the attribute that separates the leaders from the followers, the innovators from the conformists, the achievers from the average. It indicates an ability to set your own direction and move to your own beat rather than to the rhythm of others.

The ability to operate independently and with confidence is a skill often developed through the examples of others or honed over time as success in one independent action leads to other trailblazing actions. This is the skill demonstrated in the ability of those black youth, for instance, who are successful in overcoming the temptation and pressure of peers to give in to such things as drugs or sex. Such people are most often marching to the beat of another "higher power"—perhaps the high hopes of parents or their own high ambitions.

Having its roots in self-confidence, self-reliance is the quality that leads to an ability to break from the pack, to take a chance. Those with a high degree of self-reliance are the least likely to "give a damn" about what others may think. As a result, they are often the most likely to succeed.

Rhonda Strivers: Brewing It Her Way

Rhonda Strivers breathes, sleeps, eats, and drinks coffee . . . coffee beans, specifically. They are in her wallet, at the bottom of her washing machine, in the car, on her clothes, everywhere. "I smell like coffee wherever I go," says the shapely coffee-colored 37-year-old, who with her former husband owns Color Me Coffee, a chic gourmet coffeehouse in Chicago's upscale Lincoln Park. The shop, three years old in 1988, has the sort of trendy Eurostyle that appeals to a yuppie clientele, offering in addition to coffee the required quiche, croissants, mineral water, and a full line of specialty teas. But it is the coffees, specifically the rich-roasted coffee beans, exotic and flavorful, that have earned Color Me Coffee its reputation.

The shop's espresso was deemed to be "the foamiest in town" by the *Chicago Tribune,* and Rhonda Strivers, who is a former TWA flight attendant, has emerged as a new young business leader in Chicago, considered an expert in the art of the brew. "Specialty coffees, for instance, made with Arabic beans are more select," she explains, giving a brief lesson on the nuances of her product. "They're grown on higher slopes that are closer to the sun, and all are hand picked. Your commercial blends are more robust."

Color Me Coffee stocks coffees ranging from the select to the exotic, with flavorful names such as Jamaican Blue Mountain, Sumatra Mandehling, Yemen Mocha, Tanzania, Kenyan, Ethiopian, or Costa Rican. The average cup costs $1.25, and by the pound averages $30. A large part of Strivers' job is educating the buying public to the varied richness of coffee's possibilities. Both *Food and Wine* and *Fancy Food,* two highly regarded gourmet publications, have called on Strivers when looking to quote a knowledgeable source in the gourmet coffee industry.

It was Carl Icahn's takeover of TWA in 1985 that locked out the flight attendants during a bitter strike in 1986, forcing Strivers out of her job. Two years before, however, Rhonda had become interested in coffee and in the idea of opening a coffee shop. Her international flights took her around the world and she visited coffee-houses everywhere: in cities in both Western and Eastern Europe and in Asia, Africa, the Mediterranean, and the Middle East.

"I fell in love with coffeehouses and their ambience. I researched coffee for a year and a half, wrote everything on three-by-five cards, and kept the cards with me everywhere I went. I used the flash cards to learn the characteristics of coffee. I'd be sitting on the jump seat of a plane with passengers staring at me, and I'd have my flight attendant's smile on, but my brain was all coffee. Same thing on the crew bus. We would arrive in Paris at 6 A.M., and while everybody else was asleep, I'd be going over my flash cards and thinking about what I wanted to learn about the coffeehouses that I had planned to visit that day."

Rhonda Strivers' penchant for business showed itself early. "You know the stories about little kids selling lemonade for a nickel? Well, I actually did that. I taught other kids in the neighborhood how to read, charged them, and their parents actually paid me. I was teaching kids in my age group when I was in the fifth and sixth grade because I had high reading scores and won a lot of spelling bees. I charged a dollar per one-hour session. When I was fifteen, I had story reading hours. Mothers would pay me on Saturday night to babysit their kids, and instead of calling it babysitting, I called it my story hour. I served little cookies and Kool-aid and made some money." While she was a flight attendant, Strivers even had a small public relations business, called Posh.

The oldest of three children, Rhonda Strivers learned from her family the value of knowing yourself and going your own way. Her parents were both community activists and held elective and ap-pointive political posts during Rhonda's growing-up years. At one point her mother was the park district commissioner for the city of Chicago and her dad was a commissioner of streets and sanitation. The family's lives changed as a result of who was in office during any given year. "In the early seventies my mother was the highest paid black woman in the city of Chicago. By the time 1978 rolled around, she was unemployed and nobody would talk to her. A few years later, she was back in favor, then out again.

"The key," Strivers recognizes, "is to just keep the vision. That's what I try to do, and I've always admired that in my mother. She didn't just go with the flow. Whatever she stood for, that is what she stuck with." It is a quality the mother has clearly passed on to her daughter.

Note 6: Positive Self-acceptance

Positive self-acceptance is the characteristic that gives you the ability to be yourself, to embrace who you are, and to bring forward to a work setting your natural strengths. This characteristic provides an internal gyroscope that allows successful blacks to function in varying situations without getting emotionally or psychologically lost.

Successful blacks also operate from a position of racial strength. They are not trying to escape or play down either their socioeconomic background or their culture and history, nor are they trying to be or become someone who is not black. They not only accept the positive and constructive aspects of African-American heritage but integrate them into their professional lives. The offices of successful blacks, for instance, are often adorned by black artwork, books by black authors, or black music playing in the background. Such seemingly innocuous trappings are the critical cultural reference points that frequently help keep successful blacks emotionally centered and clear about who they are, regardless of where they are.

There is a great deal of personal power inherent in positive self-acceptance: the power comes from being psychologically grounded, in understanding that what you bring to a corporate setting has value and worth. Blacks who have a positive sense of their own value and worth are much less likely to be disoriented by the vicissitudes of corporate cultures or the vagaries of corporate politicking. They are most likely to succeed because they know they can.

Clarence O. Smith: Reaping the Rewards of the Risk

Clarence O. Smith went into business at a point in time when "I thought the whole damn world was about to unravel." It was 1968.

King had been killed in Memphis. Smith's sister had been killed in a train wreck with her husband, both of them 36. Robert Kennedy had been killed in Los Angeles. "It was," Smith says, echoing the sentiments of a generation, "a somewhat cataclysmic year for me."

By the end of the year, there were riots across the country that would lead to corporate America taking diverse initiatives to quell the cataclysms of black rage, and an incoming president named Richard Nixon in the White House who would promote an idea called Black Capitalism. These were the dual forces converging the night of November 8, 1968, when two men from the Shearson & Hamill investment company—one black (Russell Goings, from the investment banking division), the other white (Michael Victory, who headed the division)—convened a meeting of about fifty young black professional men to discuss why they should consider going into business for themselves, especially since Shearson was willing to assist with securing venture capital. Clarence Smith, still grieving over the loss of family and heroes, and looking for "a larger purpose in life," was one of the men in the group.

"I saw it immediately as an opportunity," Smith recalls. "My attitude was, I don't know if they are serious, but if you don't seize opportunity when it presents itself, then you have only yourself to blame. Whatever the ills were of society, here was now an opportunity, and to not take advantage of it would place the burden of failure on you." It was at that first meeting that Smith joined with three other black men around the idea of starting a magazine for black women. He was then 35, an agent with the Prudential Life Insurance Company and a registered representative with the Investors Planning Corporation. He was also the oldest one in the group and the only one married and with a child—the one with the most to risk and thus the one with the most to lose.

Yet Smith had learned from his father that "in order to make it in America you have to understand the enterprise system, and you have to understand the risk/reward system and be able to make the trade-off—to take a risk for a reward. He, more than any other person, got me to understand that," Smith says of his father, who was "an extraordinarily bright man" whose limited opportunities gave him "a sense of rage." The father passed on to his son a propensity for risk-taking. And in the opportunity to go into business, Smith saw a way to realize both his father's dream and the dream of King, the other man, after his father, by whom he has been most influenced.

"What influenced me about King is that he was able through personal conviction, belief and courage and strength, to take a whole nation of people who had difficulty finding unity and convince them they could make a difference in their lives without any of the traditional levers of power. This idea, together with my father's belief that blacks had to become businessmen and producers to make it, just all fell together when Shearson called the meeting."

Smith is the first to admit that he knew nothing about the publishing business when he and the three men who would become his partners, Edward L. Lewis, Jonathan Blount, and Cecil Hollingsworth, got together after that first Shearson meeting to talk about launching a publication. What Smith knew how to do was sell. The rest, he knew, could be learned. "I believe most people can learn to do most things," he says. "We tend to try to make what we do more complicated than it really is because I guess it gives us a sense of importance, but most people of intelligence can do what a lot of other people are apparently doing."

Smith's can-do attitude was shaped early. He grew up in the blue-collar Williamsbridge section of the Bronx in the forties and fifties, where most people were poor, black or white, but also strong, responsible, and infused with a spirit of community. "People didn't feel poor," Smith says. "We believed we could be anything we wanted, including President. Sure, you understood you were black, but that never made you think you could not do something or pursue something. We did not think in terms of having any 'boot on our neck.' "

It was this positive sense of self that fueled Smith's drive, giving him the impetus to take a chance—to quit his job to launch a new venture, to work for a year without a salary, to be in the beginning a one-man advertising department selling a magazine for black women to a Madison Avenue advertising community that seemed unable to comprehend such a thing, to survive the shakeout of two of the partners and a lawsuit by them attempting to take over the business. "I made a commitment to my wife Elaine that if I did this [went into business] I was going to make it. No matter what my three partners did—I didn't really know those guys—or didn't do, I was going to make this a success. And she believed it. So she gave me strength and support."

Today, twenty years later, Clarence Smith, cofounder of *Essence* magazine and president of Essence Communications, Inc., has reaped the rewards of the risks. The business, which currently includes, in addition to the magazine, a mail-order, book publishing, and video division, grossed $42 million in 1990, ranking eighteenth on the *Black Enterprise* annual list of top 100 black-owned industrial/service companies. Clarence Smith has proved his wife right. When he asked her why she stuck with him during those early days, she simply said, "I knew you didn't have anything, but I always knew you had the potential."

Now seated behind the rich mahogany desk in his large, cool gray office accented with two burgundy-colored couches, a signed Romare Bearden print, the collage of a lesser known black artist, and a photograph of his wife and two sons, Smith exudes the dynamism of a man whose first love is still sales and the charm and confidence of a man who knows he is both successful and handsome. With satin-smooth dark skin and the chiseled features of a regal patrician, Smith is the extroverted half of a business partnership that has survived two decades. It is that survival with his partner, Ed Lewis, chairman and chief executive officer of the company, that accounts in large measure for the success of the company.

Unlike other independently owned businesses in which management often rises and falls on the whim and temperament of an owner, the partnership at Essence has kept the business from consolidating into one ego. As Smith says of his partner, "We have an understanding that the venture is bigger than any individual that is a part of it. Therefore one's personal ego and personal fulfillment needs to be subordinated—as difficult as that is sometimes—to what is good for the venture. I view the venture as my opportunity to fulfill my goals in life, and therefore nothing short-term should be permitted to interrupt that vision."

For Smith, the fact that the venture he's become successful in is a magazine was the "bonus" to the business. "It's an opportunity to influence how people think," he explains. "That's why for me it has been such a love affair. It is a product that has its base in information, and that is a lot more compelling than manufacturing whisk brooms."

Note 7: Balance in Life

Balance in life refers to the ability to maintain symmetry between the professional and the domestic sides of life, and demands as high a priority for home and hearth as for work and career. Although few people deny the importance of having balance in life, achieving it on a day-to-day basis remains an ongoing challenge in modern America. Yet virtually all successful blacks have either achieved such balance or have it as a goal. It is this balance that gives vitality and meaning to careers and enriches personal living.

Ed Welburn: Designing the Dream

"More than three years went into the planning, development, and construction of Aerotech," proclaimed the General Motors press release in 1986 announcing the introduction of its sleek, turbocharged racing car. Aerotech turned out to be one of the most successful design programs in General Motors history, and as its reputation soared, so, too, did the visibility and fortunes of its principal designer, Ed Welburn.

"Oldsmobile had a four-cylinder engine called the Quad-4, and they wanted to design a very special car that could exploit the engine's capabilities and set a couple of world speed records. They came to me and asked me to design the chassis of the car. It was right up my alley—the kind of car that I used to dream about designing," explains the 37-year-old Welburn in 1988. "This was my ultimate high-speed, one thousand horsepower, low drag, very stable driving machine."

Ed Welburn is living the dream—both his and his father's. Designing cars has been a part of his life since the age of 4, when an uncle taught him to draw his first automobile, for which he demonstrated a natural aptitude and interest. His father, whose own ambition for car designing could not be realized during the time he came of age as a young black man, owned an auto body repair shop where his son Ed's interest in cars took root and blossomed. The father never permitted the son to learn the car repair business, however. His future held greater opportunities.

At the end of his junior year at Howard University, where he was a student in the School of Fine Arts with a double major in product design and sculpture, Ed applied for an internship at General Motors design studios. "I knew they were going to hire about a dozen designers and sculptors. I wanted to get into the program so badly that I applied as both a designer and a sculptor. I got in as a sculptor and spent more time doing design work than I did sculpting, but one summer at GM's design studios was like two years of school."

When the summer ended, GM offered Welburn a job, which he accepted after graduating from Howard in 1972. He has been with the company for the past sixteen years—virtually all of his working life.

Ed Welburn's relationship with General Motors actually began when he was a freshman in high school and already on a straight track to car designing. He wrote letters to the company, asked questions, requested information and brochures. He used officials with the car manufacturer as advisers. What were the best courses to take, the best schools to go to? "I kept communication going with them. My parents were also really involved and helped me with the letters. I wanted to go into a field in which I knew no one and there were no blacks. I think that a lot of blacks felt that I couldn't get into the field. Years later I learned that my parents shared that concern, but they never let on. I was the first black designer hired at GM. Had I known that, I might never have applied."

The loss would have been both Ed Welburn's and General Motors', however, for in his sixteen years with GM, Welburn has won numerous design awards, helped design every Oldsmobile Cutlass Supreme since 1978, designed the 1989 model entirely himself, worked on both the Calais and Ciera models, and designed two highly acclaimed Indianapolis 500 racing cars (in 1985 and 1988). Today as assistant chief designer he has total responsibility for the entire line of Oldsmobile Cutlass cars.

If Ed Welburn is doing exactly what he's always wanted to do, he is a man who also keeps success in perspective and remains anchored by family. His wife, Rhonda, herself a success in the automotive field, spent fifteen years in corporate finance at General Motors before leaving a year ago to open her own GM dealership, Welburn Buick.

Ed Welburn is now sitting in his wife's Detroit showroom, impeccably dressed in pressed jeans and a crisp white shirt. While his work is his lifelong passion, his family—a wife, two elementary school-age children, parents, and in-laws—all form a web of support that enriches his achievements. "I've had the opportunity to travel the world, receive professional recognition and social status," Welburn concedes, "but I think when you get right down to it I like to spend a lot of time at home. I have more fun there. I enjoy cooking for the kids and hate having sitters around."

Welburn also enjoys a particular closeness with both his own parents and his wife's. "I really just enjoy having the parents, both Rhonda's and mine, around. Rhonda and I have experienced an awful lot that our parents wanted to do in their day but were unable to. We want to share our successes with them now." Whether it's taking their parents to the Indianapolis 500 or sharing with them the magic of the trip to Monte Carlo that Rhonda recently won, what matters is having the opportunity to give back to the people who, as Ed Welburn puts it "have worked so hard— and so much of what they've done has been for Rhonda and me."

Note 8: Giving Back, Reaching Back

The idea of "giving back," "reaching back," has a long, noble history in the black experience. From heroic runaway slaves who worked the underground railroad in the antebellum South, returning time and time again to lead a race out from bondage, to the black professionals of today who volunteer to tutor inner-city youth, mentor a black college student, or donate time and money to a black institution, successful African-Americans are typically driven by both the desire and the need to give back—to reach back to help others of the race, as they themselves were no doubt helped along the road to achievement.

Successful blacks, perhaps more than any other achieving group in America, instinctively recognize that "There but for the grace of God go I." They understand that in a society in which success is still more often than not reduced to the lowest common denomination of race, frequently the only factor in the equation separating them from those less successful is their own good fortune. Such fortune, to be sure, is certainly the result of their own drive and ambition, discipline, training from the family, or largesse of others.

Yet just as lone survivors of great tragedies always ask "Why me?" when hit with the stinging rush of guilt, many achieving blacks find themselves wondering by what dispensation they were singled out for the blessing of success over others who may have been smarter, more talented, more worthy. Such preoccupations do not seem to trouble the achievers within the majority race in America, as Lorene Cary points out in her finely drawn book, *Black Ice,* a memoir illustrating her experiences as a black teenager in a Northeastern prep school and her motivation for returning to the school years later to teach those black students coming after her. She notes the differences between her perspective on success and that of her white, wealthy classmates:

> Taken together, these girls seemed more certain than I that they deserved our good fortune. They were sorry for people who were poorer than they, but they did not feel guilty to think of the resources we were sucking up . . . They took it as their due . . . They gave no indication that they worried that others, smarter or more worthy, might, at that very moment, be giving up hope of getting what we had.

African-Americans are the ones most likely to feel that their success represents not so much a gain ill gotten as it does an IOU still outstanding to the spirits past and present who have gone before, paving the way, paying the price. It is a sentiment uniquely African-American, indigenous to a people for whom success is often perceived to be a result of not just great acts of faith and will, but the divine intervention of grace. It is this grace that achieving blacks seek to honor, acknowledge, and reciprocate through the act of giving back, reaching back, and in so doing achieve both empowerment . . . and absolution.

Betty Winston Bayé: Coming Home Again

It is 1984, and over two thousand neighbors from the East River housing projects of New York's Spanish Harlem have turned out this warm spring day to welcome back a favorite daughter, Betty Winston Bayé, an award-winning journalist whose recently published novel, *The Africans,* is cause for celebration this sunny afternoon. Bayé is seated on the dais, overcome with emotion as she looks at the pictures of Africans hung on the fence of the basketball court and then looks into the faces of the project's young, excited children revealing the continuing line of race and ancestry.

There are so many other faces, too; familiar, black like her own, suddenly filling her with joy and pride, nostalgia and bittersweet memories. East Harlem has changed a lot since she walked these streets. There seems to be more of everything now: disease and drugs, crime and passion; faces younger and younger showing the age-old signs of strain and struggle.

Yet at the East River Housing Project on this homecoming day there are only the broad smiles and adulation of two thousand cheering well-wishers who have turned out to welcome back one of their own—the homegirl whose personal success is the occasion for great public pride, for it represents one of those shining examples of what can be achieved even if you are born black and poor.

Five years later, in 1989, Betty Bayé is sitting in the kitchen of her comfortable Louisville, Kentucky, townhouse, a thousand miles away from the streets of Harlem. Harlem, however, will always be home, for it is one of those places in a black heart that has shaped destiny and defined spirit. Bayé returned to the projects again this year, as she does every year, visiting family and friends, reaffirming the ties that bind. She was also honored again this year as a celebrity from the 'hood during the annual "East River Day" festival.

Now an assistant editor at the *Courier Journal* newspaper in Louisville, and the first African-American to hold that position in the paper's more than hundred-year history, Betty Bayé, at 44, is a petite bundle of dark chocolate dynamism and perpetual energy. She still possesses the pixie Betty-Boop bright-eyed loveliness that led her father to nickname her his "Boopy Girl" when she was growing up, the oldest and favorite of his three daughters—never even dreaming the extent to which her life would become a success.

Though both Bayé's parents worked, their jobs were menial— her father George, who had finished only the seventh grade, was a laborer in the garment district, her mother Betty had gone to college but was a dishwasher before later becoming an aide in a daycare center—making the Winston family one of those statistics classified as "working poor." George Winston drank too much. "He was an alcoholic, I guess you could say," says his daughter. "But he never missed a day of work and loved his family madly. He was a very proud man. He wanted us to be literate. He set the tone. He liked smart, independent women, which is why he married my mother. My father used to always say to us, 'I can get drunk and fall down in the street and I'll still be Mr. Winston in the morning. *You* [a woman] get drunk and fall down in the street, and you'll be a tramp.' We got these indirect messages about the way you were to carry yourself. It had nothing to do with how far we could go professionally."

Like other children of the inner city, Bayé was not encouraged by her teachers and counselors at Benjamin Franklin High School to consider going to college, despite ranking seventh in her graduating class of four hundred in 1964. It would take, nearly a decade later, a community of people—black artists and black activists—to reach back and claim the mind and spirit of a gifted native daughter, redirecting her on a path to success.

Betty Winston married shortly after high school, divorced shortly thereafter, and started her work life as a secretary at the

Opportunities Industrialization Center (OIC), the antipoverty work training program begun by the celebrated Reverend Leon Sullivan. "I was the best damned secretary that I could be," she notes. By age 21 she was working as a secretary for the Episcopalian Church where she met Gerterlyn (Lynn) Dozier, a church executive and the black woman who would help change Bayé's life.

"Lynn and the late actor Dwayne Jones were the two people who really encouraged me to go to college. Lynn was instrumental in opening doors for me and exposing me. She encouraged me to take my first trip to Europe and introduced me to all of these scholars, even taught me how to drive."

Dozier, who now teaches at Baruch College, was also active with the National Black Theatre in Harlem founded by Barbara Ann Teer, a cultural gathering place for some of the sixties' most popular black artists, activists, and intellectuals. Bayé quickly became part of the cultural collective, working at the church for a living and at the theater for an education. It was here that she met Dwayne Jones, star of the cult classic *Night of the Living Dead*. It was here that she attended seminars with Stokely Carmichael and Maya Angelou and had conversations with Martin Luther King, Jr., and his lieutenant, Jesse Jackson. "I once spent an entire day with Jackson," Bayé recalls fondly. "I was so excited and thought that he was the most handsome man I had ever seen. I can remember walking down Seventh Avenue with him and thinking, I wish somebody I know could run into me right now [and see me] with this fine man."

Bayé also worked as a volunteer with the Student Non-Violent Coordinating Committee (SNCC) during this time, interacting with and being influenced by activists H. Rap Brown, James Farmer, Ivanhoe Donaldson, John Henrik Clarke, Nikki Giovanni, Melvin Van Peebles, Felipe Luciano of the Young Lords, The Last Poets, Bobby Seale, and Ralph Featherstone. "I didn't just meet them, I was inspired by them. It was probably the most exciting period of my life."

In 1972, at age 27, Bayé, after considerable personal resistance, gave in to the peer pressure of her friend and mentor Dwayne Jones and registered for college. "I could always talk and run my mouth.

I was never afraid to say that I didn't know something. But even when I didn't know, I had something to say anyway. Dwayne always told the story about how he was talking to me about going to college one day on the corner of 125th Street and Madison Avenue. I called him a 'bourgeois nigger' and told him I didn't need to go to college because I was so accomplished already. He told me he said to himself, Let's get this bitch some education so she can have something to match her damned opinion." "I wanted to slap your little face," Jones told her later.

College was mostly part-time, and Bayé graduated from Hunter College in 1979. "I was going to undergraduate school, getting a degree in communications for no particular reason other than the fact that I needed a degree." In her junior year she was approached by Jim Aronson (now deceased), a journalism professor with whom she had taken a number of courses, who told her that her writing was excellent and suggested she consider a career in journalism. He also suggested she attend Columbia University's School of Journalism, his own alma mater, for her master's degree. Such an idea had never occurred to her, but she heeded her professor's advice, won a couple of scholarships, and took out a five-thousand-dollar loan to attend pricey Columbia, graduating in the Class of 1980 at age 34.

Bayé's first journalism job was with the *Daily Argus,* a Gannett newspaper in Mt. Vernon, New York, and the experience was a good one. "My first editor, Nancy O'Keefe, was invaluable in giving me the confidence I needed to be a professional."

Success for Betty Bayé means not just recognizing the value of the gifts she has been bestowed, but returning the gifts in kind. "I've always felt a sense of their spirit, a sense of not wanting to disappoint them," she says of those who have gone before her, helped her, encouraged her, advised her, seen her potential, and reached out to claim her. "I feel the weight of history, the weight of responsibility, which is why even as I accumulate material things [I struggle with] the whole notion of individual success. There is 'people success,' and I am obligated to reach back. It grows out of the people who reached back and got me. They never consciously said that, but that was always there. If you get this gift, you've got to give this gift."

It is a gift she gives back every time she returns home to the old neighborhood, a living role model for those coming up behind on what is possible, or speaks before youth groups or volunteers her time and energy to a black professional organization. She is humbled, awed, by just how far she has come each time she remembers the day her father, stricken with terminal cancer, accompanied her to the bank to watch her deposit the twenty-thousand-dollar advance for her novel *The Africans* in 1983. "I helped my father get dressed that day. He had looked at that check and cried. He said, 'You know, Boopy Girl, I've never made more than $7,000 a year in my life.' He didn't believe it—that somebody would give me $20,000 to write something. This was a man who pushed a rack through the garment center for years. All the way to the bank he just stared at the check. I knew that in his eyes, I was a success, that his Boopy Girl was okay."*

Note 9: Faith

Successful blacks tend to consciously acknowledge and even publicly proclaim the power that faith and spirituality give their lives. Whether they pray to a Lord named Jesus, bow to a God called Allah, chant before the altar of Buddha, or pour libations to the Ancestors, achieving blacks of every religious persuasion have "come this far by faith." Faith is the ability to trust in a higher power, to believe in "the evidence of things not seen," to be guided by not just intellect and reason, but also intuition and spirit. For blacks, faith is the force that has historically, successfully, moved mountains.

Just as important, faith has also given blacks their moral fiber, their psychic strength, their capacity for struggle and sacrifice and continuing success against the odds. Not all blacks who have a personal relationship to God are themselves successful in the secular, professional sense. Nor do all successful professional blacks

---

* In 1990 Betty Bayé won a Nieman Fellowship, awarded to journalists to do a year of independent study at Harvard University. She was promoted to an editorial writer and columnist for the *Courier Journal* when she returned to the paper in 1991.

necessarily practice a specific religion. Faith is personal, individual, nondenominational, stemming from a cosmic respect for the natural order of things—the recognition that there must be systems and balance, law and values, if there is to be purpose, meaning, and success in life.

Thomas Watson: Doing God's Will

It is Super Bowl weekend in the winter of 1990. The record cold fronts ripping through regions of the North and Midwest constitute only mildly interesting news reports in the Bonaventure Estates section of Ft. Lauderdale, Florida, this balmy January day. Here the sun is shining brightly, the temperature hovers near eighty, and the pace is slow, with residents leisurely traveling by foot or golf cart.

It is to this tiny corner of paradise that Thomas Watson retreats on the weekends. The 44-year-old certified public accountant is seated, facing East, on the floor of his condominium apartment that borders the fairway of the local country club. His salt-and-pepper hair and matching full beard contribute to his statesman-like assurance, his regal authority. Yet there is also a certain serenity and calm, a quality of inner peace suggesting a man in harmony with his inner and external worlds.

Thomas Watson is a man who lives with God actively in his life. The founder and managing partner of Watson, Rice and Company, a certified public accounting firm with offices in Washington, D.C., New York, and Cleveland, is a practicing Muslim who begins each business meeting with a prayer for assistance in doing the will of Allah. The pamphlets and brochures that lie in the reception area of his Washington, D.C., office describe the company's corporate philosophy, its culture, and reiterate a clear statement of intent to do God's will. Company managers are allowed, and even encouraged, to take time off during the business day to attend prayer services. Watson views such spirituality to be completely compatible with the company's other mission—earning profits—and points out that doing God's will has never cost him any business.

Though Watson has chosen Islam as the religion which guides his life, it really doesn't matter by what name God is called, he says, as long as a spiritual presence is evident and acknowledged. "We tend to praise the logical, rational mind and give little credence to the intuitive powers within us," says the successful Black Muslim businessman. "Having God as an adviser is one of those things that successful [white] people do but don't necessarily tell the whole truth about.

"What happens," Watson believes, "is that we [blacks] are given a different set of rules to live by. We are told about the separation of church and state—that spiritual development has no place in business. Yet if you reach into your pocket and look at the money that business is chasing, it reads 'In God we Trust.' Now who's fooling who?"

The essential message of God, by whatever name, says Watson, is that humans must be accountable, grounded at the core with a sense of right and wrong, responsible not only to themselves but to all things on earth. "If you are operating with a strong and powerful faith in an image that is powerful and constructive, and you believe that you are accountable for everything that you do, say, and think, then that will drive you in a constructive direction, and that constructive direction will make your life easier. It will allow you to attain the benefits of a comfortable life here on earth and also bring you into union with God."

Watson's initial union with God began when he was a Catholic growing up in Cleveland. He graduated from prestigious Cathedral Latin High School in 1964, though in his youth his respect for school and authority was less than reverential. "I was a good student in my freshman year, a mediocre student in my sophomore year, almost punched out during my junior year, and was an A student in my senior year," recalls the man of God who raised hell as a teenager. "I was counseled by the principal for being an obstinate nonconformist because I didn't try to be white. My parents' position was that I had to respect authority, so it didn't matter if the school was right or wrong, I had to deal with it. I felt differently. I got expelled once a year, but never even thought about leaving school. We just had a running battle the entire time."

Working part-time through high school and full-time during college, Watson received his bachelor's degree and MBA from Cleveland State University in 1974. By then he was married for the second time and the father of two children, both of whom are now in college. He became active in the Ohio Society of Certified Public Accountants, working to recruit more blacks into the profession.

In 1971 Watson founded the firm of Watson, Rice and Company. He is active on the national political scene, where he serves as commissioner of international trade with the White House Conference on Small Business and was cochair for trade of the Small Business Advisory Council of the Republican National Committee. He has also been chairman of the Department of Commerce Industry Sector Committee for Small Business Trade Policy.

The demands of a hectic business, political, and personal life makes it critical that Watson remain centered through faith. And black success still requires such centering, he insists. "It is absolutely necessary that young black professionals understand that if you ignore the intuitive power that is within you, you will not achieve as much as you could have. We as a race of people come from a culture that has traditionally recognized, respected, and developed intuitive power. We must always use it."

Note 10: Transcendence of a Racial-Victim Perspective

In the end, all notes on black success strike this final chord, the capacity to transcend a racial-victim perspective. Though they will most certainly experience racism, successful blacks seldom give in to the thinking of racial victims. They neither expect the Man to save them, nor blame the Man for all the problems and injustices in society.

Such thinking is not be confused with the head-in-the-sand denial of some blacks who say things like "I've never experienced racism," or "Race is no longer an issue," or "I'm just a professional who happens to be black." Achieving blacks know race remains an issue, for it is the issue they have nearly always managed to overcome. They recognize racism's reality and its virulence, but just don't give in to its debilitation.

CONCLUSION: REACHING THE HIGH NOTE

When the Reverend Martin Luther King, Jr., delivered his historic "I Have a Dream" speech before a quarter of a million demonstrators assembled for the March on Washington on August 28, 1963, in that defining moment he gave voice to the frustrations, hopes, and aspirations of America's disenfranchised. The hope, of course, was that a modern democracy would live up to its promise of being one nation under God with liberty and justice for all. In fits and starts, America has moved in that revolutionary direction.

The revolution for equality has always been a battle fought on two fronts, however: one political, the other personal. There is no question that integration, as a political and social movement, has had a decisive impact on black professional achievement during the last three decades. What is less often discussed is the extent to which the phenomenon of integration has defined the personal front in black America—the existential struggle to liberate the mind.

A critical lesson learned from the experience of successful blacks, these experts in the art of victory, is that the key to managing success and to personal power is in understanding that real success lies in who you become on the journey to achievement. The ability to not just overcome but to triumph in the face of obstacles, to make a way out of what appears to be no way, to wrest destiny from the seemingly arbitrary hands of fate, constitutes power that is transcendent, freedom that is supreme.

Once this power is discovered, however, the real question is whether it can be channeled to liberate a race and not just a few successful individuals within the race. To a generation that has achieved much, there is much more left to do, to struggle for, to overcome.

As we head into a new century, the tide of progress is slowly, ominously, rolling back—shifting to the right, to an era of backlash and retrenchment not unlike that which followed the first great movement for civil rights in America, the Civil War. Today's national mood, however, reflects not only the old venom of racism but the odious bile of new resentments that threaten the rights of all. Recent judicial assaults on abortion rights, freedom of religion in the classroom, protection from unwarranted search and seizure by police, and deliberate discrimination by employers are just a few of the danger signs indicating that we may be approaching the critical mass experienced by nations that erupt into fascism.

The dominant mood today is that enough has been done—for blacks and Hispanics, for women and children, for the poor and the sick. It is an attitude born of economic and spiritual deprivation in what was once the land of plenty. And it reflects what has always been the national character of America: its short attention span. If we as a nation cannot solve a problem quickly, we lose patience, move on, place blame on the shortcomings of others, rather than on our own lack of national resolve.

Yet resolve is the very quality this generation's successful African-Americans must continue to maintain in the face of three rising, daunting tasks. The first task is to mobilize for struggle against what are clearly new threats to civil rights: the defeat of the 1990 civil rights bill; the packing of the United States Supreme Court with conservatives; the dismantling of affirmative action; the unchecked rise in police brutality and racist violence. Such developments require the same diligent, militant call to action that inspired a civil rights movement thirty years ago.

The second, and in some ways perhaps more formidable, task facing this generation's Talented Tenth is to extend the parameters of black success to an increasingly isolated and polarized black underclass. The greatest casualty in the battle to integrate America has clearly been the loss of too many black role models in too many black communities; the loss of black institutions; the loss of a sense of collective black struggle, collective black identity. These are the historic strengths with which a race survived the Middle Passage, slavery, Jim Crow. They must be drawn upon again if we are to survive integration.

The challenge for any achieving black has always been in figuring out how to be a success but not a sellout: how to live anywhere you can afford and want to, but not abandon your spirit of black community; how to be a rugged individual and at the same time committed to working for the group; how to be black, yet integrated; whole, yet always a part of the struggle.

It is a burden, a responsibility, uniquely black and American. For no other class of Americans—save the black success class, the black middle class—is expected to take responsibility for saving those of its underclass, to be the solution to problems not of its making. Yet one of the key traits of successful blacks is their willingness to take such responsibility—to articulate and distinguish between what can be done *for* them and what must be done *by* them to achieve success.

The third task confronting this generation's black achievers is to successfully pass the torch of freedom to the next generation, to instill in black youth the notion of possibilities, and to also recognize that for each new generation there will inevitably be new struggles. The struggle of the civil rights generation was for access, inclusion, integration. The struggle facing the next generation is certain to be in large measure for simply holding ground. To those who have gone before lies the task of arming those who come behind with a sense of history, a sense of mission, and the recognition that in a black experience in America, to whom much is given, much is still certain to be required.

BIBLIOGRAPHY
AND REFERENCES

BOOKS

Anson, Robert Sam. *Best Intentions: The Education and Killing of Edmund Perry.* New York: Random House, 1987.

Bates, Daisy. *The Long Shadow of Little Rock.* Fayetteville, Ark.: University of Arkansas Press, 1986.

Bennett, Lerone, Jr. *Before the Mayflower.* Chicago: Johnson Publishing Company, 1962.

Branch, Taylor. *Parting the Waters: America in the King Years 1954–63.* New York: Simon and Schuster, 1988.

Breitman, George. *The Last Year of Malcolm X: The Evolution of a Revolutionary.* New York: Schocken Books, 1967.

Cade, Toni. *The Black Woman.* New York: New American Library, 1970.

Campbell, Bebe Moore. *Successful Women, Angry Men.* New York: Random House, 1986.

Cary, Lorene. *Black Ice.* New York: Knopf, 1991.

Cross, Theodore. *The Black Power Imperative.* New York: Faulkner, 1984.

Dewart, Janet (editor). *The State of Black America.* New York: National Urban League, 1991.

Davis, George, and Watson, Glegg. *Black Life in Corporate America.* New York: Anchor Books, 1982.

Douglass, Frederick. *Narrative of the Life of Frederick Douglass.* New York: Anchor Books, 1973.

DuBois, William E. B. *The Souls of Black Folk (Three Negro Classics).* New York: Avon Books, 1965.

Fanon, Frantz. *Black Skin, White Masks.* New York: Grove Press, 1967.

Foner, Philip S. *Frederick Douglass.* New York: Citadel Press, 1950.

Frazier, E. Franklin. *Black Bourgeoisie.* New York: Free Press, 1957.

Giddings, Paula. *When and Where I Enter . . . The Impact of Black Women on Race Sex in America.* New York: William Morrow and Company, 1984.

Grier, William H., M.D., and Cobbs, Price M., M.D. *Black Rage.* New York: Basic Books, 1968.

Harding, Vincent. *There Is a River.* New York: Harcourt Brace Jovanovich, 1981.

Harrigan, Betty Lehan. *Games Mother Never Taught You: Corporate Gamesmanship for Women.* New York: Warner Books, 1977.

Hughes, Langston. *The Best of Simple.* New York: Hill and Wang, 1961.

Kerner, Otto, et. al. *Report of the National Advisory Commission on Civil Disorders.* Washington: U.S. Government Printing Office, 1968.

Johnson, John H., with Bennett, Lerone, Jr. *Succeeding Against the Odds: The Inspiring Autobiography of One of America's Wealthiest Entrepreneurs.* New York: Warner Books, 1989.

Jones, Reginald L. (ed.). *Black Psychology,* 2d ed. New York: Harper & Row, 1980.

King, Coretta Scott. *The Words of Martin Luther King, Jr.* New York: Newmarket Press, 1984.

Landry, Bart. *The New Black Middle Class.* Berkeley and Los Angeles: University of California Press, 1987.

Madhubuti, Haki, *Black Men: Obsolete, Single, Dangerous?* Chicago: Third World Press, 1990.

Malcolm X. *Malcolm X on Afro-American History.* New York: Pathfinder Press, 1970.

Morris, Aldon M., *The Origins of the Civil Rights Movement.* New York: Free Press, 1984.

Sheehy, Gail. *Passages.* New York: E. P. Dutton, 1976.

Simms, Margaret C., and Malveaux, Julianne M. (eds.). *Slipping Through the Cracks: The Status of Black Women.* New Brunswick, N.J.: Transaction Books, 1986.

Steele, Shelby. *The Content of Our Character.* New York: St. Martin's Press, 1990.

Wallace, Michele. *Black Macho and the Myth of the Superwoman.* New York: Dial Press, 1978.

Williams, Juan, with the Eyes on the Prize Production Team. *Eyes on the*

Prize: America's Civil Rights Years, 1954–1965. New York: Viking, 1987.

Wilson, William Julius. *The Declining Significance of Race.* Chicago: University of Chicago Press, 1978.

Woodson, Carter G. *The Mis-education of the Negro.* Washington: Associated Publishers, 1933.

PERIODICALS

Bland, Dorothy. "Little Rock's Integration Hard-Won." *USA Today,* September 27, 1987.

Bray, Rosemary. "Managing as a Black Woman." *New York Daily News,* February 2, 1987.

Edmond, Alfred, Jr. "Dealing at the Speed of Light." *Black Enterprise,* June 1988.

Fairhall, John. "The Political Education of Kweisi Mfume." *The Baltimore Sun Magazine,* January 31, 1988.

Frank, Allan Dodds with Zweig, Jason. "The Fault Is Not in Our Stars." *Forbes,* September 21, 1987.

Gelman, David. "Black and White in America." *Newsweek,* March 7, 1988.

Joint Center for Political and Economic Studies. "Black Elected Officials in the United States." *Political Trendletter,* May 1990.

Jones, Edward W., Jr. "Black Managers: The Dream Deferred." *Harvard Business Review,* May–June 1986.

Jones, Kenneth Maurice. "A Crisis Report on the Buppies." *The Crisis,* April 1986.

Jovanovitch, Milena. "Black Women Exchange Views of Corporate Environment." *New York Times,* March 9, 1986.

King, Martin Luther. "The Ethical Demands of Integration." *Bulletin of the Religion and Labor Council of America,* May 1963.

Klein, Joe. "Race: The Issue." *New York,* May 29, 1989.

Kondracke, Morton. "The Two Black Americas." *The New Republic,* February 6, 1989.

McGhee, James D. "Running the Gauntlet: Black Men in America." *National Urban League,* August 1984.

Nelson, Jill. "The Fortune that Madame Built." *Essence,* June 1983.

Newcomb, Peter. "The Richest Entertainers." *Forbes,* October 3, 1988.

Oliver, Stephanie Stokes. "Liberation Love." *Essence,* July 1991.

Ostrowski, Marya. "Minorities in Accounting." *New Accountant,* February 1986.

Payne, Les. "Slam the Gate Behind the Chief." *Newsday,* April 7, 1991.

Perkins, Joseph. "Boom Time for Black America." *Policy Review,* Summer 1988.

Prince, Richard. "Blackout at Nightly TV News?" *NABJ Journal,* April 1991.

Reibstein, Larry. "Many Hurdles, Old and New, Keep Black Managers Out of Top Jobs." *Wall Street Journal,* July 10, 1986.

Safran, Claire. "What It's *Really* Like to Be Black." *Woman's Day,* May 28, 1991.

Seib, Gerald F. "Dukakis's Issues Director Deals With Paradoxes As He Seeks Ways to Counter Jackson Magnetism." *Wall Street Journal,* April 7, 1988.

Smith, Patricia. "Black Professionals: Achieving Success Can Come at Expense of Culture, Values." *Chicago Sun Times,* March 15, 1987.

Strickland, William. "The Future of Black Men." *Essence,* November 1989.

Updegrave, Walter L. "Race and Money." *Money,* December 1989.

U.S. Department of Commerce. "Money Income and Poverty Status in the United States: 1988." *Current Population Reports,* October 1989.

Waldrop, Judith. "Up & Down the Income Scale." *American Demographics,* July 1990.

Williams, Lena. "When Blacks Shop, Bias Often Accompanies Sale." *New York Times,* April 30, 1991.

Young, Jeffrey S. "Doctored Evidence." *San Francisco,* August 1983.

INDEX

ABC (A Better Chance) program, 219, 221
ABC (American Broadcasting Company), 69–71, 78–80, 120
Accountants, black, 58, 230–32, 246–49, 252–55, 271–73
Affirmative action, 228–29
Afro haircuts, 119–20, 121
Ailey, Alvin, 109
Allen, Debbie, 101
Alpert, Herb, 196
American Express Company, 57
Ames, Gary, 89
Amin, Idi, 209
Angelou, Maya, 269
Anger, black, 113–15, 119–24, 130, 227
Anson, Robert Sam, 220–21
A. Philip Randolph Institute, 62
Arkansas State Press, 30
Armonk (New York), 237–38
Aronson, Jim, 270
Ashmore, Anne, 172–75
Atlanta (Georgia), 15, 75, 204–5, 209
Aunt Jemima, 98–99
Automobile designer, black, 263–65
Auto salesman, black, 203–6
Avon Corporation, 18, 231–32

Baez, Joan, 250
Bailey, John, 129–31, 137 n.
Balance in life, 262–64
Baltimore (Maryland), 15, 183, 187
Banking, blacks in, 57–58, 114–15, 120–22, 124–28
Banks Brown Management Systems, 113
Baraka, Amiri, 212
Baranco, Gregory T., 203–6

Baranco, Juanita, 204
Baruch College, 247–48, 268
Bates, Daisy, 29, 32, 33, 48
Bates, L. C., 29
Bayé, Betty Winston, 266–70
BCI Holdings, 20
Beals, Melba Patillo, 1, 35
Bearden, Romare, 261
Bee Gees, the, 196
Bell, Dennis, 209
Benson, George, 196
"Big Break" (TV show), 137 n.
Birmingham (Alabama), 161, 163, 165
Bishop College, 223
Black baby boom generation, 123
Black beauty products, Madame Walker and, 17–18
Black Capitalism, 259
Black Enterprise magazine, 10, 14, 19, 86, 235–36, 261
"Black Male/Female Relationships" workshop, 181–83
Black men, 180–213
  children of, 186, 192
  physical-size problems of, 255–56
  statistics on, 181
  successful, 55–56
  white male presumption concerning, 200
  white men's fear of, 192
Black Muslims, 212
Blackness, positive sense of, 6, 136–37
Black Panther Party, 2, 208
Black politicians, 53–57, 94–99, 200–3
  statistics on, 56–57
  See also Jackson, Jesse
Black Power, 188

Black racism, 239
Black success, 3–13, 54–56
  becoming "non-black" after, 135–36
  for black women, 110–11, 151–79
  contradiction in concept of, 132–33
  dressing for, 106–8
  future of, 274–276
  integration and, 123–24
  psychology of, 240–76
    balance of life, 262–64
    faith, 270–73
    giving back, reaching back, 264–70
    GOPAs, 245–49
    high degree of self reliance, 255–58
    managing others' racial perceptions and
      reactions, 249–51
    personal responsibility/integrity, 241–45
    pioneering, 251–55
    positive self-acceptance, 258–62
    transcendence of a racial-victim
      perspective, 273
  social grooming and, 137–38
  speech and, 105–6
Black women, 110–11, 151–79
  beauty in, 109–11
  changing patterns of work by, 155–57
  economic situation of, 156–57
  households headed by, 162, 167
  increase of income among, 12–13
  in marriage, 62, 166–68
  professional black man's attitude to, 169–72
  stereotypes about, 138, 150
Blount, Jonathan, 260
Bolling vs. Sharpe, 45
Bradley, Ed, 70
Bradley, Tom, 95, 208
Branch, Taylor, 129, 133
Breedlove, Sarah (Madame C. J. Walker), 17–
  18
Briggs vs. Clarendon County, 45–46
Britton, Barbara, 169–72
Brooklyn College, 165
Brown, Elaine, 140
Brown, H. Rap, 268
Brown, Linda, 45–46
Brown, Minnijean, 35
Brown, Ronald, 112–15, 121, 123–24
Brown, Willie, 95, 99
Brown vs. the Board of Education, 29, 44–47, 58
Buffalo Soldiers, 243
Buppies, 229
Burch, Buford, 145–48
Burrell, Thomas, 223
Burris, John, 148, 150
Burris, Ramona Tascoe, 138–50
Bush, George, 208

Business
  black-owned
    Earl Graves Ltd., 235–36
    Mitchell/Titus and Company, 246–47
    recent growth, 205
    revenues of top 100, 10, 14
  blacks in
    dress, 106–8, 119–20
    executives, 81–82, 85–86, 109, 222–27,
      250–51, 262–64
    speech, 105–6
    the wealthiest blacks, 14–23
  black women in, 170–72
  dealing with racism in, 227–29

California, black elected officials in, 94–99
California, University of, 142–43, 153
  at Los Angeles (UCLA), 35
California State University, Los Angeles, 97
Camelot Entertainment, 132, 137 n.
Campbell, Bebe Moore, xii, 122
Cannon, Reuben, 120
Capital Bank of California, 122
Capital Bank of Texas, 126
Carmichael, Stokely, 165, 269
Carreras, Billy, 221
Carter, Jimmy, 62, 201, 202
Cary, Lorene, 265
Central State University, 191
Chicago (Illinois), 15, 191, 257, 258
Chicago State University, 191
Chicago Tribune, 218, 256
Cincinnati, University of, 211
Citibank, 234
Citizens Loan Corporation, 16
Civil Rights Act of 1875, 39
Civil Rights Act of 1964, 149
Civil Rights Movement, 2, 4–6, 13, 40, 113,
  133, 188, 190, 213, 275
  examples of activists within, 160–66
  women's movement and, 152, 155, 157–60
Clairol, 238
Clark, Kenneth, 46
Clarke, John Henrik, 268
Clarkson, Charles, 21
Cleaver, Eldridge, 140
Cleveland State University, 273
Clinton, Bill, 48, 63
Cobbs, Price M., 112, 114, 115, 121, 124
Coca-Cola USA, 222–26
Cole, Natalie, 137 n.
Colgate University, 134–35
Color Me Coffee, 256
Columbia University, 219, 269
Congressional Black Caucus, 180–83
Cooke, Janet, 217–21
Cornell University, 191, 219

Cosby, Bill, 9, 173
Cross, Theodore, 10

Dartmouth College, 116, 211
Davis, Benjamin O., 242
Davis vs. Prince Edward County, 45
Dillon Read & Company, 126
Dinkins, David, 208
DINKs, 229
Doctorates, black women with, 155
"Doll study" of segregation, 46
Donaldson, Ivanhoe, 165, 269
Douglass, Frederick, 42, 43, 189, 207, 208
Dowdell, Dennis, 197, 199
Dozier, Gerterlyn (Lynn), 269
DuBois, W. E. B., 3, 5, 12, 39, 202, 208,
    220
Dukakis, Michael, 200–3
DuSable, Jean Baptiste, 191
Dylan, Bob, 250

Ebony magazine, 16
Eckford, Elizabeth, 35
Economist, black, 151–55
Edley, Christopher, Sr., 201
Edley, Christopher, Jr., 199–203
Education
    higher
        blacks in, 117–19, 200
        earnings of blacks with degrees, 181
    integration of
        in *Brown* case, 29, 44–47, 58
        See also Little Rock (Arkansas)
    "separate but equal" in, 42–43
Eisenhower, Dwight D., 33
Entertainers, 9–10
Equal Employment Opportunity Commission,
    147
Equal opportunity, 228–29, 236
Essence magazine, 153, 175–76, 178, 192,
    261–62
Ewing, Bobby, 130
Eyes on the Prize (TV series), 40, 43–44

Faith, 270–73
Fancy Food magazine, 256
Fanon, Franz, 106
Farmer, James, 268
Farrakhan, Louis, 191
Faubus, Orval E., 29–32
Featherstone, Ralph, 165, 268
Ferguson, Shellie, 252–55
F.I.P. Corporation, 253–55
First Boston Corporation, 22
First Interstate Bank of California, 120
Fisher, Stanley, 252–55
Food and Wine magazine, 256

Forbes magazine, 9, 14
Ford Motor Company, 109
Fortune magazine, 86
Founders National Bank of Los Angeles,
    122 n.
Fourteenth Amendment, 39
Frampton, Peter, 196
Frazier, E. Franklin, 108
Freedom, King on, 56
Fulbright, Karen, 157

Garvey, Marcus, 189
Gasby, Clarence Alvin Daniel, 129–37
Gebhart vs. Belton, 45
General Electric Company, 82–85
General Motors Corporation, 204, 263–65
Giovanni, Nikki, 268
Gite, Lloyd, 100–5
Gittens, Anthony, 162
Gittens, Jennifer Lawson. *See* Lawson, Jennifer
Giving back, 264–70
Glass ceiling, 225, 236
Goings, Russell, 259
"Golden Girls, The" (TV show), 194
GOPAs (goals, organization, planning, and
    action), 245–49
Gordon, Ellis, 114–22
Gordon, Fred A., 242–45
Graves, Barbara, 238
Graves, Earl G., Sr., 235
Graves, Earl G., Jr., 234–39
Graves, Johnny, 237
Graves, Michael, 237
Graves, Roberta, 238
Gray, Frizzell. *See* Mfume, Kweisi
Green, Ernest, 35, 57–65
Grier, William H., 112, 124
Gumbel, Bryant, 70

Hall, Daryl, 196
Hampton, Fred, 191
Hampton College, 38
Harding, Vincent, 38
Harragan, Betty Lehan, 106
Hartford (Connecticut), 207, 253
Harvard Law School, 200–2
Harvard University, 229, 233, 235, 270 n.
Hawkins, Augustus, 95
"Heroin Trail, The" (newspaper series), 208
Hervey, Ramon, 194–99
Hibbard, O'Connor and Weeks, 124–26
Highland General Hospital (Oakland,
    California), 141–49
Hollingsworth, Cecil, 260
Hollingsworth, Perlesta (Les), 49–51, 53–56
Holly, Buddy, 195
Hollywood, blacks in, 9–10, 120, 194–95

Honeywell Corporation, 231
Hooks, Ben, 48
Horne, Lena, 96
Houston, Charles, 43
Houston, Whitney, 9
Houston (Texas), 100–2, 115, 124–25
Howard University, 38, 191, 229, 233, 263
Howell, Ron, 209
Hughes, Langston, 92, 93
Humphrey, Hubert, 187
Hunter College, 269

Icahn, Carl, 256
Idaho State University, 250
Illinois, University of, 117–19, 191
Income of blacks
  highest-earning individuals, 9–10
  household income over $50,000, 12–13
  1967–1987, 3
  poverty level, 154
  in upper middle class, 5
  women compared to men, 157
Integration
  black success and, 123–24
  as compromise, 233
  failures at, 218–22
  fantasies of, 217, 218
  meaning of, 80–81, 215, 226
  racism and, 228–29
Integration generation, 2, 48–65, 229
  "dropping out" by, 234
Integrity, 241–45
International Paper Company, 233–34
Investment banking, blacks in, 57–58, 124–28
Investors Planning Corporation, 259
Islam, 271–72

Jackson, Derrick, 209
Jackson, Jesse, 25, 183, 188–89, 200–2, 223, 268
Jackson, Michael, 9
Jamaica, black immigrant from, 246–49
Jews, 41, 133–34
"Jim Crow," 40
Johns Hopkins University, 187
Johnson, Jerry, 88–89
Johnson, John H., 14–16, 18–19, 191
Johnson, Loretta, 166–68
Jones, Dwayne, 268–69
Journalists, black
  on magazines, 14–16, 153, 175–79, 235–36, 261–62
  on newspapers, 206–10, 218–19, 267, 270 n.
  on TV, 69–80, 101–4

Karenga, Ron, 212
Kaufman, Monica, 69, 72, 75, 76
Kennedy, Robert, 259
Kent School, 229, 232–33
Kerner Commission Report, 207
KHQ (Spokane station), 73–74
King, Don, 222
King, Martin Luther, Jr., 2, 49, 56, 130, 160, 165, 188, 189, 211, 212, 259, 260, 268, 274
King, Rodney, 208
King Features, 153
King World Syndicates, 132
Kipling, Rudyard, 197
Knee-jerk reaction to racism, 227–28
Knight, Kathleen, 108–11
Koch, Edward, 208
Kohlberg Kravis Roberts, 20
Kristofferson, Kris, 130
Ku Klux Klan, 203
Kwanza (holiday), 212

Lanier, Carlotta Walls, 35
Last Poets, The, 268
Lawson, Jennifer, 160–66
Lawson, Willie D., 163, 165
Lawyers, black, 53–54, 58
Lee, Don L. *See* Madhubuti, Haki
Leevy, Redcross, and Company, 247
Lehman Brothers, 57, 65 n.
Leonard, Sugar Ray, 10
Lewis, Edward L., 260, 261
Lewis, Reginald F., 19–23
Lieberman, A. J., 208
Lifetime Television Network, 80 n.
Lincoln, Abraham, 208
Little Rock (Arkansas)
  Central High School
    Little Rock Nine in, 1–4, 27–36, 48–49, 57–62
    in 1980s, 34
  "Jewish" country club in, 61
  Mayor Shackelford of, 49–52, 54–56
  other segregation in, 52, 59–60
Los Angeles (California), 122. *See also* Hollywood
Louisville (Kentucky), 266–67
"Lower-class black life," 138
Lucas, Tucker and Company, 247
Luciano, Felipe, 268

McCall's Pattern Company, 21–22
McCartney, Paul, 195
McClain, Leanita, 217–21
McLaurin, John, 44–45
Madhubuti, Haki, 190–93
Malcolm X, 188, 189, 212, 215, 249

Malveaux, Julianne, 151–56
Managing others' racial perceptions and
    reactions, 249–51
Marriage, 62, 166–68
Marshall, Thurgood, 44, 46
Martin Marietta Corporation, 81–82, 85–86
Mary Kay Cosmetics, 18
Massachusetts Institute of Technology (MIT),
    84–85, 87–88, 153
Mattatuck Community College, 252
Mays, Richard, 49, 50, 53–56
MCI, 89
Measured response to racism, 227
Memphis (Tennessee), 129–31, 135–36
Mencken, H. L., 208
Mfume, Kweisi, 181–87
Michigan State University, 62
Middlebury College, 244
Midler, Bette, 196
Military forces, integration of, 51
Miller, Alfred, 177
Milloy, Marilyn, 209
Miscegenation, 93
Miss America contest, Vanessa Williams and,
    196–99
Mitchell, Bert N., 246–49
Mitchell, Carol, 248
Mitchell, Parren, 183, 187
Mitchell-Smith, Gloria, 229–32, 234
Mitchell/Titus and Company, 246–47
Monitor Management Incorporated, 252
Monsanto Company, 230–31
Montgomery (Alabama), 2, 160
Morgan State University, 187, 234
Morrison, Charles, 222–26
Morrison, Toni, 152
Motown, 195
Mountain Bell, 88–90
Mt. Vernon *Daily Argus,* 269
Moyers, Bill, 153
Moynihan, Daniel Patrick, 169, 235
Muhammed, Elijah, 191
Murder rate for black men, 181
Murphy, Eddie, 9
Music Television (MTV), 171

National Association for the Advancement of
    Colored People (NAACP), 2, 30, 43–
    46, 199
National Association of Black Journalists, 73
National Black Theatre, 268
National Western Insurance Corporation, 126
NBC News, 72
Negro Digest, 15–16, 19
Networking, 252
Newark (New Jersey), 211, 212
Newsday, 206–10

Newsweek magazine, 218
Newton, Huey, 140, 208
New York City, 132–35, 229–30, 247, 260,
    266
New York Futures Exchange, 126
New York Life Insurance Company, 106–8
New York State Society of Certified Public
    Accountants, 248
New York Times, 209
Nieman Fellowship, 270 n.
Night of the Living Dead (movie), 268
Nixon, Richard, 259
North Carolina, University of, 230
Northern Illinois University, 117–18
Northwestern Bell, 87
Northwestern University, 218
Nunn, Ray, 78–79

Oakland (California), 140–41, 150, 210–11
Oates, John, 196
O'Keefe, Nancy, 269
Operational trusting mode, 227–28
Operation PUSH, 222
Opportunities Industrialization Center (OIC),
    268

Pace, Harry, 15, 16
Pacific Management Systems, 115
Pacific Northwest Bell, 87
Parks, Rosa, 2
Pascal, John, 208
"Passing" for white, 100
Patillo, Melba. *See* Beals, Melba Patillo
Payne, Les, 206–10
Peat/Marwick, 247
Pennsylvania State University, 82
Penthouse magazine, 197, 199
Pepsi Cola, 224, 226, 235
Perkins, Bill, 220
Perry, Edmund, 217–21
Perry, Jonah, 219
Petry Communications, 170
Personal responsibility, 241–45
Phillips Exeter Academy, 219–21
Physicians, black, 140–50, 210–13
Pioneering, 251–55
Plessy vs. Ferguson, 39–46
Poet, black, 190–93
Poussaint, Alvin, 173
Poussaint, Anne Ashmore. *See* Ashmore, Anne
Poverty, black, 154
Power
    black male quest for, 187–89, 193–94
    intuitive, 273
Prayer, 271
Prince, 10
Prison rate for black men, 181

Procter & Gamble Company, 112, 223
Prudential Life Insurance Company, 259
Pryor, Richard, 196
Psychologist, black, 172–75
Public Broadcasting Service (PBS), 161
Public relations, blacks in, 195–99
Pulitzer Prize, 208, 209, 218

Ralston Purina Company, 231
Rape, 93
Rashad, Phylicia, 101
Reaching back, 264–70
Reagan, Ronald, 208
Ren-Mar Studios, 194
Reverend Ike, 177
Roane, Arlene, 86–90
Roane, Arnold F., 81–86, 90
Roberts, Terrance, 35
Robinson, Ruby Doris, 165
Rogers & Cowan, 195–96
Role models, 70, 275
Roosevelt, Eleanor, 32
R&S Strauss and Company, 251–52
Russell, James, 105–8

St. Louis (Missouri), 96, 229–32
Ste. Marie, Buffy, 250
San Francisco (California), 152–54
San Francisco State University, 142
Satterwhite, Edgar. *See* Sulieman, Jamil
Savings Bank of Massachusetts, 126
Sawyer, Carolyn, 69–80
Sawyer, Diane, 69
Scarsdale (New York), 238, 239
Schlitz Brewing Company, 223
Seale, Bobby, 140, 208, 268
Segregation, 39–46, 52, 64–65
Self-acceptance, 259–63
Self-reliance, 255–58
"Separate but equal," 39–46
Service Link, 86, 89
Sevareid, Eric, 139
Sexuality, 192–93
Shackelford, Lottie, 49–52, 54–56
Shearson & Hamill, 259–60
Shearson Lehman Hutton, 35, 57, 63
Signifyin' monkey, 92–93
Simms, Margaret C., 156
Simpson, Carol, 72
Singer Corporation, 231
Skin color, 93–94, 96, 99–111
"Slave" names, 187, 191
Sloan-Kettering Institute for Cancer Research, 165
Smith, Clarence O., 258–62
Smith, Craig, 229–34

Smith, Gerald B., 124–28
Smith, Graham and Company, 128 n.
Smith, Peter, 135
Soft drinks, black consumption of, 224
"Southern coping skills," 59
Sparkle Productions, 232
Spinks, Michael, 10
Sports, blacks in, 9–10, 236–37
Steele, Shelby, 138, 206
Stewart, Marsha Ann, 243
Strivers, Rhonda, 256–58
Student Nonviolent Coordinating Committee (SNCC), 2, 165, 268
Sulieman, Jamil, 210–13
Sulieman, Kathleen Carney, 210, 211
Sullivan, Leon, 268
Supreme Liberty Life Insurance Company, 15–16
Survival, black ability for, 193, 275
Swarthmore College, 201
Sweatt, Herman, 44, 45
Swift, Maurice, 207
Switching professions, 230, 234

Talented Tenth, 3, 5, 12, 275
Tascoe, Ernest, 138–40
Taylor, Susan L., 175–79
Teenage-into-manhood years, 181, 185
Teer, Barbara Ann, 268
Television, blacks in, 129–31
  in news departments, 69–80, 101–4
Texas Southern University, 116, 117
Thomas, Jefferson, 35
Thompson, Morris, 209
Times-Mirror Company, 210
Titus, Robert, 247
TLC Beatrice International Holdings, 19
TLC Group, 21–22
Training programs, 77–78, 112–13, 120–21
Transcendence of a racial-victim perspective, 273
Truman, Harry, 51
Trump, Donald, 181
Truth, Sojourner, 156
Turner, Nat, 189
Turner, Tina, 10
Tuskegee Institute, 38, 165
TWA (Trans-World Airlines), 256
Tyson, Mike, 9

Underclass, 4, 211, 275
Underground railroad, 264
Unemployment rate of black men, 181
United California Bank, 114–15, 120–21
United Nations Hunger Award, 208
United Negro College Fund, 201

United States Military Academy, 242–44
US West, 86, 88

Vann, Al, 134
Van Peebles, Melvin, 268
Victory, Michael, 259

Wair, Thelma Mothershed, 35
Walker, Alice, 208
Walker, Madame C. J., 17–18
Walker, Margaret, 208
Wallace, Michele, 158, 188
Wall Street Journal, 201
Walters, Barbara, 70
Warren, Earl, 46
Washington, Booker T., 38–39
Washington, Harold, 191
Washington, D.C., 45, 162
Washington Post, 210, 218
Washington State University, 73
Washington University, 233
Waters, Maxine, 94–99, 111
Watson, Diane, 99
Watson, Rice, and Company, 271, 273
Watson, Thomas, 271–73

WBZ-TV (Boston station), 80 n.
Wealth
  total black and white compared, 13
  of wealthiest blacks, 14–23
Welburn, Ed, 262–64
Welburn, Rhonda, 265
Westcap Corporation, 125–28
Wharton Business School, 238
"White values," 108
Williams, Juan, 40, 43
Williams, Vanessa, 196–99
Winfrey, Oprah, 9, 132
Winston, George, 267, 270
WIS (Columbia, S. Car., station), 74–75
Wisconsin, University of, 109
Woods, Alfred E., 250–51
Workshops for black and white employees,
  112–13, 121
WSB (Atlanta station), 75–76, 78

Yale University, 236, 238
Yates, Jack, 100–1
Young, Andrew, 200
Young Lords, 268

Audrey Edwards, an award-winning journalist, is currently Editor-at-Large at *Essence,* where she previously served as Editor and Executive Editor. She has been an editor at a variety of magazines, including *Family Circle, Black Enterprise,* and *Redbook.* Her work has appeared in the *New York Daily News,* the *New York Times, Ms., Ladies' Home Journal, Glamour, Redbook,* and *Working Woman.* She is the author of four books for children, and has taught writing and editing at New York and Columbia Universities.

Dr. Craig K. Polite is a clinical and industrial psychologist with nineteen years experience. He has a clinical practice in New York City where he specializes in the issues and concerns of the black middle class. He is also an organizational development consultant to industry and government. Dr. Polite hosts "The Mind's Eye," a popular radio talk show on WLIB in New York, and has frequently been interviewed as a consultant for radio and television. He received his Ph.D. from Michigan State University and his Postdoctoral Certificate in psychotherapy and psychoanalysis from New York University.